Luxemburger Juristische Studien –
Luxembourg Legal Studies

edited by

Faculty of Law, Economics and Finance
University of Luxembourg

Volume 23

Chantal Bomprezzi

# Implications of Blockchain-Based Smart Contracts on Contract Law

Nomos

Università Europea di Roma

This work is co-funded by the Department of Human Sciences of Università Europea di Roma.

**The Deutsche Nationalbibliothek** lists this publication in the Deutsche Nationalbibliografie; detailed bibliographic data are available on the Internet at http://dnb.d-nb.de

ISBN 978-3-8487-8592-6 (Print)
978-3-7489-3006-8 (ePDF)

**British Library Cataloguing-in-Publication Data**
A catalogue record for this book is available from the British Library.

ISBN 978-3-8487-8592-6 (Print)
978-3-7489-3006-8 (ePDF)

**Library of Congress Cataloging-in-Publication Data**
Bomprezzi, Chantal
Implications of Blockchain-Based Smart Contracts on Contract Law
Chantal Bomprezzi
266 pp.
Includes bibliographic references.

ISBN 978-3-8487-8592-6 (Print)
978-3-7489-3006-8 (ePDF)

Onlineversion
Nomos eLibrary

1st Edition 2021

# IMPLICATIONS OF BLOCKCHAIN-BASED SMART CONTRACTS ON CONTRACT LAW

*Dr. Chantal Bomprezzi*

*ABSTRACT*

Smart contracts are the most advanced blockchain applications. They can also be used in the contractual domain for the encoding and automatic execution of contract terms. Smart contracts already existed before the blockchain, but they take advantage of the characteristics of that technology. Namely, the decentralised and immutable characters of the blockchain determine that no single contracting party can control, modify, or interrupt the execution of smart contracts.

As every new phenomenon, blockchain-based smart contracts have attracted the attention of institutions. For example, in its Resolution of 3 October 2018 on distributed ledger technologies and blockchain, the European Parliament has stressed the need to undertake an in-depth assessment of the legal implications, starting from the analysis of existing legal frameworks. Indeed, the present study aims to verify how blockchain-based smart contracts fit into contract law. To this end, the analysis starts from the most discussed and relevant aspects and develops further considerations. Before that, it provides a detailed description and clarifications about the characteristics, the functioning, and the development of the technology, which is an essential starting point for a high-level quality legal analysis. It takes into considerations already existing rules concerning the use of technology in the life cycle of contracts, from vending machines to computable contracts, and verifies its applicability to blockchain-based smart contracts.

The work does not limit to consider the mere technology, but some concrete scenarios of adoption of blockchain-based smart contracts in the contractual domain. It focuses on the implications of blockchain-based smart contracts on contract formation, contract performance, and applicable law and jurisdiction.

# ACKNOWLEDGEMENTS

I would like to thank the University of Bologna for allowing me to attend the doctoral program in Law, Science and Technology and defend my dissertation on which this book is based. I would like to thank the members of the thesis supervision committee: the Chairman, Professor Alberto Gambino, from the Università Europea di Roma, for having decided to co-fund this publication; Professor Michèle Finck and Professor Annarita Ricci, for their questions and comments. I would also like to thank my external evaluators, Professor Valeria Falce and Professor Oreste Pollicino, for their suggestions.

Special thanks go to my Supervisor Professor Giusella Finocchiaro for her availability, advice, guidance, and expertise. It has been a great honour to work with her. I also wish to thank Professor Monica Palmirani (PhD Programme Coordinator) that managed all the activities.

I am also very grateful to the University of Luxembourg, my partner University. I found a very lively and stimulating place to conduct my research. In particular, I would like to express my gratitude to my co-Supervisor Professor Luca Ratti, for his kindness and support.

Many thanks to my colleagues of LAST-JD Giorgia, Valentina, Salvatore, and Federico, for their cooperation and help. We created a special team, and I wish to work with them in the future.

Many thanks also to all the Professors, researchers, PhD students, institutions, entrepreneurs, and other people I have encountered during the PhD period, both in Italy and Luxembourg. They enriched me as a PhD Student, and as a person.

Finally, I want to thank my family, my boyfriend and my friends for their unfailing encouragement.

# Table of contents

# INTRODUCTION

## *I. Background*

Blockchain technology is a new kind of database that originated around 2008. It is a distributed database because the same copy of recorded data is stored in various devices or nodes. Moreover, it is decentralised because the ledger updates through a system of consensus. Decentralistion means that no master node coordinates the others, but a shared protocol sets the rules for updating all the nodes. Decentralisation allows a more efficient, less costly, and more transparent way of keeping information, instead of relying on a single point of failure. However, the peculiarity of blockchain compared to other decentralised databases is its tamper-resistance. Indeed, data are represented in the form of hash. A hash is a unique string of random letters and numbers, i.e. every modification of the underlying data causes a change of the hash. Furthermore, blockchains use an append-only data structure where transactions of data are cryptographically and chronologically linked to each other; thus, every attempt of alteration becomes immediately detectable.

Because of the latter characteristic, blockchain technology is considered 'disruptive'. Digital tools allow infinite reproductions of the same data, and the distinction between the original and the copy becomes quite impossible. The fact that in blockchain data are unique and inalterable solves this problem. It is not by coincidence that blockchain technology emerged with Bitcoin and virtual currencies in general. Blockchain technology overcomes the so-called 'double spending problem', i.e. the same amount of value is spent twice.

Blockchain can store every kind of data and it can represent assets in digital forms. These digital assets, or tokens, can be native blockchain (like virtual currencies), or a representation of existing assets, both digital (e.g. intellectual property) and physical (e.g. a house). The most advanced blockchain platforms make these tokens programmable thanks to smart contracts.

A smart contract is the most advanced blockchain functionality. A smart contract is a deterministic computer program that can execute according to predetermined instructions and inputs. Therefore, blockchain platforms that can store smart contracts can perform more complex computational operations on the chain.

Smart contracts can be blockchain-based, but they were not born with the blockchain. They can also exist in traditional database architectures. Blockchain-based smart contracts take advantage of blockchain properties. Once added on the blockchain, they cannot be unilaterally changed or modified. As a result, they cannot avoid execution or execute themselves differently.

Smart contracts, despite the referral to 'contracts', are not contracts. They do not always have a legal meaning. They can automate every action or operation. Thus, they can give rise to innumerable use cases, from supply chains to the public sector. Of course, smart contracts can get legal relevance, also in the contractual domain. In the latter case, someone suggested talking about 'smart legal contracts'. Here, smart contracts are tools for performing contractual obligations automatically, without human actions. Smart contracts might also represent contractual conditions in computer language.

The use of deterministic computer programs to enter into and perform contractual agreements in place of the parties is not new. Unlike in the past, the decentralisation and tamper-resistance of blockchain prevent the parties from controlling and influencing the automatic execution of the contract. For this reason, blockchain-based smart contracts are considered self-enforcing and capable of removing the need to trust that the obliged party performs the contract. Scholars usually associate the adoption of blockchain technology for the conclusion/execution of contracts to the computer scientist Nick Szabo. In the 1990s, he envisioned that computer software could completely substitute humans in contractual activities, and reduce delays, obstacles, and disputes determined by the unreliability of people. He talked about 'smart contracts'. Probably the theories of Szabo have become a reality with the invention of blockchain technology. This study focuses precisely on the legal implications of applying blockchain-based smart contracts in the contractual environment.

## *II. Research problem*

Since Bitcoin and the first applications, blockchain experimentations are growing exponentially. Industries are making significant investments to correct technical problems and aim to mass-market adoption. Institutions have recognised blockchain potentials and are trying to spread knowledge about blockchain characteristics and suitable uses. For instance, the United Nations Innovation Network (UNIN) has published the 'Blockchain Practical Guide'.[1] It has created the Atrium, an interagency platform to study and promote blockchain development through collaboration between UN different agencies.[2] The Organisation for Economic Cooperation and Development (OECD) has the Global Blockchain Policy Centre,[3] an international reference point for policymakers on blockchain to support governments to research and analyse the impacts and opportunities of the technology.

In Europe, 30 European countries have signed the European Blockchain Partnership.[4] The signatories of the declaration commit to working together towards realising the potential of blockchain-based services for the benefit of citizens, society, and economy. In particular, they created the European Blockchain Services Infrastructure (EBSI) to develop cross-border digital public services based on blockchain technology. In February 2018 the European Commission, in collaboration with the European Parliament, launched the European Blockchain Observatory and Forum, which hosts lively debates, organises workshops, and produces reports to accelerate blockchain innovation.[5] The European Union has already spent 180 million euros to support research and innovation in blockchain.[6]

Like every new impacting phenomenon, blockchain technology needs a regulatory response. Indeed, besides the positive aspects, it might also bring risks or raise new legal questions. The above initiatives were specifically born to help countries, stakeholders, and consumers to face such challenges and find proper legal answers and protections.

Concerning smart legal contracts, legal scholars affirm that blockchain-based smart contracts could foster the development of electronic commerce thanks to automation, simplification, costs, and time saving. Via the added value of blockchain, they represent the evolution of Surden's computable contracts. However, authors have outlined several legal shortcomings and profiles regarding the entire life cycle of contracts, from

1 <https://atrium.uninnovation.network/guide> accessed 1 October 2021.

2 <https://www.uninnovation.network/blockchain> accessed 1 October 2021.

3 <https://www.oecd.org/going-digital/topics/blockchain/> accessed 1 October 2021.

4 <https://digital-strategy.ec.europa.eu/en/news/european-countries-join-blockchain-partnership> accessed 1 October 2021. In the context of Brexit, UK is no longer an active member of the partnership.

5 <https://www.eublockchainforum.eu/> accessed 1 October 2021.

6 <https://digital-strategy.ec.europa.eu/en/policies/blockchain-funding> accessed 1 October 2021.

formation to performance. On this point, the Resolution of 3 October 2018 of the European Parliament 'Distributed ledger technologies and blockchains: building trust with disintermediation'[7] stresses that the European Commission needs to undertake an in-depth assessment of the legal implications of smart contracts, in particular by use-case monitoring and conducting an in-depth analysis of the existing legal framework in the individual Member States.[8] Then, in its Resolution of 20 October 2020 'Digital Services Act: adapting commercial and civil law rules for commercial entities operating online',[9] the European Parliament considers that the European Commission should provide guidance to ensure legal certainty around the civil and commercial aspects surrounding smart contract, and make proposals for the appropriate legal framework.[10]

The European Commission has commissioned a study to examine legal and regulatory aspects related to blockchain-inspired technologies as well as the socio-economic impacts of blockchain technology. The 2020 full Study Report, entitled 'Study on Blockchains: Legal, Governance and Interoperability Aspects',[11] also focuses on some legal issues about smart contracts and contract law. Namely, it takes into consideration: the cross-border dimension of smart contracts, especially concerning the applicable law and jurisdiction; the national legal requirements on the need for a written form of the contract; consumer's protection; the problem of pseudonymous identities, for instance in determining contract capacity; the difficulty of understanding computer-coded contracts by parties without the necessary technical background, that raises the question of how they can negotiate, draft and adjudicate smart contracts. These analyses are necessary for blockchain development, to the extent that the research showed that observers regard 'legal certainty' and 'regulation clarity' as critical barriers to this end.

Member States are also starting to outline their national strategies. In Italy, the Ministry of Economic Development has set up a group of 30 experts. They have redacted a document containing some proposals for

7 <https://www.europarl.europa.eu/doceo/document/TA-8-2018-0373_EN.html> accessed 1 October 2021.

8 See paragraphs from 36 to 38 of the Resolution.

9 <https://www.europarl.europa.eu/doceo/document/TA-9-2020-0273_EN.pdf> accessed 1 October 2021.

10 See, in particular, par. 32.

11 <https://digital-strategy.ec.europa.eu/en/library/study-blockchains-legal-governance-and-interoperability-aspects-smart-20180038> accessed 1 October 2021.

an Italian strategy for blockchain technology.[12] The proposals aim, among others, to provide the country with a competitive regulatory framework. According to a study conducted by the OECD's Centre for Entrepreneurship, SMEs, Regions and Cities, one of the major obstacles to the adoption of blockchain technology in Italy is regulatory uncertainty.[13]

The United Nations Commission on International Trade Law (UNCITRAL) and the International Institute for the Unification of Private Law (UNIDROIT) can play a key role at a more international level. As intergovernmental organisations tasked with the unification of private law, they can help national legislations update to modern-day technologies. The work of UNCITRAL and UNIDROIT is still at an initial stage. On 6 and 7 of May 2019, they organised a joint workshop on legal issues arising from the use of smart contracts, artificial intelligence and distributed ledger technology. The primary purpose of the event was to identify topics for future work to ensure that legal regulations are kept up-to-date with those new technologies. On that occasion, the panellists highlighted the need to seek clarity in regulating new technologies for commercial actors. On 10 and 11 March 2020, UNCITRAL hosted the second session of the workshop.[14]

In summary, appropriate clarifications on the applicable legal framework to smart legal contracts would enhance trust among blockchain entrepreneurs and promote further investments.

## *III. Research objective and question*

The objective of the present research is to investigate the implications of blockchain-based smart contracts on contract law. In light of the need for better clarity on legal compliance of these applications, expressed above, it

---

12 *Proposte per la Strategia italiana in materia di tecnologie basate su registri condivisi e Blockchain – Sintesi per la consultazione pubblica*. The document is accessible at the following link: <https://www.mise.gov.it/index.php/it/consultazione-blockchain> accessed 1 October 2021.

13 <https://www.mise.gov.it/index.php/en/news/2039990-mise-and-oecd-on-blockchain-italy-is-the-first-eu-country-to-finance-a-study-on-startups-and-smes> accessed 1 October 2021.

14 A summary of the discussion and conclusions of both workshops is available at this link <https://unidroit.aedstudio.net/law-technology/> accessed 1 October 2021.

would like to focus on the impact of the characteristics of blockchain in contracting.

It has already been given an account of the assumptions of legal experts in this regard. It was noticed that research in this area is still relatively limited. There is indeed plenty of literature on this topic. International, European and national institutions organise conferences and workshops, involving experts or disbursing funds to undertake studies. However, on the one hand, they are confined to put in evidence problematic issues and formulate legal questions, without giving specific answers. On the other hand, they take into consideration different aspects but do not provide in-depth legal analysis. It is intended to assess in details the most recurrent observations and address the following research question:

- How blockchain-based smart contracts fit into contract law?

Indeed, smart contracts do not exist in a legal vacuum. There are contract law principles and rules, enabling or regulatory, binding, or belonging to soft law, international, European, or domestic. Therefore, it is thought that one should give priority to existing rules and legal instruments that can potentially apply and be adapted to smart contracts. The latter can provide a sufficient legal basis for smart contracts and not require any additional legislation. Further normative production might generate interpretational difficulties, complexity, and fragmentation leading to an opposite effect.

To establish if actual disciplines are still adequate, or new regulations are needed, one should wonder whether the technology raises old or new legal issues according to its specific uses and applications. In other terms, old questions do not imply new answers. In a nutshell, related sub-questions derived from the main research question would be as follows:

- Which novelties do smart contracts bring?
- Which are the same legal questions and implications?
- Which ones are new and peculiar of blockchain technology?
- For new ones, does existing regulation suffice? Or is new regulation needed?

## *IV. Methodology*

To answer the aforementioned research questions, a technical description of blockchain technology and smart contracts is firstly provided. Blockchain is still an immature technology and it is the result of a combination of pre-existing technologies. For this reason, its comprehension is not so clear, especially for non-experts.

A good understanding of blockchain functioning and characteristics is fundamental to make proper legal classification and analysis. In this respect, it is noticed that sometimes there is confusion among legal experts. This is thought not only because they move within a new field of study, but also due to an overlap between blockchain inner features and the anarchist ideology that surrounded its invention. Moreover, the same words can have different meanings in the technical or legal domain. This contributed to the spread of some false myths that this work tries to clarify. To this end, in addition to the selection of the best literature, the research period was characterised by participation in national and international conferences, attendance of courses, and individual meetings with some blockchain stakeholders, academics, and members of associations. Another relevant aspect is that there is a large variety of blockchains. It was attempted to give an overview of the various kinds of blockchain and highlight those differences that imply different legal considerations.

Secondly, the legal literature on this topic was consulted and the most recurring and discussed legal implications of blockchain-based smart contracts for contract law selected. The analysis developed by starting from the latter. Blockchain-based smart contracts were connected with current legal frameworks.

Contract law is conceived on a national basis. Rules on contracts come mostly from domestic law and the European legislature lacks a general competence for private law. There are also supranational rules on contracts. However, soft law is not binding, even though it can harmonise national contract laws. On the other hand, binding norms need ratification by States. In general, contract law is mainly under the control of the nations. Therefore, to get more high-quality work, Italian contract law was chosen as domestic law. At the same time, to make the research accessible also to a non-Italian audience, the Principles of European Contract Law (PECL), the Draft Common Frame of Reference (DFCR) and the UNIDROIT Principles of International Commercial Contracts (PICC) were applied.

Nick Szabo, the first one to coin the expression 'smart contract', considered vending machines as the ancestors of this technology. From vending machines to Electronic Data Interchange, the invention of the Internet, software agents, and artificial intelligence, scholars have started to inquire about the relationships between the use of machines for the conclusion/performance of contracts and existing legal apparatus. This process led to the interpretation of old rules to fit the new context or create new regulations when necessary. Because blockchain-based smart contracts are another step of the evolution of electronic contracts, international, European, and Italian regulations that have flourished on electronic commerce are considered. It is also verified whether the adjustments to traditional contract law to fit electronic commerce can be valid for smart contracts.

Lastly, blockchain technology can have various governance structures. Regulation should not govern technology, but aspects of its application. So, the analysis does not move from the technology as such, but from how the technology is used. Thus, it concentrates on four scenarios of the use of blockchain technology in the realm of contracts. The scenarios result from an observation about the market moves in this field, starting from some concrete examples.

## *V. Structure of the book.*

The book is composed of 7 chapters. Chapter 1 is dedicated to the explanation of blockchain technology and smart contracts. It describes blockchain properties and typologies. It illustrates blockchain origins and evolution and clarifies some false myths. Then, it moves to smart contracts, which are the most advanced blockchain applications. It focuses on Ethereum, the most famous blockchain platform for smart contracts, and depicts the various uses of smart contracting platforms.

Chapter 2 concerns the use of blockchain-based smart contracts in the contractual domain. It distinguishes between smart contract code and smart legal contracts. It talks about Nick Szabo who originated the expression 'smart contract' and the ancestors of smart contracts, starting from vending machines. It summarises the characteristics of smart legal contracts. It reports existing literature to identify the most recurring and discussed aspects, which are the subject matter of the legal analysis in chapters 4, 5, and 6. The remaining sections have regard to the different hypotheses of regulation of smart legal contracts, making a parallel with the theories that arose around the Internet, and to the first attempts of regulation by countries. It concludes by giving an account of the most suitable types of contracts that can be represented in code and by delineating four possible scenarios of use of blockchain-based smart legal contracts. As affirmed in the previous section on methodology, the study shall consider how the technology is used.

Chapter 3 focuses on the impact of technology on contract law, from vending machines to nowadays. It encompasses contract formation, contract performance and liability, jurisdiction and applicable law in cross-border contracts. For each of them, it gives an account of the problematic issues and legal responses. The chapter aims to fix existing regulations on electronic commerce as the basis of the analysis. Moreover, it is intended to identify potential similarities with the current legal debate on smart contracts. In other words, it should help to verify which implications of blockchain-based smart contracts on contract law are new, and which ones do not differ from the past. In the latter case, the same legal aspects imply identical solutions.

Chapters 4, 5, and 6 develop the main arguments. Chapter 4 is about contract formation, chapter 5 is about contract performance, and chapter 6 is about jurisdiction and applicable law in cross-border contracts.

Chapter 4 investigates contract requirements. More specifically, it deals with the agreement, the contractual intention, and the form. It investigates the exchange of offer and acceptance, their revocation, the time of conclusion of the contract, the applicability of supplementary norms set by the e-Commerce Directive and the Consumer Rights Directive on information requirements and acknowledgment of receipt. It wonders whether it can be said that the party had the intention to conclude a legally binding contract given that the average man is not capable of understanding the language of the code. For the same reason, a section considers the annulment of the contract concluded under a mistake. As regards the form, it is dwelled on the possibility for on-chain contracts to satisfy the requirement of the written form. A section explores the conclusion of smart contracts by machines, both software agents and systems of artificial intelligence. In this event, smart contracts are not only executed but also concluded 'smart'. The chapter ends with a reflection on the actual possibility to conclude contracts solely in the form of lines of code.

Chapter 5 is divided into two parts. Part 1 has regard to the self-enforcement of smart contracts and the shift from trust in the other party to trust in the code. It examines the suitability of existing rules on contractual liability to blockchain-based smart contracts. To do that, it makes some clarifications of the meanings of some terms and refers to the four scenarios. It also examines the supposed problem of identifying the liable party in case of disputes because of the pseudo-anonymity of blockchain participants. Part 2 addresses the relationship between blockchain immutability and ex-post interventions on the contract. It criticises the idea that blockchain technology is immutable, and gives some clarifications on that point; secondly, it takes into consideration some forms of legal intervention on the contract, and describes them starting from Italian contract law and by making some parallels with the general principles; thirdly, it verifies the applicability of the above remedies and rights of the parties in the field of blockchain-based smart legal contracts and gives an account of the primary technical solutions suggested by the scholars to stop or modify the execution of smart contracts. Lastly, it examines the possibility for the parties to renounce *ex-ante* to such remedies and rights.

Chapter 6 closes the analysis with the matter of jurisdiction and applicable law in disputes for cross-border contracts whose conclusion or performance occurs through blockchain-based smart contracts. Some scholars have identified incompatibilities between blockchain characteristics and existing rules. More specifically, the anonymity of the parties and problems in the exact localisation of the nodes would hinder identifying the connecting factors. It is verified whether and to what extent blockchain technology is (or is not) suitable to existing rules. It is also made a brief reference to Online Dispute Resolution mechanisms.

Chapter 7 makes a summary of the above results and some closing remarks.

# CHAPTER 1: INTRODUCTION TO BLOCKCHAIN AND SMART CONTRACTS

## 1. *Definition and functioning of blockchain.*

Blockchain is a distributed ledger technology (DLT). It is a ledger or a database, which is used to store data. It is distributed because a copy of the same data is replicated across a network of nodes.[15] Nodes are electronic devices, while a network is a group of nodes that can communicate.[16] Someone affirms that blockchain is an application layer that runs on top of the Internet.[17]

In distributed systems, nodes coordinate to achieve the same outcome. The result is that users perceive them as a single one.[18] Distributed systems emerged to overcome two main problems.[19] Firstly, they are more secure in case of shutdowns. Centralised systems have one server, while distributed systems rely on several servers that continue to operate through data replication.[20] Secondly, traditional client-server systems become overwhelmed when the data traffic is very high. The hardware has to be upgraded, which can be very expensive to face more requests. Distributed

---

15 J. Bacon, J. D. Michels, C. Millard, J. Singh, 'Blockchain Demystified', Queen Mary University of London, School of Law, Legal Studies Research Paper No. 268/2017, 4 <https://ssrn.com/abstract=3091218> accessed 1 October 2021.

16 European Commission, 'Study on Blockchains – Legal, governance and interoperability aspects' (n 11) 26–27.

17 P. De Filippi, A. Wright (eds), *Blockchchain and the law – the rule of code* (Harvard University Press 2018) 46–49. The authors explain that the Internet can be divided into five layers. At the bottom, the physical layer is represented by all hardware components and is necessary to transfer information. Then, there is the data link layer, the protocols that interface with hardware. The network layer consists of IP addresses that transmit packets of data to their destination. The transport layer ensures correct data fragmentation and reassembly. The last is the application layer, which enables people to interact thanks with online services daily. These five layers are also known as the TCP/IP model.

18 I. Bashir (ed), *Mastering Blockchain* (2nd edn Packt 2018) 38.

19 De Filippi, Wright (n 17) 17.

20 They provide fault tolerance, i.e., ensure that the system works if some nodes fail and become unresponsive.

systems are more efficient and less costly because more computers hold the same information.

In distributed ledgers, consensus algorithms ensure that all nodes return the same latest version of the data. They set the rules to update the system.[21]

Not all DLTs are blockchains.[22] The peculiarity of blockchain is that the records of the transactions -the most granular piece of information that can be shared among a blockchain network – are grouped to form a block. The blocks are so linked to form a chain. The term 'blockchain' derives from this particular way to collect transactions. Blockchain is an append-only ledger, which means that data can only be added.[23]

The consensus protocol provides that each node adds the same new block to its local version of the database in the blockchain. There are different consensus protocols, depending on the type of blockchain and application.[24]

A hash represents each block. A hash is a unique string of random letters and numbers of a fixed length. Every change in the underlying data results in a variation in the corresponding hash. A block is usually composed of two parts: the header and the body. The header contains the hash, the hash of the preceding block, and some metadata, such as a timestamp (*Figure 1*). The body incorporates the transactions. In the body, each transaction has its hash. All hashes of a block recreate a Merkle Tree, where the hashes of the single transactions are the leaves, and the hash of the block is the root.

---

21 M. Finck (ed), *Blockchain regulation and governance in Europe* (Cambridge University Press 2018) 19–20.

22 Bacon *et al.* (n 15) 4–5.

23 Others include 'block-less blockchains', where transactions are not grouped into blocks, but chained together in a way that only allows the addition of data. See G. Hileman, M. Rauchs, '2017 Global Blockchain Benchmarking Study' (*SSRN*, 22 September 2017) 21 <https://ssrn.com/abstract=3040224> accessed 1 October 2021.

24 See below Section 5.

The hashes of the leaves are hashed in couples to produce an internal hash until a single hash is calculated, representing the root of the tree (*Figure 2*).

*Figure 1: representation of three chained blocks showing the content of every block*

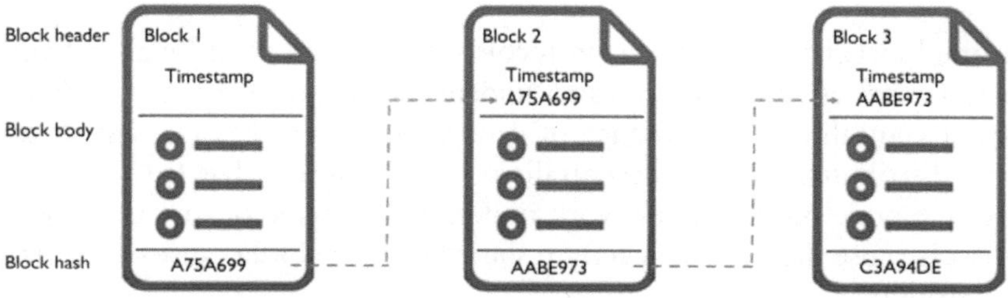


Source: Bacon et al (n 15) 8.

*Figure 2: a Merkle Tree*

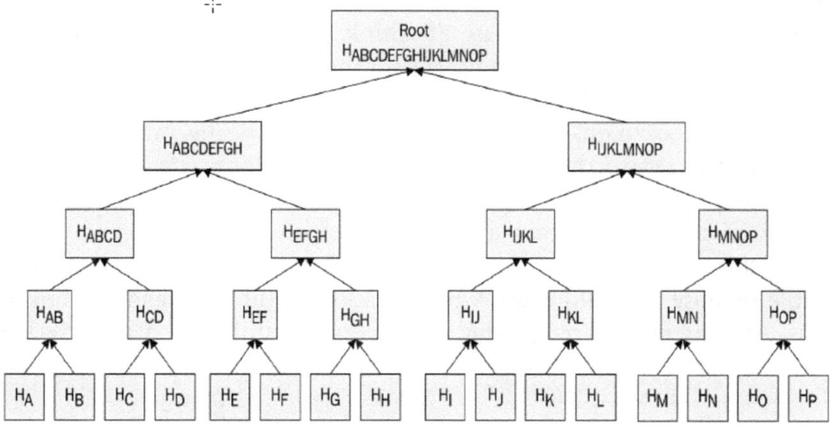


Source: Bashir (n 18) 199.

Each user has a pair of keys: one is private, and the other is public. The public key acts as a sort of public address and the other users use it to send transactions to the key owner. The private key has to be kept secret because it serves to add transactions.

The user signs the transaction with her private key. The transaction is broadcasted to the validator nodes. Validator nodes are nodes in charge of processing the transaction and assembling new blocks. They validate the block according to pre-set rules (the consensus algorithm).[25] Then, the block is added to the blockchain.[26]

## 2. *Properties of blockchain.*

In the blockchain, consensus protocols – i.e. software run by all network nodes – pre-establish the rules to update the ledger. Thus, the updating is not centralised. The absence of central control makes the system not only distributed but also decentralised.[27] One can say that trust is not in a single node but in the network nodes. Nodes agree on the truth of an event because they agree on certain shared rules.[28] Not because of arbitrary imposition.

The single version of the truth guarantees that data are shared in a more efficient, less costly, and more transparent way. Indeed, instead of maintaining different databases, it is as if the parties share a single ledger because there is an assurance that everyone stores and sees the same data. Moreover, the system avoids expensive and error-prone reconciliation processes between isolated databases.[29] Think, for example, to parties that have to share their information because of their business, such as banks.

The peculiarity of blockchain is its tamper-resistance. As already described, in blockchain, data are hashed. It is practically impossible that different data return the same hash value. So, hashing safeguards the integrity of the data. Hashes of the single transactions and the various blocks are linked together to form a Merkel Tree (inside a block) or a chain (of blocks). Consequently, any unauthorised change will be immediately visible–because it would cause a modification of the hash and the linked ones. Any attempt of re-hashing could be successful only if the attacker

25 European Union Blockchain Observatory and Forum, 'Legal and Regulatory Framework of Blockchains and Smart Contracts' (thematic Report, 27 September 2019) 38 <https://www.eublockchainforum.eu/reports> accessed 1 October 2021.

26 Finck (n 21) 20.

27 Distributed ledgers are a subset of distributed databases. The difference is that distributed ledgers operate in an adversarial environment (i.e. assuming not every participant is honest), and are designed to be Byzantine fault-tolerant (which means that they can run even if a certain number of nodes are acting maliciously). See Bacon *et al.* (n 15) 23.

28 Finck (n 21) 7.

29 Hileman, Rauchs (n 23) 16.

re-hashes all the subsequent blocks, and if the majority of nodes collude to change the current state of the ledger.[30] Even changes are theoretically possible in practice, they would be complicated and costly. Validator nodes primarily continue to add new transactions and blocks to the chain, so every following hash must be recalculated before validator nodes process recent transactions. This operation becomes harder the longer the chain is, and the older is the block subject to modification.[31] Moreover, reaching a new consensus is more or less likely or convenient depending on the typology of blockchain.[32] For this reason, it is assumed that blockchain is immutable.

Blockchain combines hash functions and asymmetric cryptography.[33] Asymmetric cryptography – i.e. the private and the public key that every user holds to transact – is resistant to unauthorised data access and preserves the confidentiality of the data. Indeed, in asymmetric cryptography, the key that is used to encrypt the data differs from the key used to decrypt it. So, asymmetric cryptography is more secure than symmetric cryptography because it is not necessary to share a key to decrypt a message.[34] Moreover, asymmetric cryptography allows the verification by the receiver of the provenance and integrity of the received message. The sender encrypts the data with her private key and sends both the encrypted message and its hash. The receiver decrypts the message with the sender's public key. If the result is identical to the hash, the recipient is ensured that the message originated from the sender and was not modified by third parties.

The time-sequential order of data in concatenated blocks, hashing functions, and asymmetric cryptography make blockchain very secure.[35] Besides, the same characteristics render it non-repudiable, in the sense that it provides incontrovertible evidence that an event occurred at a determined time and from a specific address. Hence, non-repudiation enhances the transparency of the blockchain.

---

30 De Filippi, Wright (n 17) 25.

31 De Filippi, Wright (n 17) 36.

32 See below Section 5.

33 Bashir (n 18) 154–155.

34 In symmetric cryptography, the encryption key coincides with the decryption key. In asymmetric cryptography, the sender encrypts the message with the recipient's public key. The recipient decrypts the message with her private key, which is kept secret by the receiver.

35 Bashir (n 18) 47.

### *3. Origins.*

Blockchain technology originated from a group of crypto-anarchists, called 'The Cypherpunk Movement', whose manifesto suggested the use of information technology to defend everybody's privacy, safe from government institutions, relying on cryptography and anonymous systems for sending e-mails, digital signatures, and electronic money.[36] They wanted to recreate a sort of 'new universal order', free from classic third-party intermediaries who verified people's identity or ensured payments among strangers.[37] They had the idea that machines could substitute humans, and provide more reliability and trust.[38]

In 1983, the cryptographer David Chaum proposed a system for creating and transferring electronic cash that was anonymous and untraceable.[39] In 1994 he launched his company, DigiCash.[40] DigiCash relied on Chaum's digital signatures based on asymmetric cryptography. DigiCash was still centralised because Chaum's company validated every transaction via a client-server model.[41] Instead, the ultimate goal of the movement was to eliminate the need for centralised forms of control. In particular, they had to overcome the 'double spending' problem.[42] Indeed, digital cash can be easily copied without a central bank or other trusted intermediaries. So, in the absence of a third party, a subject would have sent the same amount to more recipients.

---

36 E. Hughes, 'A Cypherpunk's Manifesto' (1993) <https://www.activism.net/cypherpunk/manifesto.html> accessed 1 October 2021.

37 D. Chaum, 'Security without Identification: Transaction Systems to Make Big Brother Obsolete' (1985) 28(10) Communications of the ACM 1030.

38 T. C. May, 'The Cyphernomicon: Cypherpunks FAQ and More, Version 0.666' (1994) <https://hackmd.io/@jmsjsph/TheCyphernomicon> accessed 1 October 2021.

39 D. Chaum, 'Blind Signatures for Untraceable Payments' in D. Chaum, R. L. Rivest, A. T. Sherman (eds), *Advances in Cryptology: Proceedings of Crypto 82* (Springer 1983), 199.

40 P. H. Lewis, 'Attention Internet Shoppers: E-Cash Is Here' (*New York Times*, 19 October 1994) <http://www.nytimes.com/1994/10/19/business/attention-internet-shoppers-e-cash-is-here.html> accessed 1 October 2021.

41 J. Brodesser, 'First Monday Interviews: David Chaum' (*First Monday*, 5 July 1999) <http://journals.uic.edu/ojs/index.php/fm/article/view/683/593> accessed 1 October 2021.

42 U. W. Chohan, 'The Double Spending Problem and Cryptocurrencies' (*SSRN*, 19 December 2017) <https://ssrn.com/abstract=3090174> accessed 1 October 2021.

In 2008, Satoshi Nakamoto[43] published an article[44] where he described a peer-to-peer electronic cash system that relied on a network of computers instead of ~~on~~ a centralised operator to validate transactions.[45] The system, called Bitcoin, was launched in 2009 and represented the first blockchain application.

In Bitcoin, anyone can get access to the platform and start to transact.[46] People interact by using a wallet where they keep the digital coins (the bitcoins).[47] People can store their wallets online or offline[48] and sign their operations through their private key. The private key is secret, while the public key is public and links the transactions to a Bitcoin address. In Bitcoin, identities are unknown, according to the Cypherphunks' dream.[49] Bitcoin functions as data storage replicated on an indefinite number of computers spread across the world. The network can continue to grow because access is not subject to restriction. Transactions – i.e. exchanges

---

43 The name Satoshi Nakamoto is a pseudonym.

44 S. Nakamoto, 'Bitcoin: A Peer-to-Peer Electronic Cash System' (2008) <https://bitcoin.org/bitcoin.pdf> accessed 1 October 2021.

45 In the abstract of the article, Nakamoto affirms: 'We propose a solution to the double-spending problem using a peer-to-peer network. The network timestamps transactions by hashing them into an ongoing chain of hash-based proof-of-work, forming a record that cannot be changed without redoing the proof-of-work. The longest chain not only serves as proof of the sequence of events witnessed, but proof that it came from the largest pool of CPU power. As long as a majority of CPU power is controlled by nodes that are not cooperating to attack the network, they'll generate the longest chain and outpace attackers. The network itself requires minimal structure. Messages are broadcast on a best effort basis, and nodes can leave and rejoin the network at will, accepting the longest proof-of-work chain as proof of what happened while they were gone.'

46 On Bitcoin, see A. M. Antonopoulos (ed), *Mastering Bitcoin* (2nd edn O'Reilly 2017). Bitcoin is a permissionless blockchain. On permissionless blockchains, see below Section 5.

47 Bitcoin, with the capital letter, refers to the protocol, while bitcoin with the lowercase letter indicates the exchanged units of value.

48 There are wallet service providers that offer online wallets, accessible online ('hot wallets'). Users can also maintain their wallets offline, e.g. in a USB flash drive ('cold wallets').

49 Eric Hughes's Chyperpunk's Manifesto declares: '...privacy in an open society requires anonymous transaction systems. Until now, cash has been the primary such system. An anonymous transaction system is not a secret transaction system. An anonymous system empowers individuals to reveal their identity when desired and only when desired; this is the essence of privacy... We the Cypherpunks are dedicated to building anonymous systems. We are defending our privacy with cryptography, with anonymous mail forwarding systems, with digital signatures, and with electronic money'.

of bitcoins from one address to another – are grouped in blocks and chronologically ordered through hashes, as described above.[50] The protocol searches through all previous transactions to avoid the double-spending problem and verifies that a user has enough bitcoins to send. If it is the case, the transaction is valid and is added to a block. Otherwise, the network rejects the transaction. The code substitutes central trusted authorities.

### 4. *Evolution.*

After Bitcoin, other similar platforms have developed for the exchange of crypto-currencies. Up to date, there are more than twelve thousand kinds of virtual currencies,[51] and they are continuously growing.[52]

Then, blockchain has gone beyond the trading of crypto-currencies. It has made it possible to transfer other digital assets than just digital currency. Digital assets are the digital representation of goods or rights, such as votes, equities or diplomas. Theoretically, everything can be stored on a blockchain. For example, in 2012, the launch of the Colored Coin protocol[53] enabled parties to log other digital elements in addition to bitcoins.[54]

The most advanced blockchain platforms are equipped to store computer programs, called 'smart contracts'. Smart contracts can run automatically upon the occurrence of a specified condition according to prespecified functions. Every resulting change (transaction) is stored in the blockchain. These smart contracts – as the name suggests – are used in the field of contracting for the automatic execution of contractual conditions.[55]

---

50 See above Sections 1 and 2.

51 <https://coinmarketcap.com> accessed 1 October 2021.

52 Virtual currencies have attracted the attention of the financial institutions that have warned about the related risks (e.g. high volatility, risk of fraud, anti-money laundering). Such worries are primarily due to the novelty of these products that need proper regulation. The work does not deepen these aspects because it focuses on smart contracts and contract law.

53 <https://en.bitcoin.it/wiki/Colored_Coins> accessed 1 October 2021.

54 M. L. Perugini, P. Dal Checco, 'Smart Contracts: A Preliminary Evaluation' (*SSRN*, 8 December 2015) 17–18 <https://ssrn.com/abstract=2729548> accessed 1 October 2021.

55 Analysing the implications of blockchain-based smart contracts on contract law is the research topic of the work.

Therefore, blockchain has evolved, and the complexity of operations that can be done on it has increased. To stress blockchain development, someone differentiates blockchain platforms into three main categories: Platforms 1.0, 2.0, and 3.0.[56] Platforms 1.0 are digital currency protocols. Platforms 2.0 are Colored Coins and those where users can transact more than only crypto-currencies. Platforms 3.0 are the ones that manage the storage of smart contracts.

Another classification takes into consideration the sectors with investments in blockchain solutions. An author elaborated three categories: Blockchain 1.0, Blockchain 2.0, and Blockchain 3.0.[57] Blockchain 1.0 is about currencies, such as currency transfers and remittances. Blockchain 2.0 is about financial contracts[58] and applications. Blockchain 3.0 is about blockchain applications beyond finance, particularly in government, health, science, literature, culture, and art. In 2017, the European Parliament tried to identify the main areas of application of the blockchain.[59] The study lists eight fields: currency, digital content, patents, e-voting, smart contracts, supply chains, public services, and decentralised autonomous organisations.[60] In its more recent Resolution of 2018,[61] the European Parliament has highlighted that DLT-based applications 'could potentially affect all sectors of the economy'.[62] Because of its versatility, somebody compares blockchain to an operating system, such as Microsoft Windows or macOS, where many applications can run.[63] Blockchain applications are called DApps, which stands for Decentralised Applications (given that blockchain is a decentralised system).

---

56 Perugini, Dal Checco (n 54) 18.

57 M. Swan (ed), *Blockchain. Blueprint for a new economy* (O' Reilly 2015) IX.

58 The financial sector is dedicating huge experiments and funds to blockchain technology.

59 P. Boucher, 'How blockchain technology could change our lives – In-depth Analysis' (*EPRS European Parliamentary Research Service*, February 2017) <https://www.europarl.europa.eu/RegData/etudes/IDAN/2017/581948/EPRS_IDA(2017)581948_EN.pdf> accessed 1 October 2021.

60 Decentralised autonomous organisations (DAOs) are forms of organisations that rely on blockchain technology and smart contracts as their primary source of governance. See below Section 10.

61 European Parliament resolution of 3 October 2018 on distributed ledger technologies and blockchains: building trust with disintermediation (2017/2772(RSP)) P8_TA-PROV(2018)0373.

62 Par. 3.

63 M. Gupta (ed), *Blockchain for dummies – IBM Limited Editions* (John Wiley & Sons 2017) 6.

Since its initial conception in 2008, blockchain has expanded rapidly all around the world. Even though most applications are in their preliminary stage, it is expected to become mature around 2025.[64] According to the World Economic Forum, blockchain will represent 10 % of the GDP in 2025.[65] The European Union Blockchain Observatory and Forum has confirmed this trend in a report.[66]

Blockchain is considered a revolutionary invention, like was the Internet in the 1990s.[67] It is believed that blockchain characteristics fit the needs of the market. This might be the cause of its success.[68] In the age of information society and globalisation, transaction volumes are growing exponentially worldwide. There is a strong necessity for safe, transparent, and trustworthy systems considering the risks of long-distance negotiations between unknown parties. At the same time, the recourse to traditional client-server and centralised systems can be costly and time-consuming, and the advantages of technology (i.e. fastness and simplicity) can be lost. The properties of blockchain technology, described above,[69] might help to face these needs.

### 5. *Typologies.*

There is a large variety of blockchains. Differences have regard to the different types of permission granted to network participants. Namely, the permission to read (i.e. to access the ledger and see its transactions), to write (i.e. to generate transactions and send them to the network), and to commit (i.e. to update the state of the ledger).[70]

---

64 Bashir (n 18) 35.

65 World Economic Forum, Global Agenda Council on the Future of Software & Society, 'Deep Shift – Technology Tipping Points and Societal Impact (Survey Report, September 2015) 24 <https://www.weforum.org/reports> accessed 1 October 2021.

66 European Union Blockchain Observatory and Forum, 'EU Blockchain Observatory and Forum 2018–2020 Conclusions and Reflections' (thematic Report, 25 June 2020) 12–15 <https://www.eublockchainforum.eu/sites/default/files/reports/report_conclusion_book_v1.0.pdf> accessed 1 October 2021.

67 S. Davidson, P. De Filippi, J. Potts, 'Disrupting Governance: The New Institutional Economics of Distributed Ledger Technology' (*SSRN*, 22 July 2016) 2 <https://ssrn.com/abstract=2811995> accessed 1 October 2021.

68 Gupta (n 63) 19.

69 See above Section 2.

70 Hileman, Rauchs (n 23) 20.

Concerning the right to read transactions, there is a distinction between public and private blockchains. Public blockchains have a high degree of openness because anyone can read the transactions.[71] Instead, designers of private blockchains can make transactions only visible to certain users (affected by those specific transactions).

The literature distinguishes between permissionless and permissioned blockchains, which refers to the permission to write and commit. In the former case, anyone can become a user and write transactions without pre-identification. Any computer can be a node in the network.[72] Furthermore, everyone can add new blocks and update the ledger. In the second case, only pre-selected participants can transact in the network, only authorized devices can take part as nodes and add blocks. While permissionless blockchains are general-purpose, permissioned ones are often designed to fit a specific need. Thus, permissioned blockchains are not open to everyone. For the same reason, they are usually private, while permissionless blockchains are generally public.[73] In the middle, there can be several types of blockchains (*Table 1*).

As stated above,[74] there are various consensus protocols. The choice is strictly linked with the typology of blockchain and not all consensus mechanisms are suitable for all types of blockchains.

In permissionless blockchains, the system does not belong to anyone; thus, there is a need to incentivise people to put their devices at the disposal of the network.[75] Therefore, nodes are offered to maintain the network with the promise to get a reward for their job. Moreover, free

---

71 Blockchain Explorers are used to view transactions that are similar to web browsers. For example, Bitcoin Block Explorer allows anyone to view information on the Bitcoin blockchain (<https://www.blockchain.com/it/explorer> accessed 1 October 2021). Usually, users only view the hashes of the transactions and the hashes of users' public keys. So, blockchain can guarantee a certain level of anonymity. For example, in Bitcoin, the public can see that an address is sending some bitcoins to another, but without information on real-world identities. However, this could pose some problems from a data protection perspective, considered that there are different techniques to trace back to encrypted data. Taking up the example of Bitcoin, there are different ways to discover the underlying identity, such as when the address appears in a blog, or when crypto-currencies are exchanged with money in exchange platforms.

72 Permissionless ledgers rely on open-source software that anyone can download.

73 It might also be that a permissioned blockchain is public. But it is very unlikely that a permissionless one is private.

74 Section 1.

75 De Filippi, Wright (n 17) 25.

access in permissioned ledgers is risky because malicious actors could flood the system by adding new nodes and new blocks, with the possibility to gain control of the network.[76] To prevent this, the operation to add new blocks is rendered very difficult. The nodes that are willing to participate have to compete with each other. The winning one is authorised to add the block and receives the prize.[77]

*Table 1: Blockchain types*

| Blockchain type | Explanation | Example | Visualisation |
|---|---|---|---|
| Public permissionless blockchains | In these blockchain systems, everyone can participate in the blockchain's consensus mechanism. Also, everyone worldwide with an internet connection can transact and see the full transaction log. | Bitcoin, Litecoin, Ethereum | 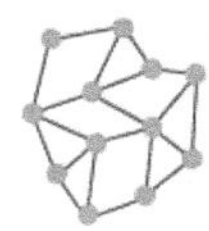 |
| Public permissioned blockchains | These blockchain systems allow everyone with an internet connection to transact and see the blockchain's transaction log, although only a restricted number of nodes can participate in the consensus mechanism. | Ripple, private versions of Ethereum | 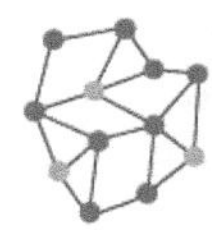 |
| Private permissioned blockchains | These blockchain systems restrict both the ability to transact and view the transaction log to only the participating nodes in the system, and the architect or owner of the blockchain system is able to determine who can participate in the blockchain system and which nodes can participate in the consensus mechanism. | Rubix, Hyperledger | 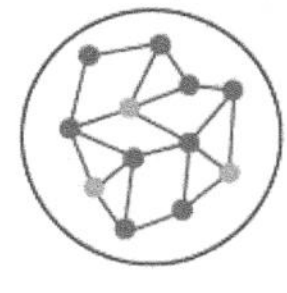 |
| Private permissionless blockchains | These blockchain systems are restricted in who can transact and see the transaction log, although the consensus mechanism is open to anyone. | (Partially) Exonum | 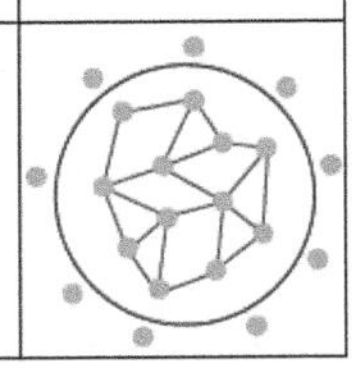 |

Source: European Commission, Joint Research Centre, 'Blockchain now and tomorrow – assessing multidimensional impacts of distributed ledger technologies' (2019) <https://ec.europa.eu/jrc/en/facts4eufuture/blockchain-now-and-tomorrow> accessed 1 October 2021.

76 This attempt of corruption is known as 'Sybil attack'. See Finck (n 21) 27.
77 The price usually consists of crypto-currencies.

The most famous consensus protocol for permissionless blockchains is called Proof-of-Work (PoW).[78] In PoW, to generate the hash of a new block, it is necessary to solve a mathematical game. The game requires finding a hash that begins with a specified number of leading zeros. The puzzle is challenging, and competing nodes – called 'miners'[79] – have to spend their computational resources to find the solution. Even though PoW is secure, it is slow and wastes enormous amounts of electric energy.[80] There are alternative consensus protocols under development to reduce costs and improve efficiency, e.g. Proof-of-Stake (PoS).[81]

In permissioned blockchains, on the contrary, since they are usually built for a specific purpose, incentives become unnecessary. Furthermore, nodes are known and generally not malicious.[82] Hence, adding new blocks is less complicated and less costly.[83] Because of pre-selection, the system is closed and the number of nodes is limited. As a consequence, consensus mechanisms are likely to be faster. A suitable consensus protocol is the Proof-of-Authority, where there are pre-authorised nodes allowed to create new blocks.[84] In general, a study[85] observed that consensus mechanisms divide into two main groups: proof-based consensus algorithms and vote-based consensus algorithms. In proof-based consensus algorithms, nodes have to show that they have performed sufficient proof to get the right to

78 Nakamoto (n 44) 3.

79 The word 'miner' puts in evidence that there is a continuous searching activity.

80 H. P. E. Vranken, 'Sustainability of bitcoin and blockchains' (2017) 28 Current Opinion in environmental Sustainability 1.

81 In the PoS, participants have to show a 'stake' in the system (i.e. to have a certain amount of crypto-currencies) to participate. Selection by account balance is combined with other selection criteria (such as the hash value or the number of days the coins have been held). Otherwise, the richest member would have a permanent advantage. See Bashir (n 18) 341.

82 Participants are held liable through off-chain legal contracts and agreements and are incentivised to behave honestly via the threat of legal prosecution in case of misbehaviour. See Hileman, Rauchs (n 23) 21.

83 H. Eenmaa-Dimitrieva, M. J. Schmidt-Kessen, 'Regulation through code as a safeguard for implementing smart contracts in no-trust environments' (EUI Working papers LAW 2017/13) 13 <http://hdl.handle.net/1814/47545> accessed 1 October 2021.

84 First, the PoA was proposed by a group of developers in 2017 (the term was coined by Gavin Wood, co-founder of Ethereum and Parity Technologies) for Ethereum. See G. Wood, 'PoA Private Chains' (*Github*, November 2015) <https://github.com/ethereum/guide/blob/master/poa.md> accessed 1 October 2021.

85 N. Giang-Truong, K. Kyungbaek, 'A Survey about Consensus Algorithms Used in Blockchain' (2018) 1 Journal of Information Processing Systems 101.

do the appending work. In vote-based consensus algorithms, nodes have to agree (i.e. to vote) about the possibility to append to the ledger. The first are usually designed for public blockchains, the second for private ones.

Permissionless and permissioned blockchains also differentiate from each other because they can guarantee a different level of immutability. As mentioned before,[86] modifications can occur only if the majority of the nodes collude to change the current state of the ledger. In permissionless blockchains, this is more difficult. Firstly, because permissionless blockchains are open to new nodes, so the copies of the blockchain grow continuously and are not easily controllable.[87] Secondly, collusion is complicated by the fact that underlying identities are unknown. However, mining pools[88] have emerged over time, because adding new blocks is usually expensive.[89] Mining pools increase the risk of a 51 % attack.[90] However, someone also argues that these consolidations of miners are not interested in altering the system because they are the ones who most financially benefit from it.[91]

Permissioned blockchains, instead, are more closed systems. Besides, the number of nodes is smaller and validators are known. All this facilitates changes.[92]

## 6. *False myths surrounding blockchains.*

There are some false myths surrounding blockchain technology.[93] The first misconception concerns decentralisation. Because blockchain is a decentralised technology, one often derives that there is not a central authority

86 Section 2.

87 Eenma-Dimitrieva, Schmidt-Kessen (n 83) 11.

88 A mining pool is the pooling of resources by miners, who share their processing power and split the rewards accordingly.

89 In terms of computing power and electricity.

90 D. Conte de Leon *et al.*, 'Blockchain: Properties and Misconceptions' (2017) 11(3) Asia Pacific Journal of Innovation and Entrepreneurship 294, 295 <www.emeraldinsight.com/doi/full/10.1108/APJIE-12-2017-034> accessed 1 October 2021.

91 Indeed, participants of mining pools increase their probability of winning the competition and get rewards. See Finck (n 21) 21.

92 Eenma-Dimitrieva, Schmidt-Kessen (n 83) 13.

93 Bacon et al (n 15) also aim to demystify blockchain. Janssen and Patti, similarly, try to demystify smart contracts. See A. U. Janssen, P. Patti, 'Demistificare gli *smart contracts*' (2020) 1 Osservatorio del diritto civile e commerciale 31.

that manages blockchain networks, but a community of peers. This statement is false.

The confusion is due to the meaning of 'decentralisation', which might refer to the technology and the governance that underlies the application running on the blockchain. The presence of a decentralised network does not necessarily imply that the governance of that network is also decentralised.[94] The difference is evident in permissioned blockchains. Permissioned blockchains are decentralised systems because they overcome the client-server model, and nodes are not dependent on a single master node. But there is an authority that governs these blockchains and uses them for its scopes.[95]

Blockchain has to be regarded as mere technology. Instead, sometimes it is considered to be as a community of people. Blockchain is somehow 'personified'. One often refers to decentralisation due to a lack of central governing authorities acting as third parties on which people trust, such as a bank. For example, in Bitcoin, the system avoids the double-spending problem without the need for a bank. For this reason, blockchain is also qualified as a 'trustless trust' system.[96] This conviction is also utopian and depends on the different significance of identical terms in computer science and the legal domain. In particular, misinterpretations have regard to the concept of 'validation' of a new block. In the legal context, validation recalls the respect of the law. From a technical point of view, the validation process is the set of rules provided by the code to update the ledger. Blockchain has not the authority to guarantee that a transaction matches with the real world, i.e. corresponds to an event that has a legal significance and is lawful.[97]

'Trust' is another misleading word. It is well known that people do not trust each other. Humans are not reliable by nature. Therefore, when leading their affairs, there is often a trusted intermediary. The law itself provides instruments against unreliability. Think, for example, to notaries

---

94 Finck (n 21) 19.

95 E.g. a consortium of banks that creates a blockchain for interbank reconciliation.

96 A. Savelyev, 'Contract law 2.0: 'smart' contracts as the beginning of the end of classic contract law', Higher School of Economics Research Paper no. WP BRP 71/LAW/2016, 11.

97 E. Mik, 'Smart contracts: terminology, technical limitations and real world complexity' (2017) 9 Journal of Law, Innovation and Technology 269, 278–279. E.g. a blockchain can record a transfer of cryptocurrencies, but cannot know if the transfer was due, as in the case when a party concluded a contract containing an obligation to make the transfer under duress.

or public registries. Judges also are intermediaries because they intervene when one party betrays another party's trust. With the rise of the Internet, commerce became even unsafer. Indeed, the Internet is an open network that permits communication between strangers that do not trust each other because they have limited means to verify the other party's identity. This gave rise to several online intermediaries (such as e-Bay, PayPal, or Amazon).[98] In this scenario, the 'trustless trust' nature of blockchain should compensate for the need for intermediaries.

In reality, this concept of trust is different from the one of the blockchain context. In the latter case, putting trust in the network nodes means no central node attests that some data were inserted at a specific date and time. Here, multiple nodes certify the same insertion contemporarily. These nodes are meant reliable because of blockchain properties. As a result, the client-server model can be overcome without renouncing the consistency of the system.

Blockchain is only a database. It is reliable in the sense that it guarantees data integrity and provenance despite being distributed. So, it does not imply that intermediaries become superfluous. In other terms, the truth inside the blockchain does not correspond to the reality outside the blockchain.[99]

Maybe, the political ideas surrounding blockchain invention contributed to misinterpretation of the meaning of 'decentralisation' and 'trust'. It has been already mentioned that blockchain originated from a group of crypto-anarchists, which wanted to build an 'open society', free from classic institutions that were seen as a form of mass surveillance.[100] To do so, they primarily needed to find an autonomous system of money-transfer that lacked centralised control. At the same time, they had to eliminate the risk of fraud, because digital cash can be endlessly copied and reproduced.[101] They had to replace the trust placed in financial institutions regarding who owns what and at what time.

---

98 *Ibid.*, 277.

99 In computer science, 'truth' means that a piece of data exists in the ledger and does not conflict with other data in the system. See M. Rauchs *et al.*, '2nd Global Enterprise Blockchain Benchmarking Study' (*SSRN*, 18 September 2019) 17 <https://ssrn.com/abstract=3461765> accessed 1 October 2021.

100 Section 3.

101 De Filippi, Wright (n 17) 19.

## 7. *Smart contracts.*

As previously stated,[102] smart contracts are the most advanced blockchain functionalities.

A smart contract is a deterministic computer program that can self-execute. A computer program is nothing but data, namely a list of instructions.[103] The instructions are written in the form of conditional 'if-then' statements.[104] They represent the rules that the smart contract must follow while executing.[105] Therefore, the smart contract performs its tasks based on predetermined functions.[106]

A computer program is deterministic when, given a specific input, it always generates the same output.[107] This means that the effects of the program are always predictable. Inputs are data that the program receives. Outputs are the results of the operation performed by the program according to input data.[108] If the conditional statement is proved true according to input data, then the program returns a positive value (*Figure 3*). Through this mechanism, the smart contract self-executes, i.e. it can determine 'if X, then Y', where the X is the input and the Y is the output. To

---

102 Section 4.

103 European Union Blockchain Observatory and Forum (n 25) 22.

104 Chamber of Digital Commerce, Smart Contracts Alliance, 'Smart Contracts: Is the Law Ready?' (2018) 10 <https://digitalchamber.s3.amazonaws.com/Smart-Contracts-Whitepaper-WEB.pdf> accessed 1 October 2021.

105 Execution in computer engineering is the process by which a computer executes the instructions of a computer program.

106 Functions are portions of code with a given purpose. See V. Gatteschi, F. Lamberti, C. Demartini, 'Technology of Smart Contracts' in L. A. Di Matteo, M. Cannarsa, C. Poncibò (eds), *The Cambridge Handbook of smart contracts, blockchain technology and digital platforms* (Cambridge University Press 2020) 43.

107 O. Rikken, S. van Heukeolom-Verhage *et al.*, 'Blockchain and Distributed Ledger Technology: definitions' in UNOPS, 'The Legal Aspects of Blockchain' (2018) 21 <https://insureblocks.com/ep-42-legal-aspects-of-blockchain/> accessed 1 October 2021.

108 T. Swanson, 'Consensus-as-a-service: a brief report on the emergence of permissioned, distributed ledger systems' (*Great Wall of Numbers*, 6 April 2015) 15 <http://www.ofnumbers.com/wp-content/uploads/2015/04/Permissioned-distributed-ledgers.pdf> accessed 1 October 2021.

put it in other words, it is not a human that decides whether a condition is met, but the code itself verifies the inputs.

Figure 3: A simple example of a smart contract.

*The smart contract is used to supply a service and the user who wants to get the service must pay for it.*

*The user is allowed to pay in instalments. When the entire amount has been paid, the service is supplied.*

```
function pay_instalment(utility, month, deposit) {
    var debt = payments[utility][month]
    debt -= deposit
    if (debt <= 0) {
        supply_service(utility, month)
    }
}
```

Source: S. Comellini, M. Vasapollo, Blockchain, Criptovalute, I.C.O. e Smart Contract (Maggioli 2019) 93.

Every time the code returns an output, the smart contract changes its state.[109] Smart contracts are 'stateful' in the sense that they can track changes in state over time.[110] They do so by encoding state transition functions, which remember the initial state and, given an input event, return an output event and the next state as a result.[111]

Smart contracts can receive input data from outside or inside the blockchain. So, smart contracts are triggered by on-chain or off-chain

109 A state is the value of a variable. In computer science, a value is a definite object that may be stored in a variable. For example, the colour of a car can vary (red, green, yellow, etc.). So, the colour of the car is a variable, and the single colours are the values. See Gatteschi, Lamberti (n 106) 43.

110 J. Dax Hansen, C. L. Reyes, 'Legal Aspects of Smart Contract Applications' (*Perkins Coie*, May 2017) 3 <https://www.virtualcurrencyreport.com/wp-content/uploads/sites/35/2017/05/Perkins-Coie-LLP-Legal-Aspects-of-Smart-Contracts-Applications.pdf> accessed 1 October 2021.

111 V. Buterin, 'Ethereum Platform Review: Opportunities and Challenges for Private and Consortium Blockchains' (*R3CEV*, 2016) 1 <http://www.smallake.kr/wp-content/uploads/2016/06/314477721-Ethereum-Platform-Review-Opportunities-and-Challenges-for-Private-and-Consortium-Blockchains.pdf> accessed 1 October 2021.

events, depending on whether input data come from.[112] On-chain data are less (e.g. a smart contract calls another smart contract), while off-chain events are the majority. Indeed, blockchain is 'deaf and blind', meaning it cannot directly retrieve information except dictated by the protocol (e.g. the transfer of crypto-tokens).[113] Oracles provide external data to smart contracts. An Oracle is an interface that delivers data from an external data source[114] to smart contracts.[115]

Blockchains contain a sequence of smart contract transactions. The first transaction concerning a smart contract is uploading a new smart contract on the blockchain, where it is associated with an address. Then, the smart contract can execute according to the received inputs. Every time the smart contract runs an operation it moves from the current state to the next one. Thus, the subsequent smart contract transactions represent smart contract changes of state. Every transaction is submitted to the network and is validated through the blockchain consensus protocol. Namely, every node re-executes the same operation to verify that it gets to the same state. In case of a positive answer, the transaction is validated and is added to the chain (i.e. all copies of the smart contract change their state).[116]

Smart contracts can live on a distributed ledger like the blockchain, but they also exist in traditional database architectures.[117] Blockchain-based smart contracts take advantage of blockchain properties.[118] So, the differ-

---

112 Mik (n 97) 295.

113 O. Rikken *et al.*, 'Smart contracts as a specific application of blockchain technology' (2017) 17 <https://dutchdigitaldelta.nl/uploads/pdf/Smart-Contracts-ENG-report.pdf> accessed 1 October 2021.

114 Depending on the provenance of the data source, oracles can be software, hardware, or humans. Software oracles extract information from web sources (e.g. a website), whereas hardware oracles gather data from the physical world through sensors (e.g. data coming from the Internet of Things). Finally, the human can directly feed the oracle with the required information by cryptographically signing them. Some oracles do not send data to smart contracts but the output of smart contracts to external sources. For example, when the smart contract has to connect to a smart lock to unlock it. For this reason, it is further distinguished between inbound and outbound oracles. See Gatteschi, Lamberti, Demartini (n 106) 36; V. Mou, 'Blockchain Oracles Explained' <https://academy.binance.com/blockchain/blockchain-oracles-explained> accessed 1 October 2021.

115 Bashir (n 18) 411.

116 Sillaber C., Waltl B., 'Life Cycle of Smart Contracts in Blockchain Ecosystems' (2017) 8 Datenschutz und Datensicherheit 497, 499.

117 In traditional database architectures, they are called 'stored procedures'. See Hileman, Rauchs (n 23) 57.

118 European Union Blockchain Observatory and Forum (n 25) 22.

ence is that blockchain-based smart contracts acquire some additional characteristics because they run on a blockchain.

As explained earlier,[119] in contrast with traditional databases, in distributed ledgers nodes update on a peer-to-peer basis through predetermined and shared rules to achieve coordination. There is a 'single version of the truth' among the nodes of the network. Instead of having multiple isolated databases, there are several copies of a single ledger. Parties do not have to trust that all the databases keep identical. Moving to smart contracts, while it usually is necessary to rely that same sets of code running on different network infrastructures do not differ, in blockchain all nodes execute blockchain-based smart contracts in the same way.[120]

Besides, as already indicated,[121] the added value of blockchain compared to other distributed ledgers is that it can guarantee reliable coordination among nodes, thanks to its tamper-resistance. Links between the blocks through hashes make the system resistant to malicious nodes. Hence, it is impossible to alter or modify a smart contract code unilaterally once added to the blockchain. As a consequence, smart contracts cannot avoid execution and/or execute incorrectly. This property does allow not only identical execution but also reliable identical execution.

## 8. *Limitations of pre-existing blockchain platforms versus smart contracting platforms.*

Blockchain platforms that store smart contracts are 'stateful' systems, while others are 'stateless' systems. 'Stateless' systems are limited in their ability to perform complex computational operations on the chain.[122]

Stateless systems are state transition systems in a certain sense.[123] For example, in Bitcoin, the state is the ownership status of all existing bitcoins. Transactions are the requests to move bitcoins from one address to another. The state transition function takes the state, the transaction, and

---

119 Section 2.

120 S. A. McKinney, R. Landy, R. Wilka, 'Smart contracts, blockchain, and the next frontier of transnational law' (2018) 13 Washington Journal of Law, Technology & Arts 313, 315.

121 Section 2.

122 Hileman, Rauchs (n 23) 58.

123 V. Buterin, 'A next-generation smart contract and decentralized application platform' (2013) 5 <https://translatewhitepaper.com/wp-content/uploads/2021/04/EthereumOrijinal-ETH-English.pdf> accessed 1 October 2021.

outputs the result. More specifically, the state is the number of bitcoins in one account. The transaction is a request to move those bitcoins to another address. The output is that bitcoins decrease from the sending address and increases in the receiving address. Alternatively, if the quantity of bitcoins in the sending address is insufficient, the state transition function returns an error. This mechanism is the same as smart contracts. However, the scripting language has some limitations.[124]

Firstly, it lacks Turing-completeness, which means that it cannot solve all computational problems. In particular, it does not support loops.[125] Secondly, it is value-blind. For instance, it does not permit to move a desired number of bitcoins from one address to another, but only the ones received and not spent yet.[126] Thirdly, states are missing. Bitcoins can only be spent or unspent. This is a weak version of a smart contract because it cannot be used to perform more complex operations.

On the contrary, smart contracting platforms are Turing-complete. Indeed, smart contracts are written in 'general-purpose' languages[127] instead of 'fixed-purpose' languages enabling a limited range of operations.[128] Moreover, they are based on values. Smart contracts are essentially a set of attributes and a set of operations over them. The value assigned to every attribute at any moment in time defines the state of the smart contract at that time.[129] The peculiarity of these systems is that they can save state, i.e., detect state changes and remember them over time.[130]

---

124 *Ibid.* 12–13.

125 In computer science, a loop is a sequence of instructions that is continually repeated until a specific condition is reached (<https://computersciencewiki.org/index.php/Loops> accessed 1 October 2021). For this reason, loops are timesaving and more efficient for programmers, because they permit them to run a piece of code many times instead of rewriting the same piece of code.

126 Suppose to have 2 bitcoins that were received from a previous transaction. If the owner of the 2 bitcoins wants to move one bitcoin, she cannot do that and she can only move 2 bitcoins.

127 Some systems have developed their languages (e.g. Solidity for the Ethereum platform), whereas others leverage existing languages (e.g. Java).

128 Rauchs *et al.* (n 99) 68.

129 Gatteschi, Lamberti (n 106) 43.

130 C. Dannen (ed), *Introducing Ethereum and Solidity* (Apress 2017) 2.

### *9. Ethereum.*

Ethereum is the first and most famous blockchain smart contracting platform.[131] Vitalik Buterin first proposed Ethereum in 2013.[132] Its Turing-complete programming language is Solidity. To upload a smart contract on the blockchain a wallet application is needed. Wallets are software applications that hold the pair of keys used to read and write data in the blockchain. A person or an external server holds the keys. The public key corresponds to an account, allowing the connection to the network with an Ethereum client. Addresses are strings of random letters and numbers. There are several client applications, and the most useful (because it can execute smart contracts) is the Mist browser. The private key allows access to the account and must be kept secret. In Ethereum, this account is called 'externally owned account'. It is capable of sending transactions to the smart contracts but does not directly hold the code. Another type of account, the 'contract account', contains the smart contract code. The externally-owned accounts can trigger the smart contract code by sending a transaction. Alternatively, other contract accounts can send a message to the smart contract code.

Smart contract uploading and execution have a cost. These costs are expressed in units called gas. Gas costs are paid in ethers, the virtual currencies of Ethereum.[133] The more the smart contract is complex, the more gas is needed. Every transaction has to indicate the gas limit that the user is willing to pay for the execution of the transaction. If the gas is not enough, the transaction will fail. Moreover, users have to pay a fee to reward miners for the computational effort of running each smart contract. Also, the price is expressed in gas.

---

131 On Ethereum, see Dannen (n 130). Other blockchain platforms that support smart contracts are, for instance, Monax (<https://monax.io> accessed 1 October 2021), Lisk (<https://lisk.io> accessed 1 October 2021), Counterparty (<https://counterparty.io> accessed 1 October 2021), Stellar (<https://www.stellar.org> accessed 1 October 2021), Hyperledger fabric (<https://www.hyperledger.org/projects/fabric> accessed 1 October 2021), Corda (<https://www.corda.net> accessed 1 October 2021), Axoni core (<https://axoni.com/technology/> accessed 1 October 2021).

132 Buterin (n 123).

133 There are different ways to get ethers: converting bitcoins in ethers inside the Mist wallet; mining; buying ethers with fiat currency through an exchange platform.

The steps to upload a new smart contract are the following: downloading and installing the Mist browser;[134] creating an account; copying and pasting the code[135] in the box labelled 'Solidity Contract Source Code'; setting some parameters (e.g. the name of the contract); deploying the smart contract by clicking the 'Deploy' button.

Transactions can upload new smart contracts or trigger existing ones. A transaction contains: a recipient address;[136] a signature identifying the sender; the value field, indicating how many ethers are sent (if some ethers are sent); an optional data field, which contains the message to trigger a smart contract; a STARTGAS value, indicating the maximum number of computational steps the transaction is prepaid; a GASPRICE value, representing the fee the sender is willing to pay for gas.

Ethereum is a permissionless and public blockchain.[137] Every transaction is publicly visible. The consensus mechanism is the Proof of Work (PoW), even though the second release – called Serenity, or Ethereum 2.0 – adopts Proof of Stake (PoS).[138]

## *10. Use cases.*

As previously mentioned,[139] the main difference between blockchain and other distributed databases is tamper evidence. Indeed, in traditional distributed databases there is the danger that peer-to-peer nodes act malicious-

---

134 The Mist browser can be downloaded from <https://github.com/ethereum/mist/releases> accessed 1 October 2021.

135 The source code is written in a programming language (e.g. Solidity) in any text editor.

136 Specifying no recipient and attaching smart contract data is used for upload new smart contracts. If this is the case, a contract address is returned to access the contract in the future.

137 About blockchain typologies, see Section 5.

138 For a detailed description of the Ethereum 2.0 roadmap, see European Union Blockchain Observatory and Forum, 'Blockchain Ecosystem Developments and Trends' (November 2020) 4 <https://www.eublockchainforum.eu/sites/default/files/reports/1st%20EUBOF%20Trend%20Report_November%202020.pdf> accessed 1 October 2021. The first phase of the release, called Beachon Chain, went live on 1st December 2020. See W. Foxley, 'Ethereum 2.0 Beacon Chain Goes Live as 'World Computer' Begins Long-Awaited Overhaul' (2020) <https://www.coindesk.com/ethereum-2-0-beacon-chain-goes-live-as-world-computer-begins-long-awaited-overhaul> accessed 1 October 2021.

139 Section 2.

ly, in the absence of a central authority. Instead, blockchain combines the consensus mechanism with an append-only data structure composed of a chain of cryptographically linked blocks that can detect any improper alteration of the data. So, blockchain can guarantee the benefits of distributed systems[140] with a higher level of reliability.

Users can take better advantage of this peculiarity with smart contracting platforms because they can perform more complex computational operations. Thanks to their extended ledger functionalities, smart contracting platforms can be used in various ways.

One way is to represent assets in digital forms through the process of 'tokenisation'. Tokens are digital assets that can be exchanged on-chain.[141] Blockchain solves the 'double-spending' problem, i.e. it prevents the same digital file is duplicated and spent twice without the need for a trusted central authority.[142] Blockchain makes intangible digital assets 'tangible': unique, inalterable, non-reproducible, non-counterfeitable, and irrevocably transferable. Tokens can be a representation of existing assets, both digital (e.g. intellectual property) and physical (e.g. a house), or native blockchain assets (e.g. virtual currencies).[143] Smart contracts make these tokens programmable, e.g. they can represent bonds that make dividend payments automatically.[144]

Another way is to encode organisations' rules into smart contracts and create so-called 'Decentralised autonomous organisations' (DAOs). Governance rules are encoded in a smart contract or a bundle of smart contracts, automatically enforced and executed through blockchains. A DAO can adopt a mediating role between different parties in a decentralised but ultimately human-controlled organisation, or it can constitute a more fully autonomous organisation that is controlled entirely through algorithms.[145]

---

140 As stated in Section 1, distributed systems are more efficient and less costly.

141 European Commission, Joint Research Centre, 'Blockchain now and tomorrow – assessing multidimensional impacts of distributed ledger technologies' (2019) 58 <https://ec.europa.eu/jrc/en/facts4eufuture/blockchain-now-and-tomorrow> accessed 1 October 2021.

142 Section 3.

143 The major juridical questions arise with native blockchain assets because they are new to define and regulate. There are three main categories of native blockchain tokens: payment tokens, to make payments; investment tokens, to make investments; utility tokens, to access a specific product or service based on a blockchain platform.

144 European Union Blockchain Observatory and Forum (n 25) 26.

145 Some authors name Decentralised Organisations (DO) the ones that rely on human-inputs, while DAOs are fully automated. See Bashir (n 18) 97.

DAOs were born to support the deployment and the development of public and permissionless distributed ledgers.[146] The basic idea was to build communities of peers, whose rules are encoded in a computer program and not influenced by a governing authority or groups of people. But one can also imagine such organisations in permissioned blockchains. In this case, the rules defined by the smart contract code derive from pre-defined contractual agreements between different members. Blockchain technology ensures the respect of such rules.[147]

As the name suggests, smart contracts can also acquire relevance in the contractual domain to encode contractual agreements that execute automatically. This is the research topic of the present work that is deepened in the following chapters.

All these smart contracts can be applied in innumerable fields, giving rise to as many use cases. In general, they can help to automate processes. Through the blockchain, the execution of such processes becomes verifiable and auditable by all involved parties. For example, blockchain-based smart contracts could facilitate interactions in supply chains, from producers to consumers in the industrial sector They also have the potential to transform the public sector. For instance, the distributed registration and exchange of citizen records, such as birth certificates, land titles, or criminal records.[148] In particular, it seems that blockchain technology has had a great impact on the finance[149] sector.[150]

---

146 For example, a DAO, called The DAO, was created to launch the Ethereum project in 2016. It acted as a venture capital fund to crowdfund Ethereum. Contributions were paid in bitcoins and returned in ethers. The owners of ethers became part of the Ethereum community. See W. C. Usman, 'The Decentralised Autonomous Organisation and Governance Issues' (*SSRN*, 4 December 2017) <https://ssrn.com/abstract=3082055> accessed 1 October 2021.

147 On the contrary, the legal qualification of DAOs that run on permissionless blockchains is the object of debate. It might result from a partnership agreement, civil law partnership agreement, unincorporated joint venture agreement, or other types of agreement. See European Union Blockchain Observatory and Forum (n 25) 28.

148 For an in-depth analysis of the impacts of distributed ledger technologies in the various sectors, see European Commission (n 141).

149 Blockchain-based smart contracts applications in finance range from cryptocurrencies and Initial Coin Offerings to financial instruments and payment systems.

150 European Union Blockchain Observatory and Forum (n 66) 15.

# CHAPTER 2: BLOCKCHAIN-BASED SMART CONTRACTS IN THE CONTRACTUAL DOMAIN

## 1. *Smart contract: a misleading expression.*

One usually associates the term smart contract with contracts. It is misleading because it recalls contracts.

As described in the previous chapter,[151] a smart contract is a deterministic computer program that can automatically execute on a blockchain once it establishes the satisfaction of its conditions.[152] So, a smart contract is a mere technology. As already clarified,[153] there are innumerable ways of use of smart contracting platforms. So, the application of this technology does not necessarily constitute a contract in a legal sense.

Smart contracts *per se* have no legal meaning. Smart contracts can automate every action or operation. For instance, one could think of a smart thermostat that regulates the temperature inside a house according to predetermined settings. Smart contracts can also manage processes, i.e. a series of actions taken to achieve a result (e.g. a business process).[154]

On the other hand, smart contracts can play a role in various legal domains. Firstly, a smart contract can perform legal acts other than contracts or even represent that act.[155] For example, in the private law domain, there are unilateral private law acts that do not involve multiple parties.[156] Additionally, these legal acts can be private and public, issued by administrative

---

151 Chapter 1, Section 7.

152 The European Union Blockchain Observatory and Forum (n 25) 22 gives the following definition of a smart contract: 'In the blockchain context, it generally means computer code that is stored on a blockchain and that can be accessed by one or more parties. These programs are often self-executing and make use of blockchain properties like tamper-resistance, decentralised processing, and the like'.

153 Chapter 1, Section 10.

154 As illustrated in Chapter 1, Section 10, blockchain-based smart contracts can help to enhance the transparency and efficiency of processes that involve multiple actors, e.g. in supply chains.

155 Rikken *et al.* (n 113) 19.

156 E.g. a testament or a promise.

bodies, and subject to administrative law.[157] In all these hypotheses, smart contracts can be the manifestation of the act in a digital form, or they automatically execute the rights and obligations of an external legal act.

Secondly, smart contracts can perform legally relevant processes, where the law states specific legal requirements and mandatory steps to follow.[158] In this context, smart contracts can support both private and administrative activities. For instance, one can consider the process for issuing a loan commitment for a residential mortgage loan.[159] To arrive at a final decision about the lending, there are many subjects involved.[160] With blockchain, all data coming from different parties can be tracked in a single and trustworthy ledger. The smart contract can decide whether to approve or reject the loan commitment based on the acquired information and according to pre-set parameters. In the public sector, one could imagine programming the legal steps of an administrative process to obtain a permit.[161] The blockchain can collect input data and the smart contract can evaluate compliance with legal requirements and respect of given deadlines.

Smart contracts have legal implications even when they are programmable tokens. When tokens represent existing (digital or physical) assets, the applicable laws are the same as traditional assets.[162] When they are native of the blockchain, there is the need to identify appropriate rules.[163] The same considerations apply to DAOs.

Smart contracts can also belong to the contractual domain. In this case, somebody suggested referring to this specific application of the technology as 'smart legal contracts', to denote the relevance for contract law.

---

157 E.g. an administrative penalty or a temporary authorisation for the occupation of public property.

158 *Ibid.* 33.

159 Chamber of Digital Commerce, Smart Contracts Alliance (n 104) 38–39.

160 E.g. the seller, the buyer, the buyer's financial institution, a real estate agent, the lender, a surveyor, an appraiser, governmental institutions.

161 Rikken *et al.* (n 113) 33–34.

162 European Union Blockchain Observatory and Forum (n 25) 26. In particular, the explanatory note to the 2017 UNCITRAL Model Law on Electronic Transferable Records clarifies that the rules apply to various types of electronic transferable records based on the principle of technology neutrality, enabling the use of various models whether based on registry, token, distributed ledger or other technology. See UNCITRAL, 'UNCITRAL Model Law on Electronic Transferable Records' (United Nations, 2017) <https://uncitral.un.org/en/texts/ecommerce/modellaw/electronic_transferable_records> accessed 1 October 2021.

163 Chapter 1, Section 10.

Instead, he named the technology itself as 'smart contract code'. In one of its reports,[164] the European Union Blockchain Observatory and Forum revokes the expression 'smart legal contracts'. It also puts in evidence the other fields of legal relevance for smart contracts – apart from contract law – in a specific section of the report called 'Smart contracts with legal implications'.[165]

The following paragraph addresses the possible relationships between 'smart contract code' and 'smart legal contracts', which is the research topic.

## 2. *'Smart contract code' versus 'smart legal contracts'.*

According to the author who first distinguished between 'smart contract code' and 'smart legal contract', a 'smart contract code' is 'code that is stored, verified and executed on a blockchain'. In contrast, a 'smart legal contract' is 'the use of code to articulate, verify, and enforce an agreement between parties'.[166] The section illustrates smart contracts from a contract law perspective by starting from the latter definition.

First of all, a smart contract can represent the tool to articulate contracting parties' will.[167] Here, the code represents contractual conditions in the form of computer language. The contractual will can be expressed directly in code,[168] or the smart contract can be the translation of a pre-

164 European Union Blockchain Observatory and Forum (n 25) 23.

165 *Ibid.* 25ff.

166 J. Stark, 'Making Sense of Blockchain Smart Contracts' (*CoinDesk*, 7 June 2016) <https://www.coindesk.com/making-sense-smart-contracts> accessed 1 October 2021.

167 M. Durovic, A. Janssen, 'The Formation of Blockchain-based Smart Contracts in the Light of Contract Law' (2019) 6 European Review of Private Law 753, 760.

168 There are already several projects that aim at expressing and implementing legal contracts in software, e.g. Common Accord (<http://www.commonaccord.org/> accessed 1 October 2021), Legalese (<http://www.legalese.com/> accessed 1 October 2021), and the Ricardian Contract (<https://iang.org/papers/ricardian_contract.html> accessed 1 October 2021). See C. D. Clack, V. A. Bakshi, L. Braine, 'Smart Contract Templates: foundations, design landscape and research directions' (2016) arXiv: Computers and Society, 2 <https://arxiv.org/abs/1608.00771> accessed 1 October 2021. See also L. Cervone, M. Palmirani, F. Vitali, 'The Intelligible Contract' (Proceedings of the 53rd Hawaii International Conference on System Sciences, Maui, Hawaii, USA, 7–10 January 2020) 1780 <https://hdl.handle.net/10125/63959> accessed 1 October 2021.

existing contract.[169] If there is not still a contract at the moment of the uploading of the smart contract on the blockchain, the smart contract (in combination with the blockchain) can be the instrument to express the uploading party's will. In this event, a contracting party takes advantage of the blockchain to transmit her contractual will to one (or more) potential counterparty (or counterparties).[170]

As seen in the previous chapter, the peculiarity of smart contracts is that they are stateful, i.e. they can save state changes.[171] A smart contract changes its state every time it receives input and returns the corresponding output. The functions of a smart contract correspond to the conditions under which the code has to perform some tasks. As already described,[172] smart contracts execute by themselves according to the inputs they receive. Consequently, when smart contracts perform contractual obligations, they verify and enforce agreements. Namely, they execute agreements automatically, without the need for human actions.[173] In this hypothesis, the smart contract is the tool to perform a contract.

If the code replaces the natural language contract, the smart contract is contemporarily the tool to express and execute the contractual will of the parties. As already seen, however, the smart contract can only be used to automate a traditional contract's execution.[174] There is a hybrid model in the middle where some contractual terms are expressed in digital form while others are expressed in natural language.[175]

Indeed, not all contractual obligations can be translated into the language of the code. This is due to the inflexibility of the code compared to the flexibility of legal language.[176] In contracts, such flexibility is necessary.

---

169 Mik (n 97) 287.

170 Durovic, Janssen (n 167) 760 affirm that contracts can be concluded either off-chain or on-chain.

171 Chapter 1, Section 8.

172 Chapter 1, Section 7.

173 Rikken et al (n 113) 22; McKinney, Landy, Wilka (n 120) 321.

174 Chamber of Digital Commerce, Smart Contract Alliance (n 104) 25 illustrates different smart contract models. In particular, in the external model, the code merely automates the performance of the parties' legal agreement. In contrast, the code forms the entire legal agreement or a part of it in the internal model.

175 De Filippi, Wright (n 17) 78.

176 Natural language is described as 'wet code', whereas computer language is known as 'dry code'. See M. Cannarsa, 'Contract Interpretation' in Di Matteo, Cannarsa, Poncibò (n 106) 111. The language of the code is 'dry' because it cannot have several meanings. As reported in P. Catchlove, 'Smart Contracts: A New Era of Contract Use' (*SSRN*, 1 December 2017) 8 <https://ssrn.com/abstrac

The presence of performance standards like 'good faith' or 'best efforts' can help evaluate a contract's correct performance without specifically defining adequate performance at the moment of drafting.[177] A contract can be duly performed depending on the context.[178] Moreover, ambiguous terms avoid predicting all future circumstances that can affect the performance of a contract, which is impossible.[179] Ambiguity necessarily implies human judgements, while computerised systems have no ways to interpret contractual conditions by the context.[180] This could be a challenge for future advancements in technology, especially in artificial intelligence and machine learning.[181]

---

t=3090226> accessed 1 October 2021 'Smart contracts are codified using Boolean logic. Boolean logic involves a computation that resolves in a value as either true or false. Simply put, the computer coding does not permit ambiguity, something either does or does not happen, or is or is not triggered, as a result of the code'.

177 J. M. Sklaroff, 'Smart contracts and the cost of inflexibility' (2017) 166 University of Pennsylvania Law Review 263, 281.

178 According to De Filippi, Wright (n 17) 77 'For example, a contracting party may promise to act in "good faith" because it might be difficult to precisely define what constitutes appropriate performance, while another party may promise to use "best efforts" to fulfil his or her obligations, because the most cost-effective or efficient manner of performance might not yet be foreseeable'.

179 Parties deliberately include vague terms to be open to future circumstances. This is the theory of relational contracts, as opposed to the classical formalistic theory. This vagueness can result in more efficient contracts because parties can save *ex-ante* costs of drafting and negotiating contracts over precise terms. See C. J. Goetz, R. E. Scott, 'Principles of Relational Contracts' (1981) 67 Virginia Law Review 1089; R. Macneil, 'Relational Contract: What We Do and Do Not Know' (1985) Wisconsin Law Review 483; *id.*, 'Relational Contract Theory: Challenges and Queries (2000) 94 Northwestern University Law Review 877. In general, contracts are incomplete when they contain gaps. Incompleteness and vagueness of contracts imply *ex-post* interpretation. About incomplete contracts, see O. Hart, J. Moore, 'Foundations of Incomplete Contracts' (1999) 66 Review of Economic Studies 115; R. E. Scott, G. G. Triantis, 'Incomplete Contracts and the Theory of Contract Design' (2005) 56 Case Western Law Review 187; in Italy, A. Fici, *Il contratto incompleto* (Giappichelli 2005).

180 Flexibility of natural language requires contract interpretation according to interpretation rules. About contract interpretation and automated contracts, see Cannarsa (n 176) 102–117.

181 K. Werbach, N. Cornell, 'Contracts Ex Machina' (2017) 67 Duke Law Journal 313, 366 admits that this challenge 'is unlikely to be solved any time soon. Despite great advances in machine learning, computers do not have the degree of contextual, domain-specific, subtle understanding required to resolve contractual ambiguity. In this regard, smart contract platforms like Ethereum are

Furthermore, not all contractual conditions are operational, i.e. provide specific actions that the obliged parties must perform and that smart contracts automatically execute. There are non-operational contractual conditions, such as the rules to apply in case of breach of the contract, or to determine the applicable law and jurisdiction.[182]

These technical limitations favour the recourse to smart contracts in some contract types instead of others.[183]

The above assumptions are the starting point to deepen the analysis of the impact of blockchain-based smart contracts on contract law.

## 3. *Nick Szabo's theories.*

The computer scientist Nick Szabo[184] coined the term 'smart contract' in the 1990s. In 1994 he defined a smart contract as 'a computerized transaction protocol that executes the terms of a contract'. His idea was to embed in hardware and software many kinds of contractual clauses, 'in such a way as to make breach of contract expensive…for the breacher'.[185]

---

also vastly less sophisticated than state-of-the-art artificial intelligence systems like IBM's Watson.' Alternatively, the same authors (page 365, n 221) suggest encoding in the smart contracts proxies, formulas, or framing mechanisms used by human courts and juries to evaluate imprecise terms. They also propose reintroducing humans, like human oracles (to assess performance) or arbitrators (to resolve uncertain cases). Even these two proposals have some limits. The first, because 'reduces but does not eliminate the grey areas around imprecise terms. And even when it offers a precise answer, something is lost in the conversion process from analogue to digital. The second 'transforms the smart contract into a conventional contract', subject to human intervention. Also Cannarsa (n 176) 114 concludes that 'it is implausible to believe that current technology is able to capture the broader aspects of contracting (context) and the existence of unpredictable events that occur subsequent to the coding of contract'.

182 Mik (n 97) 294.

183 See below, Section 7, in this chapter.

184 The following information on Nick Szabo are available on Wikipedia <https://en.wikipedia.org/wiki/Nick_Szabo> accessed 1 October 2021: 'Nick Szabo is a computer scientist, legal scholar and cryptographer known for his research in digital contracts and digital currency. He graduated from the University of Washington in 1989 with a degree in computer science and received a law degree from George Washington University Law School. He holds an honorary professorship at the Universidad Francisco Marroquìn'.

185 N. Szabo, 'Formalizing and Securing Relationships on Public Networks' (1997) 2(9) First Monday <https://firstmonday.org/ojs/index.php/fm/article/view/548> accessed 1 October 2021.

In particular, 'the general objectives' were 'to satisfy common contractual conditions (such as payment terms, liens, confidentiality, and even enforcement), minimize exceptions both malicious and accidental, and minimize the need for trusted intermediaries. Related economic goals include lowering fraud loss, arbitration and enforcement costs, and other transaction costs'.[186] Nick Szabo's theories conceive a new way of contracting through protocols.[187]

The use of electronic means to enter into and perform contractual agreements was not something new at the time Nick Szabo elaborated his studies. Since the 1970s, industries have been using electronic data interchange (EDI) to manage their commercial relationships.[188] EDI is a form of computer-to-computer communication for the exchange of different kinds of documents (e.g. purchase orders or invoices).[189] By eliminating paperwork, EDI enabled more rapid negotiations and performance and, consequently, significant transaction costs savings.[190]

Nick Szabo considered EDI a 'primitive forerunner to smart contracts',[191] because it can facilitate the contracting process. Nevertheless, according to Szabo, EDI was still a limited system because it only passes from paper to an electronic format being nothing more than 'simple message-passing of static forms'.[192] It did not change how parties enter and perform commercial obligations. Using Szabo's words, 'it renders traditional static business forms in cyberspace, and maintains the dependence on traditional controls'.[193]

Instead, Nick Szabo envisioned that computer software could substitute humans in contractual activities.[194] Basically, he desired to overcome the lack of trust between contracting parties that causes delays, obstacles, and supplementary costs. Traditionally, trust is put in so-called intermediaries, i.e. third parties distinct from contracting parties that act in different

186 N. Szabo, 'Smart Contracts' (1994) <http://www.fon.hum.uva.nl/rob/Courses/InformationInSpeech/CDROM/Literature/LOTwinterschool2006/szabo.best.vwh.net/smart.contracts.html> accessed 1 October 2021.
187 De Filippi, Wright (n 17) 73.
188 Werbach, Cornell (n 181) 320.
189 About EDI, see Chapter 3, Section 1.
190 De Filippi, Wright (n 17) 73.
191 Szabo (n 186).
192 Szabo (n 185).
193 Szabo (n 185).
194 Werbach, Cornell (n 181) 323.

phases of the life cycle of a contract.[195] For example, a credit agency is an intermediary, as it evaluates individuals' creditworthiness to help potential lenders to decide whether concluding a loan agreement. Another intermediary might be a judge that has the power to apply existing remedies for non-performance. By rendering software capable of acting autonomously, Nick Szabo wanted to reduce at the minimum the need of those intermediaries.[196]

Nick Szabo lacked a technology that could enable him to move from theory to practice.[197] Even the rise of the Internet did not contribute to considerable advancements. Of course, the Internet has enhanced the potentials of electronic commerce by allowing mere consumers to negotiate by electronic means, but electronic contracts still depend on humans. They are electronic only because of their form.[198]

Technological advancements aimed at exploring ways to express contract terms as computer data to be processable by a computer system. Harry Surden has named this extended capability of computers to 'read' contractual clauses as 'data-oriented contracting'.[199] Data-oriented contracts led to the creation of 'computable contracts', namely the possibility that a computer is given 'computer-processable instructions that approximate what is that the parties are intending to do in their contractual arrangement'.[200] By following those instructions, computers can act in place of parties.[201] Surden states that software can make only '*prima-facie* determi-

195 Szabo (n 185) affirms: 'Smart contracts often involve trusted third parties, exemplified by an intermediary, who is involved in the performance, and an adjudicator, who is invoked to resolve disputes arising out of performance (or lack thereof). Intermediaries can operate during search, negotiation, commitment, and/or performance'.

196 *Ibid*: 'In smart contract design we want to get the most out of intermediaries and adjudicator, while minimising exposure to them'.

197 M. Giancaspro, 'Is a 'smart contract' really a smart idea? Insights from a legal perspective' (2017) 33(6) Computer Law & Security Review 825.

198 Werbach, Cornell (n 181) 320–321.

199 H. Surden, 'Computable Contracts' (2012) 46 U. C. Davis Law Review 629.

200 *Ibid.* 658.

201 For example, a financial option contract may grant the right to purchase a stock at a given price, and expire on a certain date. A data-oriented contract would represent that arrangement in computer code. A brokerage house could direct its computer system to transfer the security to the buyer's account and debit the current sum. In computable contracts, the brokerage house computer system itself could evaluate whether the price and timing of a proposed purchase meet the terms of the option. This example is taken from Werbach, Cornell (n 181)

nations':[202] if parties are not satisfied with the results of the assessments of computers, they can refuse them. Parties maintain the system under their control. So, one cannot say that computers substitute completely them.[203]

Nick Szabo considers the 'humble vending machine' as the 'primitive ancestor' of smart contracts.[204] Indeed, the machine automatically dispenses the desired products if anybody inserts the necessary number of coins. Moreover, the lockbox and other security mechanisms protect it from attackers, so that 'the amount in the till should be less than the cost of breaching the mechanism'.[205] In other terms, breaching the contract is inconvenient. In essence, the vending machine is not limited to *prima facie* decisions.[206]

There is an increasing interest in smart contracts after blockchain invention,[207] to the point that blockchain platforms exist that support smart contracts.[208] The previous chapter provided an in-depth explanation of blockchain peculiarities, mainly its decentralised character and its tamper resistance.[209] Decentralisation means keeping identical information in the various nodes without needing a master copy. Tamper resistance refers to the ability of blockchain to prevent unilateral alteration thanks to its chain structure. Decentralisation and tamper resistance ensure reliable identical execution of blockchain-based smart contracts.[210] When smart contracts are used as smart legal contracts, someone asserts that no single party is in absolute control of the blockchain, and cannot interrupt or modify the execution of the smart contract code.[211]

Smart contracting platforms (like Ethereum) are more sophisticated than platforms for the mere exchange of virtual currencies (like Bitcoin), as already described.[212] They are also general-purpose, i.e. they can do more than just moving digital cash between accounts. Indeed, they are being

---

321,322. Smart contracts are very common in the financial field (see Chapter 2, Section 7, n 268).

202 Surden (n 199) 658.

203 Werbach, Cornell (n 181) 322–323.

204 Szabo (n 186).

205 *Ibid.*

206 Werbach, Cornell (n 181) 324.

207 De Filippi, Wright (n 17) 74.

208 Chapter 1, Section 4.

209 Chapter 1, Section 2.

210 Chapter 1, Section 7.

211 De Filippi, Wright (n 17) 74–75.

212 Chapter 1, Section 8.

experimented with contracts, as Szabo imagined 20 years ago.[213] For this reason, when we hear about smart contracts today one usually refers to blockchain technology.

## 4. *Characteristics of smart legal contracts.*

Having regard to the above, authors attribute to smart legal contracts some characteristics.

The first characteristic is self-execution or automation. Smart contracts are deterministic computer programs.[214] They behave according to the instructions provided by the code. They activate when they receive input. Input data give the smart contract the necessary information and the smart contract reacts with an output. In the contractual domain, automation implies that it can substitute the contracting party once the program is instantiated. Namely, the code makes actions instead of a human and understands whether and how to act. As results from the preceding section, however, self-execution is not a novelty.[215] It is what Harry Surden names 'computable contracts'.[216] Smart contracts can exist without the blockchain.[217] In fact, they have been operating for several years.

Self-enforcement is another characteristic that distinguishes smart legal contracts from the past. This characteristic is linked with blockchain technology. As explained in part in the previous section, decentralisation and tamper resistance of the blockchain determine that no single party is in absolute control of the blockchain and cannot interrupt or modify the execution of the smart contract code. This can be better clarified with an example.[218]

A seller of a car has installed an immobiliser that allows the starting of the car after payment by the buyer. The immobiliser connects with the vendor's bank to verify whether the buyer has effectively paid. If yes, the

---

213 For example, the startup Trakti provides ~~a~~ contract negotiation and management platform integrated into the blockchain (<https://www.trakti.com/home/> accessed 1 October 2021).

214 Chapter 1, Section 7.

215 Werbach, Cornell (n 181) 343–344.

216 Chapter 2, Section 3.

217 Chapter 1, Section 7.

218 The example is taken from T. J. De Graaf, 'From old to new: from internet to smart contracts and from people to smart contracts' (2019) 35 (5) Computer Law & Security Review 105322, 4.

car starts. If not, the car does not start. This is a traditional 'computable' contract. The immobiliser receives information from the bank about the payment and acts accordingly. The immobiliser is under the seller's control that can instruct the immobiliser not to start the car even though the payment has been made. Instead, decentralised execution and tamper resistance with the blockchain prevents the seller from altering the immobiliser's functioning.

It is considered that blockchain technology removes the need to trust the other party.[219] Before the blockchain, parties had to rely on the other party's computer system. With blockchain, every user shares the same code and controls its execution on a peer-to-peer basis.[220] So, the other party cannot refuse the results of the processing. In other terms, she cannot infringe the rules of the code. If the code rules are the representation of contractual clauses, the other party has not to intervene to guarantee the respect of those clauses. There is no need for enforcement. For this reason, one talks about self-enforcement of smart legal contracts.[221]

The third characteristic is self-sufficiency. The latter is strictly related to self-enforcement.[222] If smart contracts remove the need of trust between parties because there is not the possibility to violate the rules of the code – and consequently, there is no more the need for the parties to invoke the applicable rules in case of betrayal of trust – the rules of the code are the law that govern the parties. The presence of a smart contract is sufficient and lives by its own rules. Smart contracts are considered part of a parallel and independent legal system.[223]

---

219 Swan (n 57) 16.

220 McKinney, Landy, Wilka (n 120) 314.

221 Savelyev (n 96) 15.

222 *Ibid.*

223 On the contrary, Thomas Hobbes believed that binding agreements are impossible without the law. He wrote: 'If a covenant be made wherein neither of the parties perform presently, but trust one another, in the condition of mere nature (which is a condition of war of every man against every man) upon any reasonable suspicion, it is void: but if there be a common power set over them both, with right and force sufficient to compel performance, it is not void. For he that performeth first has no assurance the other will perform after, because the bonds of words are too weak to bridle men's ambition, avarice, anger, and other passions, without the fear of some coercive power... But in a civil estate, where there a power set up to constrain those that would otherwise violate their faith... he which by the covenant is to perform first is obliged so to do'. See T. Hobbes, *Leviathan* (1st ed 1651) para. 18–19. Indeed, an essential requirement of a contract is the intention of the parties to be legally bound by the agreement. This means that parties agree that the agreement is binding for the law, i.e.

### 5. Summary of existing legal literature.

This section summarisies existing literature on the legal implications of smart legal contracts on contract law. Evaluations by authors highlight both advantages and shortcomings of smart legal contracts.

Starting from the strengths, legal scholars affirm that smart legal contracts could significantly reduce costs, time, and disputes.[224] Indeed, self-execution guarantees a high level of automation of legal agreements.[225] It helps to save time and money in manual monitoring and execution.[226] Additionally, self-enforcement implies that parties cannot disregard their promises.[227] Moreover, the language of the code impedes different interpretations, as is with the ambiguity of natural language.[228] So, it is more unlikely that they have to spend time and economic resources to resolve

each of them can go to court and enforce it. See J. M. Smits (ed), *Contract law-a comparative introduction* (Edward Elgar 2017) 63ff.

224 Eenma-Dimitrieva, Schmidt-Kessen (n 83) 74.

225 P. Cuccuru, 'Beyond Bitcoin: an early overview on smart contracts' (2017) 25 International Journal of Law and Information Technology 179, 188.

226 *Ibid.* 188.

227 *Ibid.* 186–187. According to the author, in particular, 'the risk of online fraud would be largely minimized, as the performance of the obligations is ideally simultaneous, compliance on side A being subordinated to compliance on side B. It is not possible, for instance, for one of the party to keep payment x without delivering asset y, nor that x could be reversed once y is obtained (the so-called 'chargeback frauds')'. Savelyev (n 96) 17 highlights the difference between smart contracts and vending machines. In the latter case, 'although performance is automated, the seller – owner of the vending machine has the discretion regarding the performance of the contract: he may interfere in the process of functioning of such machine (e.g. by shutting it down) and thus, change the outcome of the deal. In Smart contract it is not possible for a party to it to change the outcome by shutting down its computer – all the transactions continue to exist and be processed in cyberspace'.

228 Savelyev (n 96) 13–14.

disputes.[229] Self-enforcement also avoids the high costs of contract drafting.[230] This turns out into increased contractual efficiency.[231]

As concerns the negative aspects, the authors mainly focus on contract formation and execution. The first question is whether a smart legal contract can represent a legally binding contract.[232] Such a question can receive a positive answer in the presence of all legal requirements. Otherwise, the contract is invalid. In particular, a valid contract requires the will of the parties. Here, two major problems arise. The first has regard to identity and the second to the language of the contract.

In the blockchain, the identities of the parties are likely unknown. The impossibility to link an account to a specified identity could be relevant. For example, the contracting party might be not legally capable.[233] Or he/she might entrust the other party's identity to start a dispute.[234] Furthermore, a mistake about the underlying identity might invalidate the contract.[235]

Broad discussions concentrate on the unusual language of the contract. Many reflect on the comprehensibility of the meaning of the computer instructions uploaded in the blockchain. The risk is that a party does not properly understand the content of the contract.[236] Or it might happen that he/she entrusts a programmer to translate the agreement,[237] and the

229 Cuccuru (n 225) 187. M. Raskin, 'The Law and Legality of Smart Contracts' (2017) 1 Georgetown Law Technology Review 305, 312 observes that 'the opportunity to ensure performance ex ante is a preferable situation if the expected value of the costs of litigation outweigh the expected value of the contract'.

230 Savelyev (n 96) 18 concludes that 'all the legal regime associated with the notion of "obligations" is not applicable: mode of performance (place and time of performance, performance by third party, etc.), consequences of non-performance, etc'. Cuccuru (n 225) 187 states that 'The role of litigation-related clauses – eg competent forum or applicable law for the resolution of disputes—is therefore minimized'.

231 Eenma-Dimitrieva, Schmidt-Kessen (n 83) 74.

232 Savelyev (n 96) 10; R. O' Shields, 'Smart Contracts: Legal Agreements for the Blockchain' (2017) 21 N.C. Banking Inst. 177, 185; Werbach, Cornell (n 181) 338;

233 For instance, Giancaspro (n 197) 828 refers to minors.

234 McKinney, Landy, Wilka (n 120) 329.

235 Giancaspro (n 197) 828–829.

236 Cuccuru (n 225) 188–189. The author underlines that judges also do not usually understand (and cannot interpret) the code.

237 Cuccuru (*ibid* 188) notes that 'transaction costs would simply shift from enforcement and monitoring phase to design phase'.

translation does not correspond to the party's will by mistake or even intentionally.[238]

Another important requirement is the contract form when the law requires a specific one.[239] Consequently, smart contracts need signatures. Signature should ensure that the content is attributable to a determined person to be recognised equivalent effect of a handwritten signature.

Moving to contract performance, if, on the one hand, self-enforcement might be positive, on the other hand, it might be an obstacle because immutability eliminates all kinds of *ex-post* interventions.[240] This means there is no room for manoeuvre for parties or courts even when contract law recognises some remedies or allows some modifications or termination of the contract.[241]

Another difficulty is the identification of the jurisdiction and applicable law in case of controversies. Blockchain-based smart contracts are a global phenomenon, with the possibility to conclude transnational contract. In this hypothesis, blockchain might render complex the application of the necessary legal parameters, such as the location of the nodes or the identity of the parties.[242]

The following chapters discuss and deepen these issues.

## 6. *Applicable form of regulation.*

Section 4 of this chapter states that one of the characteristics of smart legal contracts is self-sufficiency, i.e. the independence from the legal system. Code is declared as a parallel body of law. A more realistic point of view

---

238 Savelyev (n 96) 14; Giancaspro (n 197) 829; Mik (n 97) 282.

239 Savelyev (n 96) 12.

240 Unless the code does not include these possibilities. Sklaroff (n 177) 291; Mik (n 97) 282.

241 For instance, the remedies for non-performance of the contract, like termination or specific performance. It might be that a party wants to exercise the right of withdrawal. Change of circumstances or supervening events might allow termination of the contract or its renegotiation. Interventions might also remedy the invalidity of the contract. See: Savelyev (n 96) 18; Cuccuru (n 225) 190–191; Mik (n 97) 282.

242 O'Shields (n 232) 191; McKinney, Landy, Wilka (n 120) 329; B. Cappiello, 'Dallo *"smart contract" computer code* allo *smart (legal) contract*. I nuovi strumenti (para) giuridici alla luce della normativa nazionale e del diritto internazionale privato europeo: prospettive *de jure condendo*' (2020) 2 Rivista del commercio internazionale 477, 512ff.

considers that the law of the code and the countries' law cannot coexist.[243] Nobody would invest in something that is not compliant with the law. Nobody would renounce going in front of a court or applying existing legal remedies if something goes wrong.[244]

Another point is to directly replace the current legal framework with the law of the algorithms. Somebody makes a parallel with the Internet in its early days.[245] Indeed, at the beginning, the Internet was conceived as a technological alternative to the legal system. An extreme faction proclaimed the independence of cyberspace from the law. But, after an initial period, once the Internet evolved and users started using it for e-commerce, it became evident that contracts formed via the Internet must be treated like traditional contracts and subject to real-world jurisdiction.[246]

There are three modes of regulation conceived for the Internet.[247] A first approach aims to substitute the legal system, proclaim anarchy, or build a particular and separate order for the Internet. Barlow represented the anarchic approach. In 1996 he wrote the manifesto 'A Declaration of the Independence of the Cyberspace' where the Internet was depicted as a new world populated by 'netizens' which would have organised on a decentralised network without being subject to central authorities.[248] Instead, in 1998 Reidenberg spoke of 'Lex Informatica', an alternative normative system made by technical rules.[249] The ones who supported this thesis believed that technical choices could influence the actions performed on the Internet and thus influence human behaviour. It is a form of regulation by code.[250] The second and third approaches are similar because both aim

243 Boucher (n 59) 15.

244 Mik (n 97) 284.

245 Savelyev (n 96) 16.

246 Mik (n 97) 284.

247 G. Finocchiaro 'Lex mercatoria e commercio elettronico. Il diritto applicabile ai contratti conclusi su Internet' in V. Ricciuto and N. Zorzi (eds), *Il contratto telematico* (Cedam 2002), 22.

248 J. P. Barlow, 'Declaration of Independence for Cyberspace' (1996) <https://www.eff.org/cyberspace-independence> accessed 1 October 2021.

249 J. R. Reidenberg, 'Lex Informatica: The Formulation of Information Policy Rules Through Technology' (1998) 76 Texas Law Review 553.

250 In his writings, Reidenberg compares Lex Informatica to Lex Mercatoria. In the Middle Age, there was the problem of regulating international trade. The rules of the kingdoms were no more sufficient. Merchants established a system of common rules that could apply regardless of their geographical location. They created their private ordering. The transnational character of the Internet posed the same problem of the absence of a system of law beyond the national boundaries. Technology is regarded as another form of regulation. Its rules derive

to regulate the Internet without refusing the legal framework. As for the second, it is sufficient to apply existing rules and interpret them to face innovation. The third considers the introduction of specific rules besides existing ones.

As already mentioned, the first position had no practical application. Conventional law was applied by analogy to the Internet. Contract law still exists and regulates commerce on the Internet with additional rules to face the peculiar ways of contracting by digital means.[251] Discussions around blockchain regulation are essentially following the same path.

Blockchain technology originated from a group of crypto-anarchists. In 1993 Hughes wrote 'A Cypherpunk's Manifesto' where he suggested using cryptography and anonymous systems to recreate a new anarchic order free from governments.[252] De Filippi and Wright observed that blockchain might regulate human behaviours by setting technical rules administered through smart contracts and decentralised autonomous organisations. They called this body of law 'Lex Cryptographia' to underline the similarity with Reidenberg's 'Lex Informatica'.[253]

Most of the literature concludes that traditional contract law continues to apply to smart contracts.[254] The desire to substitute the classic way people lead their affairs with technology characterised every period of technological developments.[255] In the present age, smart contracts and algorithms are preferred to humans because of their speed, efficiency, and reliability.[256] But the interpreters consider that it could be hazardous to renounce to the legal system. There is a need to exercise control over

---

from the design of online platforms. The technical characteristics determine what users can or cannot do. So, they are technical rules elaborated by technicians and followed by users on the Internet, independently of their provenance. Lawrence Lessig supported this idea of 'Code is Law'. He sustained that there are four modes of regulating individuals' actions: the law of the States; social norms; market forces; the architecture that shapes both the physical and digital world. See L. Lessig (ed), *Code: Version 2.0* (New York: Basic Books 2006).

251 See Chapter 3.

252 Chapter 1, Section 3.

253 A. Wright, P. De Filippi, 'Decentralized Blockchain Technology and the rise of Lex Cryptographia' (*SSRN*, 10 March 2015) <https://ssrn.com/abstract=2580664 > accessed 1 October 2021; De Filippi, Wright (n 17).

254 Boucher (n 59) 14–15.

255 Sklaroff (n 177) 266.

256 Werbach, Cornell (n 181) 381.

algorithms. Otherwise, there might be the danger that algorithms govern people without any safeguards.[257]

---

257 De Filippi,Wright (n 17) 174–175 claim that Lawrence Lessig's 'Code is Law' (n 250) is also valid for blockchain-based systems. Indeed, blockchains are decentralised networks like the Internet. On page 207, however, they distinguish Lex Cryptographica from Lex Informatica because the code operates autonomously in the former. As Wright and De Filippi (n 253) 40–44 point out, people could choose their alternative techno-regulatory framework. This, on the one hand, could be capable of regulating society more efficiently, reducing the costs of law enforcement, and allowing for a more customised system of rules personalised to every citizen. But, on the other hand, self-enforcement could result in decreased freedom and autonomy of people. Indeed, after a choice has been made, users can no longer deviate from those rules. This could lead to a modern totalitarian regime under the exclusive control of self-enforcing contracts (i.e. of the private companies or governments that ordered to develop the underlying software). This would be even riskier in case of bugs. For instance, Slock.it developed a DAO for Ethereum (n 146). In this DAO, people could invest in the project by depositing ethers in exchange for tokens. Because of a bug, a hacker could drain funds from the DAO (3.6 million ethers, the equivalent of $ 70 million). The DAO hack should not have been perceived as abuse if the code were law, despite the DAO's smart contract failing to reflect the parties' will. Instead, the Ethereum foundation proposed a hard fork to retrieve the stolen ethers. Moreover, smart contracts are executed thanks to input data that often come from outside the blockchains through oracles. For example, if a person willing to lose weight instructs the code not to purchase caloric products until his/her weight has returned to a determined number, the person would not be free to buy a caloric product even though he/she has not reached his/her goal.

258 At a European level, the European Parliament resolution of 3 October 2018 on distributed ledger technologies and blockchains: building trust with disintermediation (n 61) dedicates paragraphs 36 to 38 to smart contracts. It emphasises that there is a need to undertake an in-depth legal assessment of the legal implications and an-in depth analysis of the existing legal frameworks in the Member States. The aim is to provide legal certainty that could be enhanced also by means of legal coordination and mutual recognition between the Member States. In its Resolution of 20 October 2020 'Digital Services Act: adapting commercial and civil law rules for commercial entities operating online' (n 9), the European Parliament considers that the European Commission should provide guidance to ensure legal certainty around the civil and commercial aspects surrounding smart contract, and make proposals for the appropriate legal framework.

At a more international level, in 2019 and 2020 the United Nations Commission on International Trade Law (UNCITRAL) and the International Institute for the Unification of Private Law (UNIDROIT) organised two joint workshops to discuss about regulating new technologies.

Supranational institutions, too, are supporting the regulation of smart legal contracts using existing legal systems.[258] Some countries have even issued special norms.[259]

It seems that, as happened for the Internet, a legal analysis of the implications of blockchain technology on contract law should follow the second and the third approach. Self-sufficiency of smart legal contracts is refused for the reasons expressed above. It remains to be seen whether the characteristics of blockchain-based smart contracts need new norms, or an interpretation of actual norms is sufficient. Before proceeding in this study, the next chapter gives an account of how contract law evolved with technological development, and applicable sources of law in technological contracts.

---

259 For instance, the Arizona House Bill No. 2417 (available at <https://www.azleg.gov/legtext/53leg/1R/laws/0097.htm> accessed 1 October 2021) provides that: 'B. A record or contract that is secured through blockchain technology is considered to be in an electronic form and to be an electronic record'; 'C. Smart contracts may exist in commerce. A contract relating to a transaction may not be denied legal effect, validity or enforceability solely because that contract contains a smart contract term'; 'E(2). 'smart contract' means an event-driven program, with state, that runs on a distributed, decentralized, shared and replicated ledger and that can take custody over and instruct transfer of assets on that ledger'. Similarly, the Tennessee Senate Bill No. 1662 (<https://legiscan.com/TN/text/SB1662/2017> accessed 1 October 2021) states that 'a record or contract that is secured through distributed ledger technology is considered to be in an electronic form and to be an electronic record' (47–10–202. (b)); moreover, it declares that 'smart contracts may exist in commerce. No contract relating to a transaction shall be denied legal effect, validity, or enforceability solely because that contract is executed through a smart contract' (47–10–202. (c)). The California Assembly Bill 2658 amending Section 1633.2 of the Civil Code (<https://legiscan.com/CA/text/AB2658/id/1732549> accessed 1 October 2021) has prescribed that "contract' includes a smart contract' (1633.2. (e)). The 2018 Malta Digital Innovation Authority Act (available at <https://mdia.gov.mt/legislation/> accessed 1 October 2021) defines a smart contract as 'a form of innovative technology arrangement consisting of: (a) a computer protocol; and, or (b) an agreement concluded wholly or partly in an electronic form which is automatable and enforceable by execution of computer code, although some parts may require human input and control, and which may be also enforceable by ordinary legal methods or by a mixture of both'. In Italy, Law no. 12 of 11 February 2019 converting Decree no. 135 of 14 December 2018 (*Legge 11 febbraio 2019, n. 12, di conversione del decreto legge 14 dicembre 2018, n. 135, recante disposizioni urgenti in materia di sostegno e semplificazione per le imprese e la pubblica amministrazione*), also called 'Simplification Decree' (*Decreto Semplificazioni*), at Article 8-*ter*(2) defines smart contracts and determines when they satisfy the requirement of the written form.

## 7. *Types of contract.*

Due to the technical obstacles of codification of contracts, not all contracts are considered suitable for smart contracts, at least for now.

Not all contractual conditions can be represented in code. For this reason, as happened with EDI agreements, smart legal contracts are only being used for the self-performance of some contractual conditions.[260] For the same reason, they are being developed for agreements with objectively measurable 'if' conditions.[261] Moreover, many contracts are long-term and often remain open-ended because the parties cannot foresee all events or changes over time.[262] These contracts are incompatible with the immutability and unstoppable character of smart contracts on blockchain technology. So, they are seen as more suitable for standard agreements rather than one-off contracts.[263]

Smart legal contracts are being especially tested in the financial sector.[264] There are several areas of application of blockchain-based smart contracts for financial institutions.[265] They are considered 'an ideal testing ground for blockchains'[266] for three main reasons: standardised terms and measurable variables, which have always allowed a high level of digitalisation; the need of processing a huge amount of data daily; various intermediaries that exchange such data. Smart contracts and blockchain technology might

---

260 De Filippi, Wright (n 17) 78. Cannarsa (n 176) 116 states that 'For the near future, automated contracts will be limited to effectuating parts of language contracts and perform more simplistic and narrow types of contracts in specific areas, such as flight-delay insurance contracts'. Insurance is a promising area for blockchain-based smart contracts, as it is described below in this section.

261 K. Levy, 'Book-Smart, Not Street-Smart: Blockchain-Base Smart Contracts and the Social Workings of Law' (2017) 3 Engaging Science, Technology, and Society 1, 11.

262 De Filippi, Wright (n 17) 84.

263 Boucher (n 59) 14. O. Borgogno, 'Usefulness and Dangers of Smart Contracts in Consumer Transactions' in Di Matteo, Cannarsa, Poncibò (n 106) 294 writes that 'Agreements used on a large scale and containing standardized terms and conditions is currently the best and most appropriate way to optimize smart contracts', because of the drafting and design costs.

264 Cuccuru (n 225) 193.

265 Namely: cryptocurrencies, Initial Coin Offerings, financial instruments and payment systems. See European Commission, Joint Research Centre (n 141) 55–66. This growing interest in blockchain and smart contracts for finance is called Decentralised Finance (DeFi). See European Union Blockchain Observatory and Forum (n 66) 15.

266 Cuccuru (n 225) 193.

help cut costs and processing time of exchanged data by sharing a standard, secure, transparent ledger.[267]

In the realm of contracts, smart contracts can be used for financial agreements.[268] In particular, smart financial instruments (e.g. stocks, bonds, options, etc.) attract the most attention.[269] Blockchain-based smart contracts might enhance the settlement and clearance of securities and derivatives.[270] Some limitations affect post-trading activities: the presence of many intermediaries that increase costs and time needed for executing their tasks; limited transparency of the processing workflow because transaction data and logs of each intermediary's activities reside on their separate platforms that hinder the traceability of the life cycle of the security; limited interoperability of intermediaries' systems. Blockchain technology has the potential to provide all the intermediaries with a common data layer. The latter bypasses the need for data reconciliation, reducing related times and costs, and potential mistakes. Smart contracts incorporate the

267 *Ibid.* 193–194.

268 De Filippi, Whright (n 17) 89. All over the world securities markets have started using algorithms (independently of any blockchains) in trade and post-trade management processes since the 1990s. Algorithmic Trading (AT) and High-Frequency Trading (HFT) refer to transactions made by automated algorithms. HFT is the evolution of AT. It distinguishes itself from AT because of the possibility to perform transactions in a very short time, thanks to increased data collection and calculation ability. The aim is to maximise the competitive surplus value generated by their speed. Additional information on AT and HFT can be found in F. Di Ciommo, 'Smart contracts and (non)law. The case of financial markets' (2018) 7(2) Law and Economics Yearly Review 291, 304–321.

269 One representative initiative is R3 (<https://www.r3.com> accessed 1 October 2021), a bank consortium now transformed into an enterprise software firm to develop blockchain applications for financial services on Corda, an open-source blockchain platform, and Corda Enterprise, a commercial version of Corda for enterprise usage. Stock markets are also experimenting. For example, in 2015 NASDAQ launched the project 'Nasdaq Linq' to grant private companies the ability to manage and trade their stocks through blockchain technology (<http://ir.nasdaq.com/news-releases/news-release-details/nasdaq-launches-enterprise-wide-blockchain-technology-initiative> accessed 1 October 2021). The Swiss Exchange is building a fully integrated issuance, trading, settlement, and custody infrastructure for digital assets, named SIX Digital Exchange (<https://www.sdx.com/en/home.html> accessed 1 October 2021).

270 De Filippi, Wright (n 17) 89–96; S. McJohn, I. McJohn, 'The Commercial Law of Bitcoin and Blockchain Transactions', Suffolk University Law School Legal Studies Research Paper 16–13, 22 November 2016, 10 <http://ssrn.com/abstract=2874463> accessed 1 October 2021; European Commission Joint Research Centre (n 141) 62–64.

instructions to carry out the operations that concern securities.[271] The execution of the operations is allowed for authorised external agents according to the provisions of the smart contract code.[272] Blockchain technology records the state changes of the smart contract securely and transparently.

The trade finance industry is also interesting to test smart contracts. Its inefficiencies are similar to those enlisted above: mainly, high level of intermediation and manual activity.[273] Furthermore, buyers and sellers (often coming from different countries) do not trust each other: buyers want to ensure that their purchases arrive in good condition before making the payment; sellers want to be sure to receive the payment. For this reason, in long-distance sale contracts, banks issue letters of credit and parties conclude escrow agreements.[274] With a letter of credit, the buyer's bank (which issues the letter) guarantees the payment to the seller upon the delivery of the goods. Escrow agreements are concluded between buyers and sellers that involve an escrow agent to hold the money until the specified conditions of the contract are met. Although these services reduce the counterparty's risk, the exchange of paper documents between many actors lengthen the entire process and enhance the risk of fraud. It is believed that blockchain and smart contracts can alleviate these pain points.[275] In both cases, a smart contract can be programmed to transfer the funds automatically. Blockchain reduces time and costs and increases transparency because all parties access the transaction records by sharing a common ledger. The fact that letters of credit and escrow agreements are highly standardised contracts, whose conditions can be easily translated into code, enables smart contracting platforms. Even here, there are plenty of projects.[276]

Another promising sector is insurance. A recent study shows that finance has launched nearly half of live blockchain networks in combi-

---

271 E.g. the purchase, the transfer of the security, or the execution of payment obligations.

272 E.g. the security's buyer, seller, or broker.

273 European Union Blockchain Observatory and Forum, 'Blockchain in trade finance and supply chain' (thematic Report, 9 December 2019) <https://www.eublockchainforum.eu/sites/default/files/report_supply_chain_v1.pdf> accessed 1 October 2021. On pages 15–16 the Report enlists the challenges of trade finance.

274 Borgogno (n 263) 300.

275 *Ibid.* 300–301.

276 The EU Blockchain Observatory and Forum Report (n 273) 31–32 provides a list of current initiatives in this field.

nation with insurance industries.[277] Indeed, insurance companies might benefit from blockchain technology and smart contracts to cut down management red tape. They might act as a simplification and dematerialisation factor in the contract life cycle. Indeed, claims processing and settling are usually complex, not always fair, and lengthy. This lowers insured people's trust in their insurance companies. On the other hand, insurance still involves many manuals and paper-based processes. Moreover, it is a heavily intermediated industry (e.g. brokers, reinsurance companies). Insurers have to make many controls to verify that the payment is effectively due. There is a high risk of claim fraud. For these reasons, the costs are very high. With smart contracts, on the contrary, the code verifies if there are the conditions to perform the insurer's obligations. The policyholder does not have to start the claim procedure, nor does the insurance company appoint any employee. Everything is automated.[278] Blockchain technology helps to reduce costs and time further because all involved parties can interact on a single database, as highlighted above.[279]

Insurance institutions and companies realise the potential of blockchains and smart contracts.[280] Someone is conducting studies and

---

277 Rauchs *et al.* (n 99) 32–33.

278 As an author observes, insurance contracts are suitable because claims handling and payouts can be easily automated. Indeed, the insured event can be represented in binary data form. See A. Borselli, 'Smart Contracts in Insurance. A Law and Futurology Perspective' (*SSRN*, 19 January 2019) 9–10 <https://ssrn.com/abstract=3318883> accessed 1 October 2021.

279 For further analysis of current challenges faced by the insurance industry and expected benefits of blockchain technology see: M. Mainelli, C. von Gunten, 'Chain of a lifetime: how blockchain technology might transform personal insurance' (*Long Finance Report*, December 2014) <https://papers.ssrn.com/sol3/papers.cfm?abstract_id=3676416> accessed 1 October 2021. About insurance contracts and blockchain-based smart contracts: J. Evans, 'Curb your enthusiasm: the real implications of blockchain in the legal industry' (2018) 11(2) Journal of Business, Entrepreneurship and the Law 273, 294–296; Borselli (n 278). On the same topic, see also my contribution in Italian C. Bomprezzi, 'Blockchain e assicurazione: opportunità e nuove sfide' (*Diritto Mercato Tecnologia*, 7 July 2017) <https://www.dimt.it/la-rivista/articoli/blockchain-e-assicurazione-opportunita-e-nuove-sfide/> accessed 1 October 2021.

280 E.g., see: Organisation for Economic Cooperation and Development (OECD), 'Financial Markets, Insurance and Pensions: Digitalisation and Finance' (2018) 62–63 <https://www.oecd.org/finance/private-pensions/Financial-markets-insurance-pensions-digitalisation-and-finance.pdf> accessed 1 October 2021; European Insurance and Occupational Pensions Authority (EIOPA), 'EIOPA InsurTech Roundtable – How Technology and data are reshaping the insurance landscape. Summary from the roundtable organised by EIOPA on 28 April 2017' <https://

experimentations to test the effects of this technology in this area.[281] The final aim is to improve competitiveness and customer experience.

The next section attempts to identify some concrete ways of development of smart contracts solutions for the above contract types.

---

register.eiopa.europa.eu/Publications/Reports/08.0_EIOPA-BoS17-165_EIOPA_InsurTech_Roundtable_summary.pdf> accessed 1 October 2021. On 29 April 2021, EIOPA published a discussion paper on blockchain and smart contracts in insurance (<https://www.eiopa.europa.eu/media/news/discussion-paper-blockchain-and-smart-contracts-insurance-eiopa-invites-comments-0_en> accessed 1 October 2021).

281 The Blockchain Insurance Industry Initiative (B3i) (<https://b3i.tech> accessed 1 October 2021) is a consortium composed of insurance and reinsurance companies from all over the world to explore the potential use of blockchain technology and smart contracts for the reinsurance industry and to develop common standards, protocols, and network infrastructures. In 2018, the consortium incorporated B3i Services AG, a software company entirely owned by 18 insurance market participants around the world, that offers development, testing, and commercialisation of blockchain solutions for insurance and reinsurance industries. InsurETH by the start-up Oraclize, Fizzy by AXA insurance company, and Etherisc are smart flight insurance contracts for automating claims and refunds for flight delays or cancellations. Smart contracts receive data from the websites of airports regarding flight status through oracles. About InsurETH, see M. L. Perugini, P. Dal Checco (n 54) 22–23; more information about Fizzy can be found at the following link: <https://www.axa.com/en/magazine/axa-goes-blockchain-with-fizzy> accessed 1 October 2021. About Etherisc, see <https://fdd.etherisc.com> accessed 1 October 2021. In 2018, The Italian National Association of Insurance Companies (ANIA), the Italian Institute for Insurance Supervision (IVASS), the Research Centre on Technology, Innovation and Financial Services of Università Cattolica del Sacro Cuore in Milan and the company Reply started a collaboration and created the Insurance Blockchain Sandbox (<https://www.insuranceblockchainsandbox.com/> accessed 1 October 2021) to experiment real use cases of smart insurance contracts in a limited and protected environment. As can be seen in the official IBS website, three use cases were developed on travel insurance: one is about risks of bad weather; the second is for flight delays or cancellation; the third is for lost luggage. The website is in Italian. For information in English, open this link: <https://www.reply.com/en/content/insurance-companies-start-experimenting-with-blockchain-technology> accessed 1 October 2021.

*8. Concrete scenarios.*

The present section aims to outline some concrete scenarios of use of smart contracts in the contractual domain. To do that, two preliminary distinctions are made.

The first distinction is between permissionless and permissioned blockchains. As explained in the previous chapter,[282] everyone (without pre-identification) can hold a node and become part of the blockchain network in permissionless blockchains. For this reason, the blockchain does not belong to anyone that decided to invest in setting up to set up and maintain the technological infrastructure (hardware and software). On the other hand, permissioned blockchains are specifically built to fit a specific purpose. For this reason, not everyone is authorised to take part as a node, to transact, or to add new blocks.

The second distinction has regard to nodes and users. Nodes are electronic devices that store copies of the blockchain.[283] They are the units of the blockchain network. Users are the individuals or entities that use a blockchain-based application. Nodes and users are not synonyms. There can be some nodes that are not users. For example, miners can be interested in runningto run a node to compete for adding new blocks and be rewarded. But they are not obliged to write new transactions.[284] Similarly, not all users run a node. They can interact with the distributed ledger both directly, by running a node, or indirectly, through the interface of a blockchain-based application.[285]

Having clarified this, and by cross-referencing permissionless/permissioned blockchains and nodes/users, the following four concrete scenarios may be envisaged:

1) Permissionless blockchain/network participants.

   Users get access to a permissionless blockchain (that supports smart contracts) by running a node and use the platform for the conclusion/execution of contracts.

   For instance, OpenBazaar[286] is a blockchain-based decentralised marketplace for peer-to-peer e-commerce, both for private users and busi-

282 Chapter 1, Section 5.

283 Chapter 1, Section 1.

284 As explained in Chapter 1, Section 5, given that the system does not belong to anyone it is necessary to incentivise people to maintain and update it.

285 Hileman, Rauchs, (n 23) 27–29.

286 <https://openbazaar.org> accessed 1 October 2021.

nesses. Anyone can use the platform anonymously and there are no restrictions on the object of the trade. Participants can transact by running a node where to install the application.

2) Permissionless blockchain/application users.
This is mainly a B2C scenario, where the business develops services for its customers and uses a permissionless blockchain as backend. The front-end is a blockchain-based application for users that do not run a node of the permissionless blockchain.
For example, Fizzy[287] is an initiative by the insurance firm AXA that uses the Ethereum platform to record smart contracts that keep track of flight status and provide automatic compensation in case of delays or cancellation. Users conclude the insurance contract by getting access to a dedicated website. Users do not run a node, but they can see the address of the smart contracts and the transactions using a blockchain browser like Etherscan.[288]

3) Permissioned blockchain/network participants.
This scenario is suitable for B2B contractual relationships, for two main reasons. Firstly, because they have the economic power to create their own blockchain, as opposed to consumers. Secondly, because permissioned blockchains are closed ecosystems, thus businesses consider them safer for their affairs.[289] Here, there are multiple parties, each holding a node.

---

287 (n 281). Axa terminated Fizzy at the end of 2019, after almost two years of experimentation. The project head Laurent Benichou declared that there is not sufficient market appetite for the product, despite its innovative nature. Axa also reported that the right distribution channels do not yet exist for Fizzy. It added, however, that it will continue to test parametric insurance products, taking advantage of the experience gained with this project (https://coinrivet.com/axa-drops-ethereum-based-flight-insurance-platform/) accessed 1 October 2021). Nevertheless, it is one of the most cited examples of smart contract applications, and one of the first that was put into production. For these reasons, the present work cites it.

288 Ethereum is a public blockchain and anyone can read the transactions.

289 As rightly pointed out by V. Gatteschi, F. Lamberti, C. Demartini, 'Technology of Smart Contracts' in Di Matteo, Cannarsa, Poncibò (n 106) 42 these kinds of blockchains 'have the advantage of lowering validation time and costs, as network nodes are known and trusted. Furthermore, as read rights can be controlled, they provide greater privacy. Finally, it must be underlined that in cases of emergency (e.g. hacker attacks, bugs) these two latter types of blockchains could be easily modified or reverted to a previous state by making all network nodes agree on a previous version of the blockchain'.

An example can be the Spunta project, promoted and coordinated by the Italian Banking Association (ABI), which aims to implement the blockchain in interbank reconciliation. Every node corresponds to one of the involved banks, the network participants.[290]

4) Permissioned blockchain/application users.
   As for scenario 2, being a user does not mean owning a node. This case differs from scenario 2 because of the presence of a permissioned blockchain under the control of the business. A business may create a ermissioned blockchain to offer its services to end-users.

To facilitate this parallel, it is cited the Insurance Blockchain Sandbox (IBS),[291] which is similar to Fizzy by Axa (the use of blockchain for smart travel insurance contracts) except for the type of blockchain adopted as back-end.

The research aims at studying the implications of blockchain-based smart contract on contract law. In this regard, it is believed that legal analyses should start from concrete (albeit theoretical) scenarios,[292] and not from the technology itself. Regulation should not govern technology, but aspects of its application. Instead, authors usually restrict their dissertations to the dichotomy permissionless/permissioned blockchains, based on technical features.[293] They do not usually clarify the difference between network participants and application users, nor the fact that the characteristics of blockchain technology do not directly affect the governance

290 The interbank reconciliation procedure in Italy aims to reconcile the transaction flows that generate accounting entries in the mutual accounts of Italian banks, and manage pending transactions. The process follows the rules of an interbank agreement created in 1978, revised in 1987, and further amended in the '90s. This agreement has been recently updated allowing the adoption of DLT for the entire sector. Till now, over 100 banks have been operating on Spunta. For more details, see I. Ferraro, 'La pazienza della blockchain' (2019) Press release English version 88 ff <https://bancaforte.it/articolo/un-e-book-sulla-pazienza-della-blockchain-RB97945k> accessed 1 October 2021.

291 The IBS is also described in note 281.

292 These four scenarios were elaborated by observing how the market is developing smart legal contracts. Indeed, for each scenario, a real example is provided. However, taking into account the youth of the technology, it is difficult to foresee how the market will develop in the future. The cited examples are themselves still new. One of them has been interrupted (Fizzy); another is a sandbox initiative (IBS). Hence, in the following chapters, it was decided to contemplate only the scenarios, setting aside specific use cases.

293 Permissionless and permissioned blockchains distinguish by the permission to write new transactions, update the ledger, and add new blocks (Chapter 1, Section 5).

of the applications that run on the blockchain.[294] As already remarked, blockchain has to be regarded as mere technology.

By adopting this approach, it is intended to reconsider the most relevant legal assumptions about the impact of smart legal contracts on contract law, summarised above.[295]

294 E.g., as stated in Chapter 1, Section 6, the presence of a decentralised network does not necessarily imply that the governance of that network is also decentralised, like when a permissioned blockchain is developed by a business to offer its products or services to application users/consumers.

295 Section 5.

# CHAPTER 3: FROM VENDING MACHINES TO SMART CONTRACTS

## 1. *The historical impact of technology on contracts.*

Blockchain-based smart contracts are not the first technology that impacted traditional contract law. On the contrary, contract law had to face several steps of technological development.[296]

First of all, vending machines are considered the ancestors of smart contracts.[297] Vending machines are automatic machines that dispense goods or provide services. The 1880s are considered the beginning of the vending machine era. They first appeared in the USA and then arrived in Europe. They dispensed cigarettes, chewing gums, candies, soft drinks, and other low-cost items that could be easily consumed on the spot. They were (and are) located in attractive locations for consumers, such as offices, rail stations, and other public places. These devices have been existing for two thousand years. The earliest reference dates back to 219 B.C. in the book *Pneumatika* by the Greek physicist and engineer Hero of Alexandria. He described a machine that dispensed holy water for vending sacrificial water in Egyptian temples. The user had to put a coin in a spot. The coin would trigger a lever that opened a valve and the machine dispensed the water. After Hero, other vending machines appeared in the 17th century. Snuff and tobacco boxes activated by the insertion of coins appeared in taverns and inns in England around the year 1615. In 1822 the British bookseller Richard Carlile invented the book-dispensing machine against censorship. He wanted to avoid liability of the bookseller by arguing that the contract was between the buyer and the machine. Initially born as experiments, and thanks to technical advancements, they began to be used in commerce between the end of the XIX and the beginning of the XX century. They allow significant cost savings (staff, shops, advertising, *etc.*)

---

296 M. Granieri, 'Technological contracts' in P. G. Monateri (ed) *Comparative Contract Law* (Edward Elgar 2017) 1–2 <https://papers.ssrn.com/sol3/papers.cfm?abstract_id=2666191> accessed 1 October 2021.

297 Chapter 2, Section 3.

because they only need an initial investment to buy the machines, for periodical refilling and maintenance.[298]

The extraordinary spread of vending machines also enhanced their legal relevance. In that period, some authoritative legal experts wondered how these apparatus could fit existing legal systems and highlighted the need for appropriate legal protection.[299] From a legal point of view, the novelty of the vending machine was that commercial relations could be carried out in the absence of suppliers. The consumer could select the desired products and/or services and obtain them through a machine. The studies focused on the legal nature of the interactions with vending machines and the role of the device. In particular, academics conducted their research on the qualification of positioning a vending machine, inserting coins, and dispensing products or services. They wondered about the legal consequences of malfunctions of the vending machine, the absence of any products inside it, the insertion by the consumer of counterfeit currency or another similar object capable of making the machine work equally.

With technological development, businesses started to utilise electronic communications via electronic networks.[300] These networks allowed the exchange of data messages between information systems. The most famous is the Electronic Data Interchange (EDI), developed in 1965 by the U.S. Army Master Sergeant Edward Guilbert for sending cargo information between the American company DuPont and its carrier Chemical Lehman Tank Lines.[301] According to the nature of the exchanged information, they were used to perform obligations under pre-existing contracts or to enter

---

298 About the history of vending machines, see K. Segrave (ed), *Vending Machines: An American Social History* (McFarland & Company 2002); G. R. Schreiber (ed), *A Concise History of Vending in the U.S.A.* (Vend 1961).

299 The first author was the German W. Auwers, *Des Rechtsschutz der automatischen wage nach gemeinem Recht*, dissertation printed in 1891 by the bookseller of the University of Göttingen W. F. Kastner (Hansebook 2016). He was followed by F. Günther, *Das Automatenrecht*, dissertation printed in 1892 by the bookseller of the University of Göttingen W. F. Kästner (Kessinger 2010); K. Schels, *Der strafrechtlicheSchutz des Automaten*, Dissertation in Erlagen, München, 1897; F. Schiller, *Rechtsverhältnisse des Automaten*, Dissertation in Zurich, 1898; P. Ertel, *Der Automatenmissbrauch und seine Charakterisierung als Delikt*, dissertation printed by Wilhelm Pilz, Berlin, 1898; H. Neumond, '*Der Automat. Ein Beitrag zur Lehre über die Vertragsofferte*' (1899) *Archiv für die civilistische Praxis* 166 ff.

300 C. Reed, 'Electronic commerce' in C. Reed (ed), *Computer Law* (7th edn Oxford 2011) 267–268.

301 De Filippi, Wright (n 17) 72–73.

into binding agreements.[302] Concerning the former, another example is the Electronic Funds Transfer Systems (EFTS). EFTSs have been created since the end of the 1960s. They are 'telecommunication networks that move information about in the Banking Industry in order to perform a financial transaction'.[303] They originated in 1968 with the formation of a Special Committee on Paperless Entries (SCOPE) in California to consider the possibilities of using computer entries to replace paper checks and deposit slips between members. From there onwards, many systems developed, also for international transfers.[304] As was for vending machines, they allowed businesses to reduce costs and time. They are closed networks, used by commercial entities.[305]

The legal issues connected with closed e-commerce encompassed the formation, the performance of the contract, and the applicable law and jurisdiction. About formation, questions arose primarily about the time and place of the conclusion of the contract. Indeed, contracts were concluded at a distance, and a specific amount of time passed between offer and acceptance. Moreover, negotiations occurred automatically through electronic communications. Other issues were related to mistakes affecting the validity of the contract determined by faulty transposition of the will of the parties in the computer program, and the validity of the electronic form in contracts. Moving to performance, malfunctions of the networks required identifying the responsible persons and the kind of responsibility. Finally, these contracts could have cross-border elements so there was the need to determine the applicable law and jurisdiction.

---

302 Reed (n 300) 267. Information could represent the performance of contractual obligations or declarations of negotiations.

303 J. W. Cortada (ed), *The Digital Hand: Volume II: How Computers Changed the Work of American Financial, Telecommunications, Media, and Entertainment Industries* (Oxford 2006) 73.

304 *Ibid.* p. 76, Table 2.4, provides a chronology of the major events about the emergence of EFTS in the USA. The most important pre-Internet EFTS were: the Clearing House Interbank Payments Systems (CHIPS) and the Federal Reserve Wire Network (FEDWIRE), in the USA; the Society for Worldwide Interbank Financial Telecommunications (SWIFT) for international transfers. See United States General Account Office, *Electronic Fund Transfer, Information on Three Critical Banking Systems* (Briefing Report to the Chairman, Subcommittee on Telecommunications and Finance, Committee in Energy and Commerce, House of Representatives, February 1989, GAO/IMTEC-89–25BR).

305 Reed (n 300) 267–268.

Electronic commerce increased exponentially with the Internet.[306] People started to conclude contracts by sending e-mails or accessing websites. Contrary to other electronic networks, the Internet is an open network that permits worldwide connectivity.[307] Thus, the Internet opened electronic commerce to business-to-consumer (B2C) contracts.[308] The points of major legal interest were the same as traditional e-commerce over proprietary networks,[309] plus other aspects due to the peculiar characteristics of the Internet. Namely, the fact that the Internet is an open network allowed communications between strangers. This led to a lack of trust in the online market. So, there was a need for identifying underlying identities. Identities are important in contract law for establishing the legal capacity of the parties, attributing responsibilities, determining the jurisdiction and the applicable law. Furthermore, the Internet is a virtual space, so it became difficult to establish the place of contract conclusion. Another important matter is consumers' protection. A specific profile has regard to the coincidence between the parties' will and the contract's content, given that consumers began concluding agreements by browsing web pages and clicking some online buttons provided by businesses.

Information systems do not limit themselves to transmit exchanges of data messages between contracting parties. Some of them can automatically conclude contracts on behalf of the parties. This became commonplace in securities markets worldwide since the 1990s.[310] Information systems matched purchase proposals with sale proposals according to preset parameters regarding price, date, and time. The legal debate concentrated on the imputation of contractual declarations, and consequential responsibility in case of non-performance. More recently, this discussion extended and became even more complex with artificial intelligence.[311]

306 The prototype of the Internet is ARPAnet (Advanced Research Projects Agency Network). The U.S. Department of Defense invented it in the late 1960s. About the history and functioning of the Internet, see J. Abbate (ed), *Inventing the Internet* (MIT Press 2000).

307 Reed (n 300) 268.

308 *Ibid.* 268. R. Pyle. 'Electronic commerce and the Internet' (1996) 39(6) Communications of the ACM 23 distinguishes between 'traditional electronic commerce' and 'electronic commerce on the Internet'.

309 *Ibid.* 268.

310 With Algorithmic Trading and High-Frequency Trading. See Di Ciommo (n 268).

311 The term 'Artificial Intelligence' (AI) was first adopted in 1956 by the American computer scientists John McCarthy, Marvin Minsky, Nathan Rochester, and Claude Elwood Shannon, who organised the Dartmouth Conference. See J.

This kind of technology consists of non-deterministic computer programs that can learn and behave in a way that their creators cannot predict.[312] It is the contrary of deterministic computer programs, where software actions are based on predetermined instructions, and whose outputs are foreseeable.[313]

## 2. *Sources of law in technological contracts.*

As already described, vending machines spread in many countries in the world. However, related legal discussions developed on a national basis.[314] Indeed, when a consumer uses a vending machine, there are not cross-border elements. As a consequence, regulation flowed from national contract law sources.

Instead, electronic legal acts were often exchanged between subjects coming from different countries. For this reason, numerous attempts were made to regulate the phenomenon at a supranational level.

In the European Union, European contract law sources place themselves just above national sovereignty. But the European legislature lacks a gen-

---

McCarthy, M. Minsky, N. Rochester, C. E. Shannon, 'A proposal for the Dartmouth Summer Research Project on Artificial Intelligence' (1956) <http://www-formal.stanford.edu/jmc/history/dartmouth.html> accessed 1 October 2021. However, experimentations were extremely difficult in that field, because AI applications needed large amounts of data that were not available at that time. AI developed from the late 1990s thanks to the Internet. About the history of AI, see J. Nilsson (ed), *The Quest for Artificial Intelligence – A History of Ideas and Achievements* (Cambridge University Press 2010).

312 There are many artificial intelligence technologies and solutions: Natural Language Processing, Speech Recognition, Virtual Agent, Machine Learning, AI-optimized Hardware, Decision Management, Deep Learning, Biometrics, Robotic Process Automation, Text Analytics, to name a few. See B. Purcell *et al.*, 'Tech Radar: Artificial Intelligence Technologies and Solutions, Q1 2017' (*Forrester*, 18 January 2017) <https://www.forrester.com/report/TechRadar+Artificial+Intelligence+Technologies+And+Solutions+Q1+2017/-/E-RES136196> accessed 1 October 2021.

313 About the meaning of 'deterministic computer program', see Chapter 1, Section 7.

314 As seen above under footnote 299, the first scholars who have studied the interrelations between vending machines and contract law came from Germany, and they considered German law.

eral competence in private law.[315] So, it does not produce bodies of law that replace national contract laws, although it is an instrument to reach harmonisation among the Member States. There are also supranational rules to harmonise national contract laws. International Conventions are binding instruments, but soft law also plays an important role.[316]

Electronic contracts represent a challenge for national regulation, especially after the invention of the Internet.[317] The Internet has given an extraordinary boost to the development of e-commerce, giving the possibility to anyone to commerce all around the world in a cheap manner. It has already been observed that the recourse to technology in the contractual domain has brought huge advantages reducing time and costs. In this scenario, national legislations have been perceived as a threat to the advantages that technology can bring to commerce. National fragmentation augments transaction costs and time so that it may nullify the added value of technology.[318] For this reason, supranational sources of contract law have flourished in this field.[319] In particular, the increase of international traffic and the progressive erosion of the monopoly of the States – even before the Internet era – favoured the rise of a 'new *lex mercatoria*'.[320] The expression refers to soft law rules developed by private organisations and

---

315 N. Jansen, R. Zimmermann, 'General introduction European contract law. Foundations, Commentaries, Synthesis' in N. Jansen, R. Zimmermann (eds) *Commentaries on European contract laws* (Oxford 2018) 2.

316 Soft law can take various forms. For example, guidelines, codes of conduct, resolutions, action plans, principles, and model rules are informal rules. Soft law is important because it can influence future legislations or be a reference point to draft contracts. See J. M. Smits (n 223) 33–37.

317 O. Pollicino, M. Bassini, 'Internet Law in the Era of Transnational Law' (2011) EUI Working Papers RSCAS 2011/24 <https://cadmus.eui.eu//handle/1814/16835> accessed 1 October 2021; O. Pollicino, M. Bassini, 'The Law of the Internet between Globalization and Localization' in M. Maduro, K. Tuori, S. Sankari (eds), *Transnational Law – Rethinking European Law and Legal Thinking* (Cambridge 2014), 346.

318 Granieri (n 296) 5.

319 Someone believed that the Internet would have substituted the present legal system. As seen in Chapter 2, Section 6, this approach had no practical application.

320 About the ancient *lex mercatoria* that developed in the Middle Age, see Chapter 2, Section 6, n 250. On the new *lex mercatoria*, developed by the end of the Second World War, see D. R. Johnson, D. Post, 'Law and Borders: The Rise of Law in Cyberspace' (1996) 48 Stanford Law Review 1367; F. Dely, 'Lex Mercatoria (New Law Merchant): Globalization and International Self-Regulation' in R.P. Appelbaum, L. F. Felstiner, V. Gessner (eds) *Rules and Networks* (Oxford, Hart 2001).

associations representing economic operators, such as general principles, standard clauses, or model contracts, to be included in international contracts.

The following subsections deepen the solutions that legal experts and regulators have given to the issues deriving from technological evolution in commercial activities, which have already been mentioned in the previous section. They provide an overview on existing norms whose knowledge is necessary to answer the research questions: Which novelties do smart contracts bring? Which are the same legal questions and implications? Which ones are new and peculiar of blockchain technology?

Legal research developed by considering the national legal systems with vending machines. Since the present work does not intend to base the analysis on comparative private law, it focuses on the Italian legal doctrine.[321]

With the advent of electronic commerce, especially through the Internet, supranational sources of law acquired much importance. Nevertheless, as clarified above the European Union cannot produce binding norms on contract law. At an international level, international binding norms need ratification by States. On the other hand, soft law is not binding even though useful for the above reasons. Mainly, contract law is still under the control of the nations. For these reasons, the study gives an account of the European and international regulations on electronic commerce and primarily considers the Italian legal system for uncovered aspects. Moreover, the general principles are applied to make the research also accessible to non-Italians. On the latter point, three main projects have attempted to identify commonalities between the legal systems and elaborated a set of rules to guide contract law interpretation and harmonisation: the Principles of European Contract Law (PECL), drafted between 1982 and 1996 by a group of academics guided by Professor Ole Lando;[322] the Draft Common Frame of Reference of European Private Law by the Study Group on a European Civil Code (DFCR), that also includes other fields of private law in addition to contract law;[323] the UNIDROIT Principles of

321 A. Cicu (ed), *Gli automi nel diritto privato* (Società Editrice Libraria 1901); A. Scialoja (ed), *L'offerta a persona indeterminata ed il contratto concluso mediante automatico* (S. Lapi 1902). German authors that first studied the topic (n 299) have inspired the Italian ones.

322 European Union, *The Principles of European Contract Law 2002 (Parts I, II and III)* (SiSU 2002) < https://www.jus.uio.no/lm/eu.contract.principles.parts.1.to.3.2002 /portrait.pdf> accessed 1 October 2021.

323 Study Group on a European Civil Code, Research Group on EC Private Law, *Principles, Definitions and Model Rules of European Private Law – Draft Common*

International Commercial Contracts (PICC) by the International Institute for the Unification of Private Law (UNIDROIT),[324] that deals explicitly with international B2B commercial transactions and contract laws of the entire world (not only European).[325]

## 2.1. Contract formation.

To verify whether and how the acquisition of products or services through vending machines could have fit the existing legal system, legal experts[326] had primarily to qualify the act of displaying the vending machine by the supplier and inserting the coin by the consumer. They agreed on the contractual nature of these acts.[327] Namely, they considered the first one as an offer to the public and the second one as an acceptance of the offer implied by the offeree's conduct. They added that by inserting the coin the offeree would have accepted the offer and performed her obligation. So, the performance of the offeree would have concluded the contract in the absence of the supplier. They regarded the vending machine as a means of concluding contracts. Finally, scholars reflected on the revocation of offer and acceptance. They argued that the offeror should publicly express the revocation of the proposal so that everyone could get informed.[328] Regarding revocation of acceptance, it might have happened until it would have been possible to pull back the coins.

---

*Frame of Reference (DFCR), Outline Edition* (sellier.european law publishers 2009).

324 International Institute for the Unification of Private Law, *Unidroit Principles of International Commercial Contracts* 2016 <https://www.unidroit.org/instruments/commercial-contracts/unidroit-principles-2016> accessed 1 October 2021.

325 These projects have been significantly inspired by the UN Convention on Contracts for the International Sale of Goods (CISG) of April 1980. The Convention applies to commercial cross-border sales contracts and 85 states have ratified it. However, because of its limited object (sales contracts), the choice was to only refer to the PECL, the DFCR, and the PICC. About the CISG, see C. Brunner, B. Gottlieb (eds), *Commentary on the UN Sales Law (CISG)* (Wolters Kluwer 2019).

326 The Italian authors that deepened these aspects are enlisted above, n 321. The following considerations are a summary of the conclusions reached by the majority of these authors.

327 After having excluded the analogy with the *jactus missilium* of Roman law that would have attributed the phenomenon to the field of property rights.

328 E.g. by withdrawing the vending machine or placing a notice to inform the public about the revocation of the offer.

From what has been described up to this point, it emerges that existing contract law rules have been sufficient to regulate the conclusion of contracts through vending machines, without the need for *ad hoc* rules. Researchers interpreted traditional norms and adapted them to the case.

Legal experts have adopted the same approach in the field of electronic contracts. More specifically, they have deemed that the proposal should coincide with the expression of the contractual will of the sender of the data message. Acceptance is the expression of the contractual intention of the recipient of the message that replies to the offer by sending another data message.[329] An offer to the public is made when the computer connection is not between two users but a group of users because it is addressed to an indeterminate recipient.[330]

About the time of contract conclusion, the determination is easy if the parties are present or use an instantaneous means of communication. It is more problematic when the parties are absent and a specific time passes between offer and acceptance,[331] as with electronic contracts. In this case, the time of contract conclusion varies according to the applicable legal system. In general, there are three main rules: 1) the dispatch rule (also known as 'mailbox' or 'postal' rule), where acceptance becomes effective at the moment of sending; 2) the receipt rule, which determines that a contract is considered concluded when the offeror receives the acceptance; 3) the actual notice rule, according to which a contract is formed when the offeror acquires knowledge of the acceptance.[332] The jurisdictions that adopt the actual notice rule mitigate it by presuming that the offeror acquires knowledge of the acceptance when it reaches her address unless the offeror proves that gaining knowledge of the approval was impossible for reasons not dependent on her fault.[333] In the field of electronic contracts, proposal and acceptance are sent or received in the form of data messages through electronic addresses. So, the dispatch rule implies that a contract is concluded when the electronic communication that represents the acceptance leaves the information system under the control of the offeree.

329 G. Finocchiaro (ed), *I contratti informatici* (Cedam 1997) 66. For a further analysis of the rules on the conclusion of electronic agreements in those years, see A. Gambino, *L'accordo telematico* (Giuffrè 1997).

330 *Ibid.* 68–69.

331 G. Christandl, 'Offer and acceptance', in Jansen, Zimmermann (n 315) 324.

332 *Ibid.* 324–326. The dispatch rule is typical of Common Law. The receipt rule applies to Austria, Germany, and France and the actual notice rule applies to Italy and Spain.

333 Article 1326 (1) *Codice Civile* and Article 1262 (2) *Código civil.*

Following the receipt rule, the time of conclusion is when the electronic message that contains the acceptance reaches the offeror's information system and can be accessed by the offeror. The latter is also valid with the actual notice rule unless the offeror demonstrates that she was unable (without fault) to know about the acceptance.[334]

These rules also appeared in the main EDI model framework agreements developed by some industry associations and international organisations to guide businesses in the conclusion/execution of B2B contracts via EDI.[335] In particular, Article 4.3 of the UNECE Model Interchange Agreement for the International Commercial Use of Electronic Data Interchange,[336] and Article 3 of the European Model EDI Agreement included in Annex I of Commission Recommendation of 19 October 1994 relating to the legal aspects of electronic data interchange[337] apply the receipt rule.[338] Some common law countries have favoured the receipt rule instead

---

334 Art. 1335 *Codice Civile*. Finocchiaro (n 329) 66.

335 Finocchiaro (n 329) 69–70.

336 United Nations Economic Commission for Europe Working Party on Facilitation of International Trade Procedures (WP4), Model Interchange Agreement for the International Commercial Use of Electronic Data Interchange (1991) Trade/WP.4/R.697 <https://www.unece.org/tradewelcome/un-centre-for-trade-facilitation-and-e-business-uncefact/outputs/standards/unedifact/tradeedifactrules/part-2-uniform-rules-of-conduct-for-interchange-of-trade-data-by-teletransmission-uncid/part-2-uncid-chapter-4-annex.html> accessed 1 October 2021.

337 Commission Recommendation of 19 October 1994 relating to the legal aspects of electronic data interchange (94/820/EC) OJ 338/98.

338 Both articles provide that a contract is formed when the offeror's computer system receives the message of acceptance. The commentaries to the agreements explicitly refer to the receipt rule. Another important EDI model framework agreement is the American Bar Association Model Electronic Data Interchange Trading Partner Agreement and Commentary (1990) 45 Business Lawyer 1645. Art. 2.1 of the latter model framework agreement states that no document may create any legal obligation until received by the computer designated by the receiving party.

339 As regards technological contracts in England, acceptance becomes effective upon receipt, instead of the dispatch rule for traditional contracts (regulation 11 of the Electronic Commerce Regulations 2002). The same is in Australia. See A. Rawls, 'Contract Formation in an Internet Age' (2009) X Columbia Science and Technology Law Review 200, 207 ff; E. Mik, 'The Effectiveness of Acceptances Communicated by Electronic Means, or – Does the Postal Acceptance Rule Apply to Email?' (2009) 26 Journal of Contract Law 1, 8; Giancaspro (n 197) 825. The reason is that the dispatch rule was conceived as a compromise between the offer's free revocability until the contract's conclusion and the need to protect the offeree. Indeed, with traditional ways of communication for concluding contracts at a distance, acceptance could have taken a lot of time

of the dispatch rule in electronic commerce, also on the Internet.[339] Moreover, the PICC,[340] the PECL,[341] and the DFCR[342] apply the receipt rule.

In summary, traditional rules have been interpreted to suit the electronic context. This has also been the result of the United Nations Commission on International Trade Law (UNCITRAL).[343] The UNCITRAL has been one of the first international institutions to reflect on electronic commerce and foster progressive harmonisation of the national laws to develop international trade. In 1996 it adopted the UNCITRAL Model Law on Electronic Commerce (MLEC).[344] The MLEC established three main principles: non-discrimination, technology neutrality, and functional equivalence. According to the first principle, a document shall not be denied validity or enforceability on the sole ground that it is in an electronic form. The second principle prevents the adoption of specific rules for every technology because they would hinder technological development. The third principle is based on analysing the purposes and functions of the traditional paper-based requirement to determine how those purposes or functions could be fulfilled through electronic-commerce techniques.

Concerning contract conclusion, Article 11 of the MLEC states that an offer and an acceptance could be expressed by means of data messages. About the time of the conclusion of contracts, no specific rules have been included to not interfere with national laws. Article 15 only clarifies the time of dispatch and receipt of data messages. The combination of existing rules on contract formation with Article 15 of the MLEC has helped to establish the time of formation of electronic contracts without uncertainty.

---

before arriving at its destination. So, the offeree should have been able to accept a contract with the certainty that it would have been binding. Now, because offer and acceptance are exchanged instantaneously, the dispatch rule has lost its function.

340 Art. 2.1.6(2) PICC.

341 Art. 2:205(1) PECL.

342 Art. II. – 4:205(1) DFCR.

343 <https://uncitral.un.org> accessed 1 October 2021.

344 UNITED NATIONS, *UNCITRAL Model Law on Electronic Commerce with Guide to Enactment 1996 with additional article 5 bis as adopted in 1998* (United Nations 1999) <https://uncitral.un.org/en/texts/ecommerce/modellaw/electronic_commerce> accessed 1 October 2021. See R. Sorieul (ed), *The UNCITRAL Model Law and the Modernization of Legislation to Facilitate Electronic Commerce, Electronic Commerce Initiatives of ESCAP: Business Facilitation Needs/Economic and Social Commission for Asia and the Pacific* (United Nations 1998) 59–80; L. Castellani, 'I testi dell'UNCITRAL in materia di diritto del commercio elettronico' in G. Finocchiaro and F. Delfini (eds), *Diritto dell'informatica* (Utet 2014) 44–46.

In 2005, when the Internet had become more widely accessible, the UNCITRAL approved the United Nations Convention on the Use of Electronic Communications in International Contracts.[345] The Convention drew large inspiration from the MLEC and is based on the same principles. Similarly to Article 15 of the MLEC, Article 10 of the Convention defines the time of dispatch and receipt of electronic communication.[346] Article 11 admits that proposals made through electronic communications can be addressed to the general public. The article considers these proposals as invitations to make offers, unless they clearly indicate the intention to be bound in case of acceptance (and in the latter case, the proposal is an offer to the public).

In Europe, Directive 2000/31/CE on electronic commerce[347] requires that service providers render accessible to the recipients of the service some general information about themselves and prices of service.[348] In addition, at the moment of the conclusion of the contract, they have to give supplementary information[349] about the technical steps to follow to conclude the contract, the storage and accessibility of the contract, the technical means to correct input errors prior to the order, the languages of the contract, the relevant codes of conduct to which they eventually subscribe and how to electronically consult such codes.[350] If the recipient

345 United Nations Commission on International Trade Law, *United Nations Convention on the Use of Electronic Communications in International Contracts* (United Nations 2005) <https://uncitral.un.org/en/texts/ecommerce/conventions/electronic_communications> accessed 1 October 2021. See A. H. Boss and W. Kilian (eds), *The United Nations Convention on the Use of Electronic Communications in International Contracts: An In-depth Guide and Sourcebook* (Wolters Kluwer 2008); M. Ratti, '*La Convenzione sull'uso delle comunicazioni elettroniche: le principali disposizioni*' in Finocchiaro, Delfini (n 344) 71–85.

346 Similarly, Art. I. – 1:109 (4)(c) DFCR provides that a notice transmitted by electronic means reaches the address when the addressee can access it.

347 Directive (EC) 31/2000 on certain legal aspects of information society services, in particular electronic commerce, in the Internal Market [2000] OJ L 178/1. See G. Pearce, N. Platten, 'Promoting the Information Society: The EU Directive on Electronic Commerce' (2000) 6 European Law Journal 363; C. Hultmark Ramberg, ' The E-Commerce Directive and Formation of Contract in a Comparative Perspective' (2001) 26 European Law Review 429.

348 Art. 5.

349 Art. 10.

350 The recent Proposal for a Regulation of the European Parliament and of the Council on a Single Market for Digital Services (Digital Services Act) and amending Directive 2000/31/EC COM/2020/825 final, contains an obligation for certain online platforms to receive, store and partially verify and publish

of the service places her order, the service provider has to acknowledge the receipt of the recipient's order without undue delay and by electronic means.[351] These provisions do not affect national rules regarding contract conclusion. The duty to send an acknowledgement of receipt does not introduce a new way of exchanging offer and acceptance.[352] The receipt is intended to give certainty about the conclusion of the contract, given that the recipient is distant from the provider and cannot know if the order arrived at its destination.[353] The main EDI model framework agreements[354]

---

information on traders using their services to conclude distance contracts with European consumers (see Art. 22 of the Proposal). The latter provision aims to ensure an even safer environment for consumers. The Proposal builds on the key principles set out in the e-Commerce Directive while seeking to ensure the best conditions for providing innovative digital services in the internal market. Along with the Digital Markets Act, the Digital Services Act constitutes the Digital Services Act package, encopassing a single set of new rules applicable across the whole EU that will create a safer and more open digital space, with European values at its centre. For more information, see <https://ec.europa.eu/digital-single-market/en/digital-services-act-package> accessed 1 October 2021. For a comment on the Proposal, see (in Italian) A. Gambino, D. Tuzzolino, 'Il Digital Services Act tra responsabilità e governance. Commento alla proposta di Regolamento' (*Diritto Mercato Tecnologia*, 18 December 2020) <https://www.dimt.it/news/il-digital-services-act-tra-responsabilita-e-governance-commento-alla-proposta-di-regolamento/> accessed 1 October 2021.

351 Art. 11. A similar provision is laid down in Art. II. – 3:202 DFCR.

352 J. K. Winn, J. Haubold, 'Electronic Promises: Contract Law Reform and E-Commerce in a Comparative Perspective' (2002) 27 European Law Review 567, 575. The authors state that 'the only rule that might directly interfere with national contract law is the provision on the moment of receipt of electronic offers and acceptances'.

353 For instance, Art. 13 of the Italian implementing Legislative Decree no. 70 of 9 April 2003 (Decreto legislativo 9 aprile 2003, n. 70 'Attuazione della direttiva 2000/31/CE relativa a taluni aspetti giuridici dei servizi della società dell'informazione nel mercato interno, con particolare riferimento al commercio elettronico', G.U. n. 87, 14.4.2013, S.O. n. 61) specifies that the Italian norms on the conclusion of the contract apply when a contract is concluded electronically. See D. Memmo, 'Il consenso nei contratti telematici' in Finocchiaro, Delfini (n 344) 506 ff.

354 See Art. 3.2 UNECE Model Interchange Agreement for the International Commercial Use of Electronic Data Interchange, Art. 5 European Model EDI Agreement included in Annex I of Commission Recommendation of 19 October 1994 relating to the legal aspects of electronic data interchange, and Art. 2.2 American Bar Association Model Electronic Data Interchange Trading Partner Agreement.

and the UNCITRAL Model Law on Electronic Commerce[355] also provide similar duties for the originating party towards the receiving party.

As seen above,[356] with the advent of the Internet and the development of electronic commerce, people started to conduct their affairs without knowing the counterparty's identity and without the possibility to test the quality of desired products directly. Indeed, the Internet is an open network that permits communication between strangers leading to a lack of trust in the online market. For this reason, traditional contract law needed to be accompanied by further norms to encourage electronic contracting. Therefore, thanks to information duties, even though the parties are far away from each other, the recipient can understand whether she is concluding a contract and under which contractual conditions. Additional information and acknowledgement of receipt shall not apply to contracts concluded exclusively by an exchange of electronic mails or equivalent individual communication,[357] because it is more likely that the counterparty is already known, and the conclusion of the contract is less risky for the recipient.

For similar reasons, additional information and acknowledgment of receipt are not mandatory in B2B contracts.[358] The European legislator pays huge attention to the protection of consumers, which are the weakest contracting party. Indeed, if the contract is concluded between a company and an individual consumer (B2C), the Directive 2011/83/EU shall also apply.[359] The Directive aims to lay down standard rules for the common aspects of distance and off-premises contracts in the European Union to foster consumers' protection.[360] According to the definition provided by the Directive, a distance contract is 'any contract concluded between the

355 Art. 14.
356 Section 1.
357 Art. 10(4) and Art. 11(3).
358 Art. 10(1) and Art. 11(1).
359 Directive 2011/83/EU of the European Parliament and of the Council of 25 October 2011 on consumer rights, amending Council Directive 93/13/EEC and Directive 1999/44/EC of the European Parliament and of the Council and repealing Council Directive 85/577/EEC and Directive 97/7/EC of the European Parliament and of the Council Text with EEA relevance [2011] OJ L 304/64. See H. Hall, G. Howells, J. Watson, 'The Consumer Rights Directive – An Assessment of its Contribution to the Development of European Consumer Contract Law' (2012) 8 European Review of Contract Law 139; S. Grundmann, 'The EU Consumer Rights Directive – Optimizing, Creating Alternatives or a Dead-End' (2013) 18 Uniform Law Review, 98.
360 Recital 2.

trader and the consumer under an organised distance sales or service provision scheme without the simultaneous physical presence of the trader and the consumer, with the exclusive use of one or more means of distance communication up to and including the time at which the contract is concluded'.[361] Electronic commerce is included in this definition.[362] As concerns the formation of distance contracts, the Directive 2011/83/EU adds information requirements for the trader in favour of the consumer.[363]

Both in the Directive on electronic commerce and the Directive on consumer contracts, compliance to information requirements needs that the obligor provides all the information and that the information is given in a clear and comprehensible manner.[364] These provisions stress the importance of quality – more than quantity – of information, to ensure consumers' real understanding.

---

361 Art. 2(7).

362 Recital 20 explicitly refers to contracts concluded using mail orders or the Internet.

363 In particular, the trader has to give information to the consumer on her right of withdrawal. The norms related to the right of withdrawal are more favourable for the consumer if compared to the general provisions. According to Art. 169 of the Treaty of the Functioning of the European Union, the Union shall promote consumers' right to information. Information requirements can be also found in Art. II. – 3:104 and 3:105 DFCR.
The recent Directive (EU) 2019/2161 of the European Parliament and of the Council of 27 November 2019 amending Council Directive 93/13/EEC and Directives 98/6/EC, 2005/29/EC and 2011/83/EU of the European Parliament and of the Council as regards the better enforcement and modernisation of Union consumer protection rules [2019] OJ L 328/7 (or 'Omnibus Directive') has amended Directive 2011/83/EU. The Directive has been approved to strengthen enforcement of EU consumer law and modernising EU consumer protection rules given market development, like the norms on information requirements for distance contracts (e.g. the trader has to inform the consumer whether the price was personalised based on automated decision-making; there are additional information requirements for contracts concluded on online marketplaces, *etc.*). For a summary of the novelties brought by the Directive, see the European Commission Factsheet 'New Deal: What benefits will I get as a consumer?' available at the following link <https://ec.europa.eu/info/sites/info/files/factsheet_new_deal_consumer_benefits_2019.pdf> accessed 1 October 2021.
In Italy, legislative decree no. 206 of 6 September 2005, also known as Consumer Code (Decreto legislativo n. 206 del 6 settembre 2005, G.U. n. 235, 8.10.2005, S.O. n. 162) has implemented Directive 2011/83/EU. Article 68 of the Italian Consumer Code refers to the Italian legislative decree no. 70 of 9 April 2003 on Electronic Commerce.

364 Also Art. II. – 3:106 DFCR stresses the importance of clear information.

The literature expressed some doubts about the technical feasibility of revocation of acceptance. In the domain of electronic contracts, transmissions of data messages occur instantaneously, so it is difficult to discern whether revocation is antecedent to the conclusion of the contract.[365]

### 2.1.1. Conclusion of contracts through software agents.

In the hypotheses described in the previous section, contract conclusion takes place through an electronic medium. Parties transmit their contractual will electronically. So, the contractual agreement is attributable to the parties. Instead, when computer systems replace humans in concluding contracts, one questions whether the contractual will could be attributed to information systems.

As already seen,[366] the first application used to conclude agreements on behalf of the parties was algorithmic securities trading in the 1990s. In the following years, electronic commerce was characterised by the spread of so-called 'mobile agents', or 'software agents', computer programs able to move within the network, and perform tasks for users. They are considered extremely useful because of their capacity to manage big amounts of data. For example, they can be used to compare the prices of a good on the Internet, to make the best choice for the user according to her preferences.[367]

An international juridical debate developed on this point. The main object of discussion concerned the qualification of these algorithms as agents – which recalls the notion of agency – or as mere tools for expressing par-

365 R. Clarizia (ed), *Informatica e conclusione del contratto* (Giuffrè 1985) 159–160. This difficulty in revoking the acceptance justifies the European discipline on the right of withdrawal and the duty of the service provider to make available to the recipient appropriate, effective and accessible means (e.g. a splash screen, a pop-up window or an intermediate-review screenshot) allowing the identification and correction of input errors, prior to the placing of the order (Art. 11(2) of the Directive on e-Commerce).

366 Section 1.

367 V. A. Pham, A. Karmouch, 'Mobile Software Agents: An Overview' (1998) 36(7) IEEE Communications Magazine 26; C. Mc Gregor, S. Kumaran, 'An Agent-Based System for Trading Partner Management in B2b e- Commerce' (IEEE Proceedings of the 12th International Workshop on Research Issues in Data Engineering: engineering e-Commerce/e-Business Systems RIDE-2EC, San Jose, CA, USA, 24–25 February 2002) 84 <https://ieeexplore.ieee.org/document/995102?arnumber=995102> accessed 1 October 2021.

ties' will.[368] In this regard, the majority agreed on the thesis that software agents do not affect the law. Software agents have to be considered as simple tools to transpose the party's will – because they act based on predetermined schemes – and of which parties have to be legally responsible.

Indeed, Article 13(2) of the UNCITRAL Model Law on Electronic Commerce prescribes that 'As between the originator and the addressee, a data message is deemed to be that of the originator if it was sent: (…) b) by an information system programmed by, or on behalf of, the originator to operate automatically.' Then, the UNCITRAL has clarified that 'while the expression "electronic agent" had been used for purposes of convenience, the analogy between an automated system and a sales agent was not entirely appropriate and that general principles of agency law (for example, principles involving limitation of liability as a result of the faulty behaviour of the agent) could not be used in connection with the operation of such systems. The Working Group reiterated its earlier understanding that, as a general principle, the person (whether a natural or legal one) on whose behalf a computer was programmed should ultimately be responsible for any message generated by the machine'.[369] Moreover, the United Nations Convention on the Use of Electronic Communications in International Contracts gives a wide definition of 'automated computer system,'[370] which also covers software agents, and states that the interaction of automated computer systems may form a contract.[371]

Legal experts and legislators essentially denied the need of new norms or the presence of juridical obstacles for the automatic conclusion of contracts through software agents.[372]

---

368 G. Gitti, 'Robotic Transactional Decisions' (2018) 2 Osservatorio del diritto civile e commerciale 619, 624–625.

369 United Nations Commission on International Trade Law, *Yearbook Volume XXXII: 2001* (United Nations 2003) 240.

370 Art. 1(e): "Automated computer system' means a computer program or an electronic or other automated means used to initiate an action or respond to data messages or performances in whole or in part, without review or intervention by a natural person at each time an action is initiated or a response is generated by the system'.

371 Art. 12(1). This definition was inspired by those included in the United States Uniform Electronic Transaction Act and Canada's Uniform Electronic Commerce Act.

372 The view that considered software agents as agents under the law of agency has been subjected to criticisms. First of all, it was objected that they are not persons, i.e. they lack legal personality. Furthermore, even though they would be recognised a legal personality this could not lead to legal simplification, be-

With artificial intelligence, because software agents are not simply automated but rather autonomous and the contracting party cannot predict their behaviours, it is more doubtful to consider those algorithms as tools to transfer someone's will. As declared in the European Parliament resolution of 16 February 2017 with recommendations to the Commission on Civil Law Rules on Robotics,[373] technological advances have made them more and more similar to agents,[374] and 'the more autonomous robots are, the less they can be considered to be simple tools in the hand of other actors'.[375] Discussions about this aspect are still open.[376]

---

cause the contract would produce its effects on the principal. On the contrary, the presence of two separate patrimonies (the one of the principal and the agent) could result in some forms of abuse. For example, if the electronic agent operates more than its implied authority, the principal would not be liable for the damages caused by the agent. See E. M. Weitzenboeck, 'Electronic Agents and the Formation of Contracts' (2001) 9(3) International Journal of Law and Information Technology 204; T. Allen, R. Widdison, 'Can Computers Make Contracts?' (1996) 9(1) Harvard Journal of Law & Technology 25; G. Finocchiaro, 'La conclusione del contratto telematico mediante I 'software agents': un falso problema giuridico?' (2002) 18(2) Contratto e impresa 500.

373 European Parliament resolution of 16 February 2017 with recommendations to the Commission on Civil Law Rules on Robotics (2015/2103(INL)), P8_TA(2017)0051 <https://www.europarl.europa.eu/doceo/document/TA-8-2017-0051_EN.pdf> accessed 1 October 2021. About the actions of the institutions of the European Union on the liability of artificial intelligence and applicable civil law rules, see Section 2.2 of this chapter.

374 Paragraph Z.

375 Paragraph AB.

376 It seems that there are still two main opposite positions: on the one hand, there are those who suggest the application of the law of agency; on the other hand, someone continues to deny a parallel between software and agents. For instance, in favour of the first approach, see L. H. Sholz, 'Algorithmic contracts' (2017) 20 Standard Technology Law Review 101; in favour of the second, G. Finocchiaro, 'Il contratto nell'era dell'intelligenza artificiale' (2018) 2 Rivista Trimestrale di Diritto e Procedura Civile 441. The former affirms that a so-formed contract cannot be considered an expression of the will of the individual or company that makes use of such programs. The second believes that applying the rules of agency law would not lead to significant results because the responsibility would still lie with the user of the program. Instead, the author claims that the user expresses her will to conclude contracts by means of artificial intelligence, which determines the content of the contract.

### 2.1.2. Digital identity in electronic commerce.

Knowing the identity of the other contracting party can be legally relevant.[377]Furthermore, the law itself sometimes imposes identification procedures.[378] In electronic commerce, the other contracting party's identification is necessary to foster the conclusion of online contracts by promoting trust among users. As already seen,[379] the openness of the Internet enhanced exchanges with strangers. Before the Internet, this aspect was less important. Vending machines did not require identification means due to the low economic value of transactions.[380] Exceptions were related to the particular kind of contract. For example, insurance policy dispensing machines needed the signature of the policyholder.[381]

In traditional electronic commerce, even though commercial relations were maintained through closed networks, parties could agree on identity verification procedures.[382] In this regard, the European Union has intervened with binding norms for the Member States. Firstly, it is worth mentioning the information requirements laid down in Directive 2000/31/CE because some of them allow the identification of the supplier.[383] The same is also valid for the information requirements for traders towards consumers set by Directive 2011/83/EU.[384]

Another method of identification in e-commerce is the electronic signature. According to Article 3(1)(10) of the European Union Regulation n. 910/2014 on electronic identification and trust services for electronic

377 Section 1.

378 For instance, when the conclusion of a contract takes place in front of a notary, or the Know Your Customer (KYC) procedures established by bank or anti-money laundering regulations.

379 Section 1.

380 Scialoja (n 321) 168.

381 Schiller (n 299) 58.

382 For example, Art. 6.2 of the European Model EDI Agreement included in Annex I of Commission Recommendation of 19 October 1994 about the security of EDI messages includes the mandatory verification of the origin of EDI messages to identify the sender of an EDI message. Article 13(3)(a) of the UNCITRAL Model Law on Electronic Commerce mentions applying specific procedures previously agreed between the originator and the addressee in order to ascertain whether the data message was that of the originator.

383 E.g. the name or the geographic address of the service provider.

384 E.g. the name or the geographic address of the trader.

transactions (better known as e-IDAS Regulation)[385] ' 'electronic signature' means data in electronic form which is attached to or logically associated with other data in electronic form and which is used by the signatory to sign'. The Regulation recognises three different kinds of electronic signature: the simple,[386] the advanced,[387] and the qualified.[388] Only the latter is considered equivalent to a handwritten signature because of its higher level of reliability and trust.[389]

The same Regulation also contains an obligation of mutual recognition of national electronic identification means among the Member States. Art. 3(1)(1) of the e-IDAS Regulation defines 'electronic identification' as 'the process of using person identification data in electronic form uniquely representing either a natural or legal person, or a natural person representing a legal person', while Art. 3(1)(2) states that 'electronic identification means' is 'a material and/or immaterial unit containing person identification data and which is used for authentication for an online service'. The principle of mutual recognition establishes that every Member States can adopt its electronic identification mean that must be recognised by the others (upon the respect of some preconditions laid down in Art. 6 of the Regulation).[390] Mutual recognition is aimed to 'facilitate cross-border provision of numerous services in the internal market and enable businesses to operate on a cross-border basis without facing many obstacles in interactions with public authorities'.[391] Indeed, 'in most cases, citizens cannot

---

385 Regulation (EU) 910/2014 of the European Parliament and of the Council of 23 July 2014 on electronic identification and trust services for electronic transactions in the internal market and repealing Directive 1999/93/EC [2014] OJ L 257/73. On the eIDAS Regulation, see A. Zaccaria, M. Schmidt Kessel, R. Schulze, A. M. Gambino (eds), EU *eIDAS Regulation – Article-by-Article Commentary* (Beck Hart Nomos 2020); on the relationship between the Regulation and the Italian legal system, see F. Delfini, G. Finocchiaro (eds), *Identificazione elettronica e servizi fiduciari per le transazioni elettroniche nel mercato interno, commento al regolamento UE 910/2014* (Giappichelli 2017).

386 Art. 3(1)(10).

387 Art. 3(1)(11).

388 Art. 3(1)(12).

389 Art. 25(2). In Italy, Article 20(1-bis) of the *Codice dell'Amministrazione Digitale*, or *CAD* (D.Lgs. 7 marzo 2005, n. 82, G.U. 16 maggio 2005, S.O. n. 93) disciplines the 'firma digitale' (digital signature). It is a peculiar kind of qualified electronic signature that makes use of asymmetric cryptography.

390 The Italian electronic identification means are the SPID, *Sistema Pubblico per la gestione dell'Identità Digitale di cittadini e imprese* (Art. 64 of the CAD) and the CIE, *Carta d'Identità Elettronica* (Art. 66 of the CAD).

391 Recital 9 of the e-IDAS Regulation.

use their electronic identification to authenticate themselves in another Member State because the national electronic identification schemes in their country are not recognised in other Member States'.[392]

On 3 June 2021, the European Commission published the Proposal for a Regulation amending Regulation eIDAS.[393] The Proposal aims to overcome the limitations of the Regulation and accelerate the spread of electronic identity solutions across the EU.[394] The final objective is the setting of a European Digital Identity framework, for example through the introduction of a European Digital Identity Wallet to store identity data, credentials and attributes linked to someone's identity.[395]

At an international level, there are no rules for the mutual recognition of national electronic identification means. This could be of great help to stimulate people to carry out their transactions electronically. The UNCITRAL Working Group IV on Electronic Commerce has been working on a model law for the international cross-border recognition of identity management and trust services since 2018.[396] Until now, in the absence of such an instrument there are plenty of usernames and passwords

---

392 *Ibid.*

393 Proposal for a Regulation of the European Parliament and of the Council amending Regulation (EU) No 910/2014 as regards establishing a framework for a European Digital Identity (<https://eur-lex.europa.eu/legal-content/EN/TXT/PDF/?uri=CELEX:52021PC0281&from=EN> accessed 1 October 2021). The Proposal also provides the definition and legal effects of electronic ledgers, new qualified trust services that include blockchain technology (art. 3(53), art. 45-*nonies* and, art. 45-*decies*).

394 The explanatory memorandum of the Proposal states that 'The evaluation of the eIDAS Regulation2 revealed that the current Regulation falls short of addressing these new market demands, mostly due to its inherent limitations to the public sector, the limited possibilities and the complexity for online private providers to connect to the system, its insufficient availability of notified eID solutions in all Member States and its lack of flexibility to support a variety of use cases. Furthermore, identity solutions falling outside the scope of eIDAS, such as those offered by social media providers and financial institutions, raise privacy and data protection concerns. They cannot effectively respond to new market demands and lack the cross border outreach to address specific sectoral needs where identification is sensitive and requires a high degree of certainty'.

395 The Proposal defines a European Digital Identity Wallet as 'a product and service that allows the user to store identity data, credentials and attributes linked to her/his identity, to provide them to relying parties on request and to use them for authentication, online and offline, for a service under Article 6a; and to create qualified electronic signatures and seals'.

396 To follow the advancements of the working group, see <https://uncitral.un.org/en/working_groups/4/electronic_commerce> accessed 1 October 2021.

and other mechanisms of identification when dealing with electronic commerce.

### 2.1.3. Defects of consent: the mistake.

Defects of consent such as mistakes are vitiating factors that can make a contract voidable. The issue is not irrelevant in technological contracts because of the particular mean used to conclude contracts.

More precisely, the following circumstances can affect the validity of electronic contracts. Firstly, contractual parties that make declarations of intent may be mistaken about the content of the contract they agree to. In electronic commerce, these kinds of errors may happen because contracts are concluded at a distance. Especially in electronic commerce on the Internet, as already described, contractual relations occur between strangers without the possibility of testing desired products directly. Moreover, offer and acceptance are exchanged with instantaneous communications where the pre-contractual phase is substantially absent and revocation is essentially impossible.[397] In B2C online contracts, consumers conclude contracts by navigating on websites made available by businesses or platforms intermediaries and displaying virtual icons and buttons that may disorient users.[398] Articles 4:103 PECL, 3.2.1 PICC, and II.-7:201 DFCR refer to the discipline of error.[399] The latter is included in Articles 1427 ff. of the Codice civile (cc) in the Italian legal system.[400]

397 Chapter 3, Section 2.1.

398 Most online contracts are entered into the form of 'wrap contracts', adhesion contracts where both presentation of the terms and assent differ from traditional manners. The most common wrap contracts in the digital environment are 'click-wrap' and 'browse-wrap' agreements. In click-wrap contracts, the non-drafting party is asked to manifest her consent, even though in non-traditional ways, such as clicking on an 'I agree' dialogue box. Instead, in browse-wrap agreements, contract terms are accessible via hyperlinks to the 'terms of use' or 'legal terms'. The non-drafting party is not asked to agree to those terms, and the mere fact that she makes use of digital content or service is considered acceptance of the contract.

399 See S. Lohsse, 'Art. 4:103: Fundamental mistakes as to Facts or Law' in Jansen, Zimmermann (n 315) 657–673.

400 See C. M. Bianca (ed), *Il contratto* (3rd edn Giuffrè 2019) 601 ff. For a comparative perspective, see K. Zweigert, H. Kotz (eds), *An introduction to comparative law*, (3rd edn Oxford University Press 1998) 410 ff.

Secondly, when contracts are formed through software agents, the person's will to use the computer program may be vitiated. In contrast, the computer program works appropriately (even though it acts based on a vitiated will). Conversely, the will of the person may be not vitiated, but there may be an error in the computer program. The matter is related to the qualification of the program as an agent or as a mere tool to transpose someone's will. On this point, it has been already clarified[401] that, when computer programs are deterministic, there is a common opinion of considering the software as the expression of the will of the person on whose behalf the software was programmed. So, even when the mistake is of the program, the person making use of the program is considered in error. It has also been given an account of the actual open debate regarding using artificial intelligence solutions.[402]

Thirdly, errors may occur in the communication or transmission of a statement through computer systems. For instance, when incorrect data is entered by keystroke error or when someone clicks with the mouse on the wrong area on the computer screen. In automated systems, the computer program may make a transmission error. There may be errors in the communication system. In all these hypotheses, mistakes does not affect the contractual will but the transmission. They fall within Articles 4:104 PECL, 3.2.3 PICC and, II.-7:202 DFCR about inaccuracy (or mistake, or error) in communication.[403] The Italian corresponding rule is Article 1433 *cc*.[404] Article 14 of the UN Convention on the Use of Electronic Communications in International Contracts states that 'When a natural person makes an input error in an electronic communication exchanged with the automated message system of another party and the automated message system does not provide the person with an opportunity to correct the error, that person, or the party on whose behalf that person was acting, has the right to withdraw the portion of the electronic communication in which the input error was made (...)'. The norm aims at remedying mistakes made in entering data that bind people to vitiated contracts. Indeed, the presence of an automated system prevents correcting the error

401 Chapter 3, Section 2.1.1.

402 Chapter 3, Section 2.1.1.

403 See S. Lohsse, 'Art. 4:104: Inaccuracy in Communication' in Jansen, Zimmermann (n 315) 674–680.

404 See Bianca (n 400) 601 ff. For a comparative perspective, see Zweigert, Kotz (n 400) 410 ff.

prior to the conclusion of the contract, due to the particular functioning of the medium.[405]

Not all mistakes cause the avoidance of the contract. The interest of the mistaken party has to be balanced with the other party's reliance on the agreement. For this reason, the mistake has to be fundamental, i.e. it must concern an essential characteristic of the good or an essential quality of a person; therefore, the contract would not have been concluded if the mistaken party had known the truth. In addition, the other party's reliance on the agreement has to be unreasonable, in the sense that the other party must know, or ought to have known, that the mistake regarded a fundamental aspect of the agreement.[406]

In electronic commerce, many security procedures and technical measures have been developed to detect errors in the content of the contract and the identity of the parties. The EDI model framework agreements contain clauses on implementing security procedures and measures for verifying the origin and integrity of the message to identify the sender and ascertain the message itself is complete and has not been corrupted.[407] As seen above, European Directive on electronic commerce and Directive 2011/83/EU for the protection of consumers in distance contracts establish information requirements on the contracting party and the content of the contract.[408] The acknowledgement of receipt[409] could be another useful instrument to find errors because it can give information on the correctness of the content of the message[410] or it can contain a summary of the content of the order.[411] Then, Section 2.1.2 of this chapter has described the huge

405 For a comment of the Article, see J. D. Gregory, J. Remsu, 'Article 14. Error in Electronic Communication' in Boss, Kilian (n 345) 198–211.

406 There are many differences in the discipline of error between the national legal systems. In particular, English law rarely allows a remedy for mistakes. The above considerations refer to general principles (PICC, PECL, DFCR) and the Italian legal system.

407 An example is Art. 6 of the American Bar Association Model Electronic Data Interchange Trading Partner Agreement. It provides that, in case an error is detected, the receiver has to inform the sender within a specified time limit. The receiver shall not act upon the EDI message before receiving instructions from the sender.

408 Section 2.1.

409 Section 2.1.

410 E.g. Art. 6 of the American Bar Association Model Electronic Data Interchange Trading Partner Agreement.

411 E.g. Art. 13(2) of the Italian Legislative Decree no. 70 of 9 April 2003 implementing Art. 11 of the European Directive 31/2000 on e-Commerce.

variety of identification methods, from electronic signatures to national identification means. These mechanisms help avoid parties' mistakes. Furthermore, they constitute criteria to evaluate the apparent importance of the mistake.[412] In this respect, the familiarity of the mistaken party with computer systems is another important yardstick.

### 2.1.4. Form requirements.

With electronic commerce, electronic documents have replaced paper documents. However, according to the principle of informality, the parties are free to choose any form to conclude contracts.[413] This principle allows the conclusion of contracts in an electronic form. Another internationally recognised principle supports this statement, which is the principle of non-discrimination. As seen above,[414] the principle of non-discrimination can be found in the Model Law on Electronic Commerce[415] and the United Nations Convention on the Use of Electronic Communications in International Contracts.[416] The EDI model framework agreements also refer to it.[417] In Europe, Article 46 of the e-IDAS Regulation establishes that 'an electronic document shall not be denied legal effect and admissibility as evidence in legal proceedings solely on the grounds that it is in electronic form'.

Sometimes the law requires a specific form for the validity of contracts, or to prove their existence.[418] So, it was wondered when an electronic

---

412 For instance, if the obliged party infringes her information duties, it is more likely that the party's mistake is excusable.

413 Art. 1.2 PICC, Art. 2:101(2) PECL, Art. II. – 1:106 DFCR.

414 Section 2.1.

415 Art. 5.

416 Art. 8(1).

417 E.g. see Art. 3.1 of the European Model EDI Agreement included in Annex I of Commission Recommendation of 19 October 1994: 'The parties, intending to be legally bound by the Agreement, expressly waive any rights to contest the validity of a contract effected by the use of EDI in accordance with the terms and conditions of the Agreement on the sole ground that it was effected by EDI'.

418 About the contract form in Italy, see Bianca (n 400) 243 ff. For a comparative perspective, see Zweigert, Kotz, (n 400) 323 ff. Such formalities have the function to warn a party that she is entering a particularly important or financially dangerous contract (warning function) or informing the party before she is bound (information function). Formalities to prove the existence of the contract

contract could have been considered valid or evidenced when the law requires some formalities.[419] In this regard, the UNCITRAL has adopted the functional equivalence approach.[420] The function of the written form is to ensure: (a) the lasting character of the content of the contract; (b) the attribution of that content to a specific person. Therefore, according to the above principle, one should determine when the electronic form could be considered equivalent to the written form. This has been done considering the level of security of the adopted technical solutions, although without referring to specific technologies in line with the principle of technology neutrality.[421]

When the law requires some formalities for the validity or evidence of a contract, the parties usually have to sign the contract.[422] When the contract is in an electronic form, it can be signed with electronic signatures. Hence, the question was whether electronic signatures could be considered equivalent to handwritten signatures.

The function of signatures is to ensure that the content of a document is attributable to a specific person. Namely, they must provide evidence of the identity of the signatory, her intention to sign, and her intention to adopt the content of the document as her own. Article 2(a) of the UNCITRAL Model Law on Electronic Signatures defines electronic signatures as 'data in electronic form in, affixed to or logically associated with, a data message, which may be used to identify the signatory in relation to the data message and to indicate the signatory's approval of the information contained in the data message'. According to Article 3(10) of the e-IDAS Regulation, electronic signatures are 'data in electronic form which is attached to or logically associated with other data in electronic form and which is used by the signatory to sign'. Electronic signatures differ from traditional signatures because the latter result from a human gesture, so they are based on graphics. Electronic signatures result from

---

have the function to provide certainty about the existence and the content of contracts (evidentiary function).

419 Reed (n 300) 277.

420 On the principle of functional equivalence, see Section 2.1.

421 On the principle of technology neutrality, see Section 2.1.

422 Some contracts need to be laid down in a notarial deed in civil law. In these cases, the parties sign the deed and the notary must establish that the parties intend to be bound after having warned them about the legal consequences of their action.

a technological procedure and are based on a technique.[423] Hence, it was wondered when electronic signatures could be considered equivalent to handwritten signatures. For this reason, electronic signatures are not automatically equivalent to manuscript signatures, unless such equivalence is agreed by the parties or established by the law.[424]

Parties may agree on the equivalence of electronic signatures with traditional signatures. However, the agreement would not bind third parties. Moreover, such agreements may have a sense between B2B long-term relationships. Indeed, such provisions appeared in EDI model framework agreements.[425]

At an international level, it is worth mentioning Article 7(1) of the UNCITRAL Model Law on Electronic Commerce, which provides that 'Where the law requires a signature of a person, that requirement is met in relation to a data message if: (a) a method is used to identify that person and to indicate that person's approval of the information contained in the data message; and (b) that method is reliable as was appropriate for the purpose for which the data message was generated or communicated, in the light of all circumstances, including any relevant agreement'. Similar provisions can be found in the UNCITRAL Model Law on Electronic Signatures 2001[426] and in the United Nations Convention on the Use of Electronic Communications in International Contracts.[427]

---

423 G. Finocchiaro, *'Article 3. Definitions'*, in Zaccaria et al (n 385) 55. See also G. Finocchiaro, *Firme elettroniche e firma digitale*, in G. Finocchiaro, F. Delfini (n 344) 309ff.

424 Reed (n 300) 282.

425 E.g. Art. 3.3.2 of the American Bar Association Model Electronic Data Interchange Trading Partner Agreement states: 'Any document properly transmitted pursuant to this Agreement shall be considered, in connection with any Transaction, any other written agreement described in Section 3.1, or this Agreement, to be a "writing" or "in writing"; and any such Document when containing, or to which there is affixed, a Signature ("Signed Documents") shall be deemed for all purposes (a) to have been "signed" and (b) to constitute an "original" when printed from electronic files or records established and maintained in the normal course of business'. Art. 1.5 defines Signature as 'an electronic identification consisting of symbol(s) or code(s) which are to be affixed to or contained in each Document transmitted by such party ("Signatures")'. The same Article continues as follows: 'Each party agrees that any Signature of such party affixed to or contained in any transmitted Document shall be sufficient to verify such party originated such Document. Neither party shall disclose to any unauthorized person the Signatures of the other party'.

426 Art. 6.

427 Art. 9.

These international instruments of hard and soft law have guided the legislators of the countries. Indeed, many countries have adopted the principle of functional equivalence by setting functional requirements for an electronic signature. In particular, some legislations establish that the courts evaluate the meeting of such requirements on a case-by-case basis. Other legislations have adopted a two-tier approach. Electronic signatures based on third-party identity certification are considered equivalent to handwritten signatures; the courts have to evaluate such equivalence for the other electronic signatures[428]

At a European level, as already seen[429] the e-IDAS Regulation recognises the simple, the advanced and the qualified signatures.[430] The advanced electronic signature[431] meets the requirements set out in Article 26: (a) it is uniquely linked to the signatory; (b) it is capable of identifying the signatory; (c) it is created using electronic signature creation data that the signatory can, with a high level of confidence, use under his sole control; (d) it is linked to the data signed therewith in such a way that any subsequent change in the data is detectable. The qualified electronic signature[432] is created by a qualified electronic signature device and is based on a qualified certificate for electronic signatures.[433] According to Article 25(2), the qualified electronic signature shall have the equivalent legal effect of a handwritten signature. For the former two, evaluation about equivalence with handwritten signatures is left to courts.[434] Depending on national

428 Reed (n 300) 282.

429 Section 2.1.2.

430 Art. 25(1) applies the non-discrimination principle to electronic signatures: 'An electronic signature shall not be denied legal effect and admissibility as evidence in legal proceedings solely on the grounds that is in an electronic form or that it does not meet the requirements for qualified electronic signatures'.

431 Art. 3(11).

432 Art. 3(12).

433 The qualified electronic signature creation device must meet the requirements laid down in Annex II (Art. 3(23)). A qualified trust service provider must issue a qualified certificate for electronic signature (defined in Art. 3(20)) that must meet the requirements laid down in Annex I (Art. 3(15)).

434 The e-IDAS Regulation has repealed Council Directive (EC) 1999/93 on a community framework for electronic signatures [2000] OJ L13/12. The Directive only recognised two kinds of electronic signatures: the simple and the advanced. Electronic signatures were considered advanced if the identity of the signatory was confirmed by a qualified certificate issued by a qualified certification-service-provider and created by a secure signature-creation-device. Art. 5(1) provided that only advanced signatures could satisfy the legal requirements of a signature concerning data in electronic form in the same form as a handwritten

legislation, electronic seals disciplined by the e-IDAS Regulation may also acquire the same electronic signatures function.[435]

To sum up, electronic contracts satisfy the written form requirement when they are signed with particular kinds of signatures that the law explicitly considers equivalent to handwritten signatures. Suppose an electronic document representing a contract is signed with another electronic signature or is not signed at all, the satisfaction of the written form requirement is subjected to interpretation by the courts. About this, Article 9(2) of the MLEC provides that 'regard shall be had to the reliability of the manner in which the data message was generated, stored or communicated, to the reliability of the manner in which the integrity of the information was maintained, to the manner in which its originator was identified, and to any other relevant factor'. Article 9 of the UN Convention on the Use of Electronic Communications in International Contracts refers to the reliability of the methods to ensure the integrity of the document and the identification of the signatory. The e-IDAS Regulation does not set any evaluation parameter. This aspect is left to national legislators. For instance, in Italy Article 20(1-bis) of the Codice dell'Amministrazione Digitale (CAD) considers an electronic document to be in written form when the signatory signs it by using a digital signature,[436] a qualified electronic signature or an advanced electronic signature. [437] In addition, the same legal

signature satisfies those requirements in relation to paper-based data, and were admissible as evidence in legal proceedings.

435 Electronic seals are a novelty introduced by the e-IDAS Regulation. Like electronic signatures, electronic seals are data in electronic form, which is attached to or logically associated with other data in electronic form (Art. 3(25)). But, unlike electronic signatures, only legal persons can create electronic seals (Art. 3(24)). Moreover, they do not have the function of certifying the consent of a legal person in relation to a statement. However, there are some member States where legal persons are enabled to use electronic signatures. So, moving from Recital 24, commentators observed that the Member States may introduce additional functions to electronic seals, thus recognising electronic seals as being the same as legal persons' signatures. To deepen these aspects, see S. Gatti, 'Article 35 Legal effects of electronic seals' in Zaccaria *et al* (n 385) 276 ff.

436 Digital signature is peculiar to the Italian legal system and consists of a qualified electronic signature that makes use of asymmetric cryptography.

437 According to Art. 21(2) of the *CAD*, by contrast with Art. 20(1-*bis*), the juridical acts included in Art. 1350(1–12) of the *Codice Civile* are only valid if signed with a digital or a qualified signature. According to Art. 21(2-*ter*) of the CAD, every electronic notarial deed is valid if signed by the notary with a digital or qualified signature. The other involved parties sign the act with a digital, qualified or advanced electronic signature, or a handwritten signature digitally acquired.

value is recognised to a document formed under the requirements set by the Agenzia per l'Italia Digitale (AGID)[438] pursuant to Article 71 of the CAD, prior to the IT identification of its author, in such a way as to guarantee its security, integrity, and immutability and the fact that it is ascribable to the author, clearly and unequivocally.[439] In all other cases, the suitability of the document to satisfy the requirement of the written form can be freely assessed in court, in respect to its characteristics of security, integrity, and immutability.

Another kind of 'formality' required when concluding some contracts (especially in B2C contracts) may also be the already examined pre-contractual information duties.[440]

### 2.2. Contract performance: contractual and non-contractual liability.

The issue of non-performance in technological contracts is of huge importance, except for vending machines because of the low economic value of transactions. In that regard, the debate concerned responsibility and its attributability when the vending machine is empty or faulty. Indeed, as stressed by an authoritative jurist at that time,[441] related legal questions are easy to answer if properly qualified. Different opinions concerned the case of the empty vending machine in the absence of a publicly expressed revocation of the offer.[442] However, the application of existing norms appeared sufficient.

438 The *Agenzia per l'Italia Digitale* is the specialised agency of the Presidency of the Council of Ministers, whose main purpose is to guarantee the achievement of the objectives of the Italian digital agenda and that contributes to the diffusion of information and communication technologies, to foster innovation and economic growth <https://www.agid.gov.it/en/agency/about-us> accessed 1 October 2021.

439 It is the Italian 'signature with the SPID' whose discipline is set by the AGID through guidelines pursuant to Art. 71 of the CAD (*'Linee guida contenenti le regole tecniche per la sottoscrizione elettronica di documenti ai sensi dell'art. 20 del CAD'*).

440 Section 2.1.

441 Scialoja (n 321) 169 (n 2).

442 Some authors claimed that in such an event a contract was already formed, while others denied the presence of a contractual proposal and so the possibility to apply the rules on contractual liability. For the former opinion, see Schiller (n 299) 66. For the second, see Cicu (n 321) 26 and Neumond (n 299) 191.

In electronic commerce, the matter can be divided as follows: on the one hand, by considering whether the party makes use of an electronic means to conclude a contract or perform contractual obligations; on the other hand, by taking into account the use of automated or autonomous systems.

It has been described that the errors of computer systems may affect the validity of the contract.[443] When a contract is performed through the support of a computer system, such malfunctioning may also give rise to contractual liability if it impedes contract performance.

If the party engaged another subject to provide the computer system, traditional contract law rules about performance entrusted to another can be applied. In the Italian legal system, the applicable rule is Article 1228 *cc*. Almost identical formulations can be found in Article 8:107 PECL, Article III.-2:106 DFCR, and Article 9.2.6 PICC.[444] The basic principle is that the only person responsible for performance is the debtor. Any internal aspects of the debtor's organisation are irrelevant to the creditor of the contractual obligation.[445] Similarly, EDI model framework agreements provide that the contracting party is liable for damages arising from the intermediary engaged in performing its obligations. More specifically, Art. 11.3 of Commission Recommendation 94/820/EC states that 'If a party engages any intermediary to perform such services as the transmission, logging or processing of an EDI message, that party shall be liable for damages arising directly from that intermediary's acts, failures or omissions in the provision of such services'; Article 1.2.3 of the EDI Model of the American Bar Association provides that 'Each party shall be liable for the acts or omissions of its provider while transmitting, receiving, storing or handling Documents, or performing related activities, for such party'. Lastly, in the field of electronic fund transfer, Article 9.2 of the Model Electronic Payments Agreement of the American Bar Association[446] dictates that 'Each party shall be liable to the other for the acts or omissions of its

443 Section 2.1.3. This is only restricted to hypotheses of malfunctions of the computer system, when the will of the party that makes use of it is not vitiated.

444 See J. Kleinschmidt, 'Particular remedies for non-performance' in Jansen, Zimmermann (n 315) 1160 – 1163.

445 See B. Gardella Tedeschi, 'Art. 8:104–109' in L. Antoniolli, A. Veneziano (eds), *Principles of European Contract Law and Italian Law* (Kluwer Law International 2005) 380.

446 American Bar Association, Edi and Technological Division, Section of Science and Technology, *Model Electronic Payments Agreement and Commentary: For Domestic Credit Transfers* (American Bar Association 1992); also published in (1992) 32 Jurimetrics Journal of Law, Science and Technology 601.

respective bank(s) and Third-Party Service Providers designated hereunder with respect to their conduct in connection with such party's performance under this Agreement'.

The discipline on contract performance and the remedies for non-performance vary between countries, especially between common and civil law systems. Civil and common law react differently to breach of contracts. The position of civil law is that the debtor should be required to remedy non-performance with a second attempt to perform. So, the creditor is normally allowed to claim performance. On the contrary, the position of common law is that the creditor is directly entitled to claim monetary compensation. It takes a more economic-based approach. There are exceptions: for example, civil law excludes specific performance when the latter is impossible, or the costs are disproportionate; common law admits performance when a claim for damages would not be an adequate remedy to do justice, as when the contract provides the delivering of specific or ascertained goods.[447] Furthermore, common law generally allows remedies for non-performance on the sole basis of non-performance, while civil law requires that non-performance is also attributable to the debtor. In other terms, civil law is fault-based. The debtor is excused in case of *force majeure*, which means that performance is due to an impediment beyond the debtor's control and that was inevitable and unforeseeable at the moment of the conclusion of the contract. Conversely, in common law, liability is strict or absolute. The only way of escaping liability is to invoke the doctrine of frustration, which boundaries are rigorous (impossibility of performance because of the destruction of an essential element of the contract; death of a party who needs to perform personally; performance possible but pointless). Again, differences between common and civil law can become less strict. For instance, in civil law, when the debtor entrusts performance to another (as seen above); in common law, when the obliged party is asked to use reasonable care and skill.[448] The Italian system is a civil law system. It recognises the right to claim specific performance[449]

447 Art. 9:102 PECL adopts the civil law approach, even though it admits that, if the debtor may reasonably obtain performance from another source, no action for performance can be brought (thus coming close to the common law approach). The same is in Art. 7.2.2 PICC and Art. III.-3:302 DFCR.

448 Art. 7.1.7 PICC, Art. 8:108 PECL, and Art. III.-3:104 DFCR summarise the civil law position. For further details on non-performance and related remedies in PICC, PECL, DFCR, see Kleinschmidt (n 444) 1074–1184. For a comparative perspective, see Kweigert, Kotz (n 400) 470–536.

449 Art. 1453, 2930, 2931, 2932, 2933 *cc*.

and establishes that the debtor is liable for non-performance unless non-performance is due to a cause non-imputable to him.[450]

Computer contracts cover a multitude of commercial transactions. Indeed, computer contracts may be concluded to obtain the various components that form a computer system – mainly, hardware and software – or to supply collateral services, such as consultancy, installation, support, and maintenance. More recently, with outsourcing[451] and cloud computing contracts[452] hardware and software are provided remotely as a service through the Internet. This has raised the question of the classification of these contracts. In most cases, national legal orders apply existing contract law rules designed for other contracts.[453] Sometimes, legal experts or courts have characterised them as hybrid or *sui generis* contracts. While it is less problematic to apply the rules of contracts for the supply of goods to hardware, because of its physical substance, and to qualify maintenance, support, and the like as contracts for the supply of services, significat debates focused on software.

The law of copyright protects software, so its use requires a licence from the rights owner. For this reason, it cannot be said that the software can be sold because the rights owner only gives the user the right to use the software. In Italy, it is distinguished between software licence agreements and software development agreements. The former is a standardised contract, which allows the use of the software. Thus, it is treated as a contract

450 Art. 1218 *cc*. For further details about non-performance and remedies for non-performance in the Italian legal system, see Antoniolli, Veneziano (n 445) 357–479. In Italian, see C. M. Bianca (ed), *Diritto civile. Vol. 4: l'obbligazione* (Giuffrè, 2019) 261–273.

451 M. Lewis, 'Information technology outsourcing and services arrangements' in Reed (n 300) 203–204 defines an IT outsourcing contract as a contract that 'usually involves the transfer of all, part, or parts of the IT and related services functions of a customer's undertaking to one or more third party service providers'.

452 Cloud computing avoids investments in proprietary infrastructures. It encompasses a wide range of offerings: 'Software as a Service' (SaaS), to get access to software applications without having to download it on proprietary infrastructures; 'Infrastructure as a Service' (IaaS), that makes available remote access to IT Infrastructures where the user can run her software; 'Platform as a Service' (PaaS), that offers more services than simply giving remote access to software and hardware. See P. Mell, T. Grance, 'The NIST Definition of Cloud Computing. Recommendations of the National Institute of Standards and Technology' (2011) NIST Special Publication 800–145 <https://nvlpubs.nist.gov/nistpubs/Legacy/SP/nistspecialpublication800-145.pdf> accessed 1 October 2021.

453 Few countries have enacted specific provisions, such as the United Kingdom with the Consumer Rights Act of 2015.

for rent. With the latter, the software is specially written to meet the requirements of the customer, so it is considered more similar to a project contract or a service agreement.[454]

The categorisation of contracts acquires relevance for evaluating the attributability of non-performance according to the nature of the obligation. Obligations are distinguished between obligations to achieve a particular result and obligations to use reasonable care. But this distinction is more complex than it appears. There can be some obligations to achieve a specific result in which the debtor can free herself by proving that she has committed no fault or others in which the debtor guarantees a certain result, independently of fault. Or there can be different standards of care. Legal systems do not always categorise obligations in the same way, with the possibility of divergences according to the kind of contract.[455]

In addition to the problem of categorising computer contracts and the absence of harmonisation among nations, identifying the object of the contract is often difficult in computer contracts. Technicalities and technological advancements make it particularly complex to establish with precision which functions the system should guarantee. For this reason, contracts tend to set objective criteria for testing performance. Indeed, these kinds of contracts are usually very detailed and include technical annexes.[456] As a result, computer contracts appear not so comprehensible to users who do not have the same technical knowledge as the other contracting party. This aspect especially concerns consumers and small businesses that generally conclude standard contracts with suppliers. So, there

---

454 The present work does not intend to deepen the categorisation of every computer contract in Civil and Common law. For this study, it is sufficient to highlight the importance of categorisation for the reasons that are expressed below. For further details on this argument, see J. Newton, 'System Supply Contracts' in Reed (n 300) 3–60. In the Italian legal system, Finocchiaro, Delfini (n 344) 605–675.

455 On the nature of the debtor's obligation, see H. Beale, B. Fauvarque-Cosson, J. Rutgers, S. Vogenauer (eds), *Cases, Materials and Texts on Contract Law* (3rd edn Hart 2019) 772–795. In Italy, Bianca (n 450) 71–74.

456 For example, the European Commission Recommendation of 19 October 1994 on EDI establishes that the European Model EDI Agreement is supplemented by technical specifications provided in a technical Annex. Art. 10 of the Model states that the Technical Annex 'shall include the technical, organizational and procedural specifications and requirements to operate EDI'. In system supply contracts it is very common to add a Service Level Agreement (SLA) that precisely sets out the quantitative and qualitative targets that the supplier has to meet.

is the danger of signing contracts with unfair terms. More specifically, it is common for these contracts to contain provisions excluding or limiting the supplier's liability. However, there are already norms belonging to traditional commerce to prevent the inclusion of some of these clauses even in electronic commerce.[457]

Suppliers typically seek to exclude liability for consequential, or indirect damages. Indirect damages are those that do not affect the object of the contract directly. They are all the other economic and non-economic damages that may derive from the breach of the contract.[458] On this point, despite the differences among the states on the general law on contractual damages, in general a contractual party should only be held liable for such damage that could reasonably be contemplated as a consequence of a breach of a contract when they concluded the contract.[459] So, it appeared important to establish when indirect damages could be considered foreseeable. This task did not seem easy in the digital environment. The more our world become smarter, the more malfunctioning can cause huge and consequential losses to our property or ourselves.[460] Indeed, suppliers exclude liabilities for consequential damages essentially because the continuously evolving nature of ICT products may expose them to unforeseeable and disproportionate risks of damages. Moreover, ICT products have a 'general purpose' nature, so it is difficult to foresee how they will be used and, consequently, which damages they could cause.[461] In

457 In general contract law, one must remember the *contra proferentem rule* and the principle of good faith. Specific legislation is the Council Directive 93/13/EEC of 5 April 1993 on unfair terms in consumer contracts [1993] OJ L95/29, implemented by Art. 33 ff. of the Italian Consumer Code. In Italy, Art. 1229 *cc* states that clauses limiting liability for fraud or gross negligence on the debtor's part are void. Art. 1229 *cc* has to be read in connection with the norms concerning consumer protection (if the contracting party is a consumer) and with Art. 1341 and 1342 *cc*, stating that some clauses have to be specifically approved in writing when imposed to a party without being negotiated (for B2B contracts). See also Art. 7.1.6 PICC, Art. 8:109 PECL, and Art.III.-3:105 DFCR.

458 S. AE Martens, 'Consequential Loss' in R. Schulze, D. Staudenmayer, S. Lohsse (eds) *Contracts for the Supply of Digital Content: Regulatory Challenges and Gaps* (Hart Nomos 2017) 156–157.

459 Art. 7.4.4 PICC, 9:503 PECL, III.-3:703 DFCR. In the Italian legal system, see Art. 1223 and 1225 *cc*.

460 Martens (n 458) 158. For example, a malfunction of the software of a smart car can cause an accident that destroys the car, another car, and provoke serious injuries to the people inside the cars.

461 Reed (n 300) 37. For example, as affirmed by J. Lloyd (ed), *Information Technology Law* (6th edn Oxford University Press 2011) 510, a spreadsheet program

any case, some elements may help evaluate the presence of a causal link between non-performance and damages: for instance, if the buyer expressly or impliedly makes known a particular purpose for which she intends to use the product.

To reach a higher degree of harmonisation among the Member States, the European Union has recently intervened with Directive (EU) 2019/770,[462] which establishes some rights for consumers that conclude contracts for the supply of–digital content or services. Directive (EU) 2019/771[463] does the same with contracts for the sale of goods. Both Directives aim to foster the development of cross-border e-commerce and remedy consumers' lack of confidence. The norms have regard to the conformity of digital contents, digital services, or goods with the contract, the remedies in the event of a lack of such conformity, and the modalities for the exercising those remedies.[464]

In particular, by repealing Directive 1999/44/EC, Directive (EU) 2019/771 clarifies that the rules also apply to the sale of goods with digital elements.[465] The latter are those goods that require digital content or service to perform their functions.[466] The Directive provides a hierarchy

---

could be alternatively used for domestic accounting purposes, where the degree of financial exposure in the event of error may be minimal, or in the course of preparing a multi-million-pound construction contract, where any error might threat the financial viability of a contracting party.

462 Directive (EU) 2019/770 on certain aspects concerning contracts for the supply of digital content and digital services [2019] OJ L 136/1.

463 Directive (EU) 2019/771 on certain aspects concerning contracts for the sale of goods amending Regulation (EU) 2017/2394 and Directive 2009/22/EC and repealing Directive 1999/44/EC [2019] OJ L 136/28.

464 The Directives were proposed after the withdrawal of the Proposal for a Regulation on a Common European Sales Law that contained a draft codification (CESL) comprising not only the sales law but also general contract law, as well as contracts for the supply of digital content and ~~for~~ related services. Unfortunately, the term of office of the European Parliament ended only after a first reading of the CESL, and the new Commission decided to stop the project. The two Directives are only a small fraction of the ambitious plan of harmonisation of European contract law.

465 Recital 13, Art. 3(3).

466 According to Recital 14, 'the term 'goods' as provided for under this Directive should be understood to include 'goods with digital elements', and therefore to also refer to any digital content or digital service that is incorporated in or inter-connected with such goods, in such a way that the absence of that digital content or digital service would prevent the goods from performing their functions. Digital content that is incorporated in or inter-connected with a good can be any data which are produced and supplied in digital form, such

of remedies for lack of conformity.[467] Like Directive 1999/44/EU, this Directive adopts a civilian approach, because it provides the consumer with the possibility to get the repair or replacement of the good. But, unlike the repealed Directive, there will be further harmonisation among the Member States (especially common and civil law countries) not being able to maintain or introduce divergent provision, such as the possibility to exercise primarily the right to reject like in common law countries.[468] Another important novelty of the Directive is that it lays down subjective and objective requirements for conformity.[469] Reference to objective requirements is intended to provide better protection for consumers.[470] Some requirements are specifically formulated in relation to the digital environment (such as compatibility and interoperability).

Directive (EU) 2019/770 is specifically applicable to digital content and digital services. It applies to any contract where the trader supplies or undertakes to supply digital content or digital service to the consumer, and the consumer pays or undertakes to pay the price or provide personal data to the trader (except where the trader exclusively processes the personal data provided by the consumer to supply the digital content or digital services, or for allowing the trader to comply with legal requirements to

as operating systems, applications and any other software. Digital content can be pre-installed at the moment of the conclusion of the sales contract or, where that contract so provides, can be installed subsequently. Digital services interconnected with a good can include services which allow the creation, processing or storage of data in digital form, or access thereto, such as software-as-a-service offered in the cloud computing environment, the continuous supply of traffic data in a navigation system, or the continuous supply of individually adapted training plans in the case of a smart watch'. Art. 3(4)(a) of the Directive also clarifies that the rules on contracts for the sale of goods do not apply to any tangible medium which serves exclusively as a carrier for digital content (such as DVDs, CDs, USB sticks and memory cards), thus giving end to a debate on the nature of software supplied on a durable medium as goods or services. On the debate, see R. Bradgate, 'Consumer Rights in Digital Products' (2010) Report prepared for the UK Department for Business, Innovation and Skills (BIS) <https://assets.publishing.service.gov.uk/government/uploads/system/uploads/attachment_data/file/31837/10-1125-consumer-rights-in-digital-products.pdf> accessed 1 October 2021.

467 Art. 13, 14, 15, 16.

468 Art. 4.

469 Art. 6, 7.

470 According to Art. 7, the goods have to comply with the objective requirements in addition to the subjective requirements, unless the consumer expressly and separately accepts deviations from such objective conditions when concluding the contract.

which the trader is subject, and the trader does not process those data for any other purpose).[471] According to the Directive, 'digital content' means data which are produced and supplied in digital form, while 'digital service' means (a) a service that allows the consumer to create, process, store or access data in digital form; or (b) a service that allows the sharing of or any other interaction with data in digital form uploaded or created by the consumer or other users of that service.[472] The definition is very broad, covering computer programs, applications, video files, audio files, music files, digital games, e-books or other e-publications, and also digital services which allow the creation of, processing of, accessing or storage of data in digital form, including software-as-a-service, such as video and audio sharing and other file hosting, word processing or games offered in the cloud computing environment and social media.[473] It considers the numerous ways to supply digital content or services, such as by the transmission on a tangible medium like a CD,[474] by downloading on the consumers' devices or by access in the cloud. The Directive structure replicates the one of the Consumer Sales Directive because it establishes a hierarchy of remedies and subjective and objective requirements for conformity.

Member States are free to extend the application of the rules of both Directives to natural or legal persons that are not consumers, such as start-ups or SMEs because they can be the weakest party of the contract.[475] Both Directives do not contain any rules on damages, which are left to national contract law rules.[476]

---

471 Art. 3. Recital 24 of the Directive recognises that digital services are often supplied not in exchange for money but personal data. So, the Directive is also applicable to these kinds of contracts to extend consumers' rights.

472 Art. 2(1)-(2).

473 Recital 19.

474 As also clarified in the Directive (EU) 2019/771, the tangible medium has to serve exclusively as a carrier of the digital content. See Recital 20 and Art. 3(4) Directive (EU) 2019/770.

475 Recital 21 Directive (EU) 2019/771 and recital 16 Directive (EU) 2019/770.

476 Art. 3(6) Directive (EU) 2019/771 and Art. 3(10) Directive (EU) 2019/770. For comments to the Directives, see G. Spindler, 'Contracts for the Supply of Digital Content – The Proposal of the Commission for a Directive on Contracts for the Supply of Digital Content', in S. Grundmann (ed), *European Contract Law in the Digital Age* (Intersentia 2018) 281–313; C. Ramberg, 'Digital Content – A Digital CESL II – A Paradigm for Contract Law via the Backdoor?' *ibid* 315–328; Schulze, Staudenmayer, Lohsse (n 458); R. Schulze, 'Supply of Digital Content. A new Challenge for European Contract Law' in A. De Franceschi (ed), *European Contract Law and the Digital Single Market – The Implications of the Digital*

Other aspects are left to national contract law rules. In particular, the Directives do not affect national laws that allow the trader or the seller to pursue remedies against a person in previous links of the chain of transactions where the lack of conformity of good, digital content or service results from an act or omission of that person.[477] Moreover, the Directives do not affect non-contractual remedies for the consumer against persons in the previous link of the chain of transactions.[478] Indeed, suppliers and sellers are often the prime contractors of a chain of related subcontracts with other persons, such as producers or developers and with whom the final customer does not have a contractual relationship. In this event, the customer has mainly two other instruments: tort law and product liability law.[479]

In the realm of tort law diversities among the countries have regard to legally relevant damages, namely the types of damages that entitle the injured party to a right of reparation.[480] Nevertheless, one can affirm that all countries require the presence of a causal link between the harm and the behaviour that renders the person liable.[481] Here, as for contractual liability, some limits are placed upon the extent of the party's responsibilities by considering a criterion of reasonableness. In general, the person is held

---

*Revolution* (Intersentia 2016) 127–143; G. Howells, 'Reflections on Remedies for Lack of Conformity in Light of the Proposals of the EU Commission on Supply of Digital Content and Online and Other Distance Sales of Goods' *ibid* 145–161.

477 Recital 63 Directive (EU) 2019/771 and recital 78 Directive (EU) 2019/770. Art. 18 Directive (UE) 2019/771 and Art. 20 Directive (EU) 2019/770 recognise a right of redress of the seller or the trader.

478 Recital 18 Directive (EU) 2019/771 and recital 12 Directive (EU) 2019/770.

479 Reed (n 300) 4.

480 Some countries start from a series of specific torts (e.g. Germany), while others (e.g. France) from an overarching general basic rule. In Italy the general rule is Art. 2043 *cc*. For a comparative perspective, see Zweigert, Kotz (n 400) 595–708. For Italian tort law, see C. M. Bianca (ed), *Diritto civile. Vol. 5: la responsabilità* (2nd edn Giuffrè 2019) 543 ff. According to the DFCR, legally relevant damages are losses or injuries that result from a violation of a right otherwise conferred by the law (Art. VI.-2:201(1)(a)) or from a violation of an interest worthy of legal protection (Art. VI.-2:201(1)(c)). About non-contractual liability in the DFCR, see V. Sagaert, M. E. Storme, E. Terryn (eds), *The Draft Common Frame of Reference: national and comparative perspectives* (Intersentia 2012) 221–260. Apart from the DFCR, the Principles of European Tort Law (PETL) are a compilation of guidelines aiming at the harmonization of European tort law (accessible at the following link <http://www.egtl.org/docs/PETL.pdf> accessed 1 October 2021). Art. 2:101 PETL refers to legally protected interests. Injuries to a person or to physical property are usually considered relevant. This is not always the case for pure economic losses.

481 Art. VI.-4:101(1) DFCR. Art. 3:101 PETL.

liable only for losses of reasonably foreseeable kind could spring from her behaviour. The person also has to be accountable for the damage. Accountability is based upon intention or negligence.[482] Article VI.-3:102 of DFCR provides that negligence is ascertained if the particular standard of care provided by a statutory provision is not met, or if the conduct does otherwise amount to such care as could be expected from a reasonably careful person in such case. Similarly to contractual liability, compliance with objective parameters such as technical standards may be useful to evaluate the person's negligence.[483] Then, some countries discipline cases in which accountability arises without intention or fault.[484] The Product Liability Directive 85/374/EEC[485] has introduced specific provisions concerning liability for defective products independent from the producer's fault.[486] This was considered the only means of adequately solving the problem, peculiar to an age of increasing technicality, on a fair apportionment of the risks inherent in modern technological production.[487] The action may be brought against the producer of the finished product or of any component incorporated into the product. A producer is also considered the persons who, by putting a name or brand mark on goods produced by third party, hold themselves out as the producer, the importers into the European Union, or the supplier where the producer or the importer cannot be identified.[488] A product is defective if it does not provide the level of safety that persons generally are entitled to expect, taking into account (a) the presentation of the product (b) the use to which it could reasonably be expected that the product would be put (c) the time when the product was

482 Artt. VI.-3:101 and Art. VI.-3:102 DFCR; Art. 4:101 PETL.

483 Lloyd (n 461) 524–525.

484 Book VI, Chapter 3, Section 2 DFCR, and Chapter 5 PETL. In Italy, see Art. 2050 (damages caused by the exercise of dangerous activities), Art. 2051 (damages caused by things under someone's custody), Art. 2052 (damages caused by someone's animals), Art. 2053 (damages caused by the unsafe state of an immovable), Art. 2054 (damages caused by vehicles) *cc*.

485 Council Directive of 25 July 1985 on the approximation of laws, regulations and administrative provisions of the Member States concerning liability for defective products 85/374/EEC [1985] OJ L 210/29. In Italy, Art. 114 ff of the Consumer Code have implemented the Directive.

486 According to Art. 4, the injured person shall be required only to prove the damage, the defect, and the causal relationship between defect and damage.

487 See the Preamble of the Directive.

488 Art. 3.

put into circulation.[489] The Directive aims at establishing a presumption of defectiveness if damages occur because of a defect in the product. It is up to the producer to demonstrate that the cause was other than a defect in the product.[490] Only limited categories of damage can be compensated: personal injuries; damages to any property which is of a kind ordinarily intended for private use or consumption and which is used for such a purpose.[491]

It is questioned whether software can be considered a product Under the Directive, products are movables (except for primary agricultural products and game) even though incorporated into another movable or an immovable. Products also include electricity.[492] It seems that in Europe, the opinion in favour of software as product prevails,[493] even though the European Court of Justice has not intervened yet.

---

489 Art. 6. It is specified that a product shall not be considered defective for the sole reason that a better product is subsequently put into circulation.

490 Lloyd (n 461) 538.

491 Art. 9.

492 Art. 2. Somebody claim that because the Directive explicitly only refers to electricity, the other intangibles are excluded from its application. On the contrary, somebody argues that the referral to electricity is only an example, thus considering that the Directive applies to intangibles. For the former, see D. Wuyts,'The Product Liability Directive – More than two decades of defective products in Europe'(2014) 5(1) Journal of European Tort Law 1. For the latter, see G. Wagner, 'Robot Liability' in S. Lohsse, R. Schulze, D. Staudenmayer (eds), Liability for Robotics and in the Internet of Things: Munster Colloquia on Eu Law and the Digital Economy IV (Hart Nomos 2019). When the software is essential to the functioning of a product (e.g. a smart watch or a smart tv), whether the software is a product is of limited significance, because defects of the software make the product defective. See Lloyd (n 461) 537. When the software is given through a durable medium like a CD or USB, some legal experts distinguished the (intangible) software from the (tangible) medium and denied that the software was a product. See J. Triaille, 'The EEC Directive on Product Liability and its Application to Databases and Information' (1991) Computer Law and Practice 217, 219. Others considered the software tangible because it is inextricably linked to the medium. The European Commission supported the second thesis. See answer of the Commission of the European Communities of 15 November 1988 to Written Question No. 706/88 by Mr. Gijs De Vries (LDR/NL) (89/C 114/76) [1989] OJ C114/42. Nevertheless, today it is common practice to download the software or access it via a cloud. These forms of stand-alone software are more difficult to classify.

493 See B. Wagner *et al.* (eds), Research Handbook on Human Rights and Digital Technology: Global Politics, Law and International Relations (Edward Elgar Publishing 2019) 281: 'the recent case law of CJEU(…)' – C-128/11 Oracle v. UsedSoft [2012] OJ C287/10 – (…) on the exhaustion of the distribution right

When contracts are concluded or performed through artificial intelligence, software flaws may entail some forms of liability. If artificial intelligence is used to conclude contracts, an error of the software may bind the person on whose behalf the software is acting to unintended agreements. The person whose contract has been concluded may resort to the producer or the provider of the software. Or, if artificial intelligence has determined the breach of a contract because of a software malfunction, the obliged party that made use of artificial intelligence to perform may be deemed liable. The peculiarities of artificial intelligence have raised various questions on the applicability of existing liability rules.[494] Primarily, it has been wondered how to treat the artificial agent: as a tool, as an agent,[495] or even

---

in software under copyright law may indicate that the courts tend to liken immaterial forms of distribution to material forms, which may also indicate a certain openness to an equal treatment in other areas of the law'.

494 The present work do not intend to deep these aspects, given that blockchain-based smart contracts are deterministic computer programs. For further details, see S. Lohsse, R. Schulze, D. Staudenmayer (eds), *Liability for Artificial Intelligence and the Internet of Things* (Hart Nomos 2019); European Commission, 'Liability for Artificial Intelligence and other emerging digital technologies' – Report from the Expert Group on Liability and New Technologies – New Technologies Formation <https://op.europa.eu/it/publication-detail/-/publication/1c5e30be-1197-11ea-8c1f-01aa75ed71a1/language-en> accessed 1 October 2021. In Italy, see U. Ruffolo (ed), *Intelligenza artificiale e responsabilità* (Giuffrè 2018); M. Costanza, 'L'intelligenza artificiale e gli stilemi della responsabilità civile' (2019) 7 Giurisprudenza Italiana 1686; U. Ruffolo, 'Intelligenza Artificiale, machine learning e responsabilità da algoritmo' *ibid* 1689; A. Amidei, 'Intelligenza Artificiale e product liability: sviluppi del diritto dell'Unione Europea' *ibid* 1715. G. Finocchiaro, 'Riflessioni sugli smart contract e sull'intelligenza artificiale' (2020) 11 Giustizia Civile.Com 1.

495 Section 2.1.1.

496 Legal persons, or electronic persons, should be an additional category of legal subjects next to natural persons and legal persons. This would not determine that these agents have rights and obligations. It would only serve to hold them liable in case of damages caused by them, separately from their owners (like companies can act separately from their founders). This proposal dates from the last century. See L. Solum, 'Legal Personhood for Artificial Intelligences' (1992) 70 NC L Rev 1231. In its Resolution on Civil Law Rules on Robotics of 16 February 2017, also the European Parliament has called the Commission to explore, analyse and consider the creation of 'a specific legal status for robots in the long run so that at least the most sophisticated autonomous robots could be established as having the status of electronic persons responsible for making good any damage they may cause, and possibly applying electronic personality to cases where robots make autonomous decisions or otherwise interact with

as a legal person.[496] Secondly, how the concept of fault applies to damages caused by artificial intelligence is doubtful.[497]

Starting from the above questions, in its Resolution on Civil Law Rules on Robotics of 16 February 2017, the European Parliament has asked the Commission to submit a proposal for a legislative instrument providing civil law rules on the liability of robots and AI. In particular, the European Parliament has asked the Commission to evaluate the applicability of strict liability or a risk management approach instead of a fault-based approach, establishing a system of obligatory insurances (supplemented by compensation funds in case no insurance coverage exist). With its Communication on Artificial Intelligence for Europe, adopted on 25 April 2018,[498] the Commission announced that it would have submitted a report assessing the implications of the merging digital technologies and the existing safety and liability frameworks, to identify and examine the broader implications and potential gaps in the liability and safety frameworks for AI, the IoT and robotics, and with the support of a group of experts.[499] On 19 February 2020, the Commission has published the report focusing on preliminary findings.[500] The Commission has concluded that 'while in principle the existing Union and national liability laws are able to cope with emerging technologies, the dimension and combined effect

third parties independently' (par. 59.f). The proposal has been criticised. See European Commission, (n 494) 37–39.

497 Applications of artificial intelligence act autonomously. This means that they perform by learning from experience, modify the given-instructions, and develop new instructions, without human control. So, any subsequent choice made by the artificial intelligence may not derive from a flaw in its original design, thus making it unclear how to demonstrate the persons' fault relying on the use of such an application.

498 Communication from the Commission to the European Parliament, the European Council, the Council, the European Economic and Social Committee and the Committee of the Regions, Artificial Intelligence for Europe, COM(2018) 237 final, 24.4.2018 <https://eur-lex.europa.eu/legal-content/EN/TXT/PDF/?uri=CELEX:52018DC0237&from=EN> accessed 1 October 2021.

499 The Expert Group on Liability and New Technologies, operating in two different formations: the Product Liability Directive formation and the New Technologies formation.

500 Report from the Commission to the European Parliament, the Council and the European Economic and Social Committee, Report on the safety and liability implications of Artificial Intelligence, the Internet of Things and Robotics, COM(2020) 64 final, 19.02.2020 <https://ec.europa.eu/info/sites/info/files/report-safety-liability-artificial-intelligence-feb2020_en_1.pdf> accessed 1 October 2021.

of the challenges of AI could make it more difficult to offer victims compensation in all cases where this would be justified. Thus, the allocation of the cost when damage occurs may be unfair or inefficient under the current rules. To rectify this and address potential uncertainties in the existing framework, certain adjustments to the Product Liability Directive and national liability regimes through appropriate EU initiatives could be considered on a targeted, risk-based approach, i.e. taking into account that different AI applications pose different risks'. On 20 October 2020, the European Parliament adopted a resolution with some recommendations to the Commission on a civil liability regime for artificial intelligence and a proposal of regulation.[501] On 20 April 2021, the European Commission published its proposal for a Regulation on a European approach for Artificial Intelligence ('Artificial Intelligence Act').[502] On 30 June 2021, the EU Commission published an inception impact assessment for a future proposal for a directive to adapt the EU liability rules to the digital age and circular economy, also addressing challenges brought about by artificial intelligence.[503]

### 2.3. Jurisdiction and applicable law.

As stated above about the time of the conclusion of contracts,[504] in electronic commerce parties negotiate from different places, even from different countries, and the exchange between offer and acceptance is not simultaneous. It was necessary to establish which court had the jurisdiction and which substantive law applied for these reasons.

501 European Parliament resolution of 20 October 2020 with recommendations to the Commission on a civil liability regime for artificial intelligence (2020/2014(INL)), p9_TA(2020)0276 <https://www.europarl.europa.eu/doceo/document/TA-9-2020-0276_EN.pdf> accessed 1 October 2021.

502 Proposal for a Regulation of the European Parliament and of the Council laying down harmonised rules on Artificial Intelligence (Artificial intelligence Act) and amending certain union legislative acts COM/2021/206 final (<https://eur-lex.europa.eu/legal-content/EN/TXT/HTML/?uri=CELEX:52021PC0206&from=EN> accessed 1 October 2021).

503 Inception impact assessment – Ares(2021)4266516 (<https://ec.europa.eu/info/law/better-regulation/have-your-say/initiatives/12979-Civil-liability-adapting-liability-rules-to-the-digital-age-and-artificial-intelligence_en> accessed 1 October 2021). The proposal for a directive is planned for the third quarter of 2022.

504 Section 2.1.

In cross-border contracts, parties can agree on the jurisdiction and the law that govern their contract.[505] In the absence of choice, rules of private international law apply. In particular, the Bruxelles I-*bis* Regulation[506] and the Rome I Regulation[507] cover these matters.

According to the Bruxelles I-*bis* Regulation, which applies in civil and commercial matters,[508] the courts that have jurisdiction are the ones of the country where the defendant is domiciled.[509] Article 7 of the Regulation sets down some special jurisdiction. Namely, in matters relating to a contract, the courts that have jurisdiction are the ones of the place of performance of the contractual obligation. Unless otherwise agreed, the place of performance of the obligation in the case of the sale of goods is the place where under the contract the goods were delivered or should have been delivered, while in the case of the provision of services is the place where under the contract the services were provided or should have been provided.[510] As regards a dispute arising out of the operations of a branch, agency, or other establishment, the courts are the ones of the place where the branch, agency or other establishment is situated.[511]

When the contract is concluded between a business and a consumer, and when the consumer acts against the business, the consumer can choose between the jurisdiction of the country where the other party is domiciled[512] and where the consumer is domiciled.[513] But, if the business acts against the consumer, the only jurisdiction is that of the country where the consumer is domiciled.[514] The rule is applicable when the business pursues commercial or professional activities in the Member State of

505 Reed (n 300) 301.

506 Regulation (EU) No. 1215/2012 of the European Parliament and of the Council of 12 December 2012 on jurisdiction and the recognition and enforcement of judgments in civil and commercial matters [2012] OJ L351/1. The Regulation has repealed Regulation (EC) No. 44/2001.

507 Regulation (EC) No 593/2008 of the European Parliament and of the Council of 17 June 2008 on the law applicable to contractual obligations (Rome I) [2008] OJ L177/6. The Regulation repeals the 1980 Convention on the Law Applicable to Contractual Obligations (the Rome Convention) except for Denmark.

508 Art. 1.

509 Art. 4.

510 Art. 7(1)(b).

511 Art. 7(5).

512 Suppose the business only has a branch, agency, or other establishments in one of the Member States. In that case, it is considered domiciled in that Member State in disputes arising out of the branch, agency, or establishment (Art. 17(2)).

513 Art. 18(1).

514 Art. 18(2).

the consumer's domicile or, by any means, directs such activities to that Member State or to several States including that Member State, and the contract falls within the scope of such activities.[515] These provisions may be departed from by an agreement that is entered into after the dispute has arisen.[516]

In Italy, Law No. 218 of 31 May 1995[517] states that the jurisdiction is Italian when the defendant has her domicile, residence, or court representative in Italy.[518] The Regulation Bruxelles I-*bis* is applicable when the action covers the matters of the Regulation.

According to the Rome I Regulation on the applicable law, which applies to contractual obligations in civil and commercial matters,[519] the applicable law is that of the country to which the contract is most closely connected.[520] For instance, a contract for the sale of goods or the provision of services shall be governed by the law of the country where the seller or the service provider has its habitual residence.[521] In general, the contract shall be governed by the law of the country where the party required to effect the characteristic performance of the contract has his abitual residence.[522] According to Article 19, the habitual residence of companies and other bodies shall be the place of central administration. Instead, the habitual residence of a natural person acting in the course of his business activity shall be his principal place of business. Where the contract is concluded in the course of the operations of a branch, agency or any other establishment, or if, under the contract, performance is the responsibility of such a branch, agency or establishment, the place where the branch, agency or any other establishment is located shall be treated as the place of habitual residence.

In B2C contracts, the contract shall be governed by the law of the country of the consumer's habitual residence, provided that the professional purses his commercial or professional activities in the country where the consumer is resident or, by any means, directs such activities to that country or to several countries including that country, and the contract

515 Art. 17(1)(c).

516 Art. 19(1).

517 Legge 31 maggio 1995, n. 218, *Riforma del sistema italiano di diritto internazionale privato.*

518 Art. 3.

519 Art. 1.

520 Art. 4(4).

521 Art. 4(1)(a)-(b).

522 Art. 4(2).

falls within the scope of such activities.[523] The parties cannot derogate the protections provided to the consumer by the consumer's residence law.[524]

In Italy, Article 57 of the Law No. 2018 of 31 May 1995 refers to the 1980 Rome Convention (now the Rome I Regulation).

Once established the applicable law, the law of the country then sets the rules to identify the jurisdiction *ratione loci*. In Italy, it corresponds to the defendant's residence or domicile (in absence, the defendant's abode), if the defendant is a natural person.[525] If the defendant is a legal person, the court is where the legal person has its registered office, establishment, or an authorised representative for legal proceedings.[526] Alternatively, for cases related to obligation rights, the court may also be that of the place where the obligation was born[527] or has to be performed.[528] When one of the parties is a consumer, the Italian Consumer Code provides the mandatory territorial competence of the court where the consumer has her residence or domicile.[529]

The above criteria (location of contract formation and performance, residence, domicile, place of business, place of administration,) are territorial. Their application has revealed quite problematic in electronic commerce.

The location of contract formation typically corresponds to the place where the last act necessary to make the contract binding occurs.[530] So, the location of the contract is inferred from the rules determining the time of conclusion of distance contracts.[531] Indeed, Article 3.3 of the European EDI Model Agreement included in Annex I of Commission Recommendation of 19 October 1994 provides that 'A contract affected by the use of EDI shall be concluded at the time and place where the EDI message constituting acceptance of an offer reaches the computer system of the offeror'. The problem is that it is not usually possible to determine the location of the receiving server, not least when it comes

---

523 Art. 6(1).

524 Art. 6(2).

525 Art. 18 Italian Code of Civil Procedure (*Codice di Procedura Civile*, *cpc*).

526 Art. 19 *cpc*.

527 The location of contract formation is widely used as a ground for contract formation, for example in the People's Republic of China, Hong Kong, England, or Australia. See D. Svantesson (ed), *Private International Law and the Internet* (3rd edn Kluwer Law International, The Hague 2016) 436–437.

528 Art. 20 *cpc*.

529 Art. 66-*bis* Legislative Decree No. 206/2005.

530 *Ibid.* p. 436.

531 About the time of conclusion of contracts in the ICT domain, see Section 2.1.

to cloud computing. Nor the place of the conclusion can be identified with e-mail addresses or the domain names of websites. Indeed, they are not physical addresses but logical addresses.[532] Article 10(3) of the UN Convention on Electronic Communications dictates that 'An electronic communication is deemed to be dispatched at the place where the originator has its place of business and is deemed to be received at the place where the addressee has its place of business', 'notwithstanding that the place where the information system supporting an electronic address is located may be different from the address of the place of business' (Art. 10(4)). The UN Convention considers the place of business, independently of the location of the information system.[533] This is more clear in Article 6(4) of the Convention, according to which 'A location is not a place of business merely because that is (a) where equipment and technology supporting an information system used by a party in connection with the formation of a contract are located; or (b) where the information system may be accessed by other parties'. In line with the provisions of the Convention, recital 19 of the Directive on Electronic Commerce declares that 'the place of establishment of a company providing services via an Internet website is not the place at which the technology supporting its website is located or the place at which its website is accessible but the place where it pursues its economic activity'.

Nonetheless, problems also arise about the place of business (natural persons) or administration (legal persons). Here, as is for the place of residence and domicile, it is unknown where the party is located. The matter is inextricably linked to digital identities and the related methods of identification that have been deepened above.[534]

Similarly, determining the place where contract performance takes place is extremely difficult. For example, one can think a person that spends

---

532 E.g. '.it', '.com', '.eu'. See G. Finocchiaro, 'Lex mercatoria e commercio elettronico' in V. Ricciuto, N. Zorzi (eds), *Il contratto telematico* (Cedam 2002) 26. One has to note that Art. 5 of the Directive on Electronic Commerce having regard to the mandatory information for the service provider before the conclusion of the contract distinguishes between the geographic address and the electronic mail address of the service provider. Furthermore, Art. 6(4) of the UN Convention on Electronic Communications declares that 'the sole fact that a party makes use of a domain name or electronic mail address connected to a specific country does not create a presumption that its place of business is located in that country'.

533 See also Art. 15 MLEC.

534 Section 2.1.2.

her life in different countries during the year and has subscribed to an online streaming service.[535] More specifically, the place of performance is not suitable where products and services are supplied online. It remains appropriate if the performance takes place off-line.[536]

Moreover, as seen above both the Bruxelles I-*bis* Regulation and the Rome I Regulation provide special protection for consumers where the business has directed its activities to the consumer's country.[537] In these cases, the question is under which circumstances can one say that the business' activities are directed to the consumer when contracts are concluded via a website. On this point, there are two leading European cases: *Pammer v. Reederei Karl Schlüter GmbH & KG*[538] and *Hotel Alpenhof GesmbH v. Oliver Heller*.[539] The European Court of Justice concluded that: the mere fact that a website can be accessed from a state does not mean that the business has directed its activities to that state; it has to be apparent from the website and the business' overall activity that the business was envisaging doing business with consumers domiciled in one or more Member States, including the Member State of the consumer's domicile, in the sense that it was minded to conclude a contract with them.[540] The ECJ gave a non-exhaustive list of considering factors to make the so-called 'targeting test'.[541] It is up to the national courts to evaluate the single cases. Because of the mandatory nature of the rule, the professional cannot avoid its application by unilaterally stating that he has no intention to

535 The example is from D. Svantesson, 'Digital Contracts in Global Surroundings' in Grundmann (n 476) 64.

536 'Press Release – Geneva Round Table on Electronic Commerce and Private International Law' (Hague Conference on Private International Law, 26 June 2003) <https://www.hcch.net/en/news-archive/details/?varevent=63> accessed 1 October 2021

537 Art. 17(1)(c) Bruxelles I-*bis* Regulation and Art. 6(1) Rome I Regulation.

538 Case C-585/08, *Pammer v. Reederei Karl Schlüter GmbH & KG* ECLI:EU:C:2010:740, [2010] ECR I-12527.

539 Case C-144/09, *Hotel Alpenhof GesmbH v. Oliver Heller* ECLI:EU:C:2010:740, [2010] ECR I-12527.

540 Para. 95.

541 For example the use of different languages or currencies than the ones usually adopted in the Member State where the trader resides together with the possibility, for the consumer, to book in that language; the indication of telephone numbers including a country dialling code which foreign consumers have to dial; the use of a top-level domain different from the one applicable in the trader's country; the mention of an international clientele composed of customers domiciled in various Member States.

conclude contracts with consumers with habitual residence in some states (the so-called 'disclaimer').[542]

Besides the traditional means, Alternative Dispute Resolution mechanisms (ADR) have developed as alternative, more efficient, fast, and low-cost ways of resolving disputes. There are also some forms of Online Dispute Resolution (ODR) means, which are alternative dispute resolution means that takes place entirely online. They can be considered the online equivalent of ADR. ODRs are suitable to resolve e-commerce disputes because they use technology to put in communication parties often located in different countries. For this reason, it is believed that ODR can help overcome the problem of the choice of the jurisdiction and the applicable law.[543]

542 For more details on the targeting test, see D. Svantesson (n 535) 75–84.

543 For example, by adopting Regulation (EU) 524/2013 of the European Parliament and of the Council on online dispute resolution for consumer disputes (Regulation on Consumer ODR) the EU has created an ODR platform (<https://ec.europa.eu/consumers/odr/main/?event=main.trader.register#inline-nav-3> accessed 1 October 2021) that applies to disputes concerning contractual obligations stemming from online sales or service contracts. For ODR in Europe, see J. Morais Carvalho, J. Campos Carvalho, 'Online Dispute Resolution Platform – Making European Contract Law More Effective' in De Franceschi (n 476) 245–266. See also I. Amro (ed), *Online Arbitration in Theory and in Practice – A Comparative Study of Cross-Border Commercial Transactions in Common Law and Civil Law Countries* (Cambridge Scholars Publishing 2019). In Italy, see C. Menichino, 'Art. 19, d.lgs. 70/2003 (Composizione delle controversie)' in Finocchiaro, Delfini (n 344) 445 – 465.

# CHAPTER 4: CONTRACT FORMATION

## 1. *Are smart contracts 'contracts'?*

When discussing smart (legal) contracts, one primarily wonders whether they are contracts.[544] Researchers usually distinguish between smart legal contracts as contracts or as means to perform already existing contracts.[545] To answer the question, someone rightly starts from the legal definition of the contract.[546]

A contract is a legally binding agreement between two or more parties.[547] So, the agreement constitutes the very basis of the contract. The mutual consent of the parties (called the agreement) is reached based on the parties' exchange of an offer and an acceptance. The other fundamental requirement is the parties' expression of their intention to be legally bound by the contract. This means that the offeror and the offeree intended to enter an agreement apt to produce legal effects within a legal system. In other terms, through contracts parties change their respective legal positions by altering their duties and rights. Although simple negotiations or social arrangements are agreements, they are not considered contracts because of the absence of an intention to create legal effects.

To reach the so-called 'meeting of the minds', both parties must express their intent in some form. According to the principle of informality, in the silence of the law, the parties are free to choose any form to conclude contracts. As seen in the previous chapter,[548] this principle and the principle

544 E.g. see Werbach, Cornell (n 181) 338; J. G. Allen, 'Wrapped and Stacked: 'Smart Contracts' and the Interaction of Natural and Formal Language' (2018) 14(4) European Review of Contract Law 307, 319.

545 Chapter 2, Section 2. E.g. Rikken *et al.* (n 113) 22; Savelyev (n 96) 9; Chamber of Digital Commerce, Smart Contracts Alliance, 'Smart Contracts: 12 Use Cases for Business & Beyond (2016) 40 <http://digitalchamber.org/assets/smart-contracts-12-use-cases-for-business-and-beyond.pdf> accessed 1 October 2021. In Italy, see e.g. Finocchiaro (n 376) 443; L. Piatti, 'Dal Codice Civile al codice binario: *blockchain* e *smart contracts*' (2016) 3 Ciberspazio e diritto 325, 334.

546 Werbach and Cornell (n 181) 338.

547 See Christandl (n 331) 236–248. See also Art. 2:101 PECL, Art. II.-4:101 DFCR. In Italy, the definition of contract can be found in Art. 1321 *cc*. See Bianca (n 400) 1 ff.

548 Chapter 3, Section 2.1.4.

of non-discrimination allow the conclusion of contracts in an electronic form.[549] Consequently, contracts can also be expressed in the form of computer code. However, creating a smart legal contract does not automatically imply the conclusion of a contract in the lack of a legally binding agreement. Therefore, smart legal contracts can be contracts only in the presence of a legally binding agreement. As Sillaber and Waltl observe, 'although a smart contract has been stored on the blockchain, this fact alone should not be considered as a party's agreement to enter the contract as anybody can submit any smart contract to the blockchain indicating an obligation for any random wallet owner'.[550]

The meeting of the minds (exchange of offer and acceptance) may occur in various ways. Durovic and Janssen stress that smart legal contracts can be concluded either off-chain or on-chain.[551] The authors explain the process of the formation of on-chain contracts by referring to the upload of a proposed contract in coding language in the Ethereum platform and its following acceptance by communicating with the uploaded smart contract (for example by making a payment in ethers).

Then, it is believed that instead of talking about smart (legal) contracts as contracts or as means to perform already existing contracts, it might be more appropriate to refer to smart (legal) contracts as means to express contracts or perform already existing contracts. In this case, the object of the definition is always the software code. Alternatively, one could define smart contracts as contracts expressed in computer code and performed by computer code. The object of the latter definition is not the software but the contract; the use of the adjective 'smart' highlights the automatic execution of the contract without human intervention. Because the second definition focuses on the contract, the distinction between smart contract code and smart legal contracts becomes superfluous. The claim that smart (legal) contracts can be contracts, on one side, or means to perform already existing contracts, on the other side, might be misleading because it would imply that a contract was formed independently of any legally binding agreement.

549 For example, the Arizona House Bill 2417 and the Tennessee Senate Bill No. 1662 (n 259) provide that a contract may not be denied legal effect, validity or enforceability solely because it contains smart contract terms.

550 Sillaber, Waltl, (n 116) 498–499.

551 Durovic, Janssen (n 167) 760.

This chapter investigates the intersection between blockchain-based smart contracts and the rules on contract formation.[552]

## 2. *The 'meeting of the minds': offer and acceptance.*

The present section aims to identify offer and acceptance in smart contracts. To this end, the analysis starts from the four scenarios depicted in Chapter 2.

In scenario 1, users interact in a permissionless blockchain. Every user takes part in the blockchain by holding a node. Some authors observe that when a party uploads a smart contract on the blockchain, the uploading[553] corresponds to an offer.[554] The offer must contain all the elements of a valid contract. Otherwise, there is not an offer but an invitation to the other party to enter into negotiations.[555] On this point, Durovic and Janssen consider that 'as the 'offeror' posts his 'contract' onto the blockchain in a binary computer code which specifies precisely the terms of the transaction, it will regularly be held to constitute an offer, not an invitation to treat'.[556]

The offeror can direct her offer to one or more specific persons. Alternatively, she can address it to the general audience (proposal to the public).[557] In a blockchain, one should consider that one or more participants

552 Apart from the agreement, the intention to be legally bound, and the form (when the law requires some formalities), contract formation usually requires a sufficient agreement to form legally enforceable contracts. Sufficient agreement means sufficient determination of the content or object of the contract. In addition, many legal systems require indicia of seriousness of the agreement; this requirement is called *causa* in Civil law and consideration in Common law. The chapter focuses on the agreement, the intention to be legally bound, and the form. It does not investigate sufficient agreement and indicia of seriousness that do not seem to pose different issues.

553 The smart contract code is uploaded on a local node of the blockchain through a 'deploy' transaction. Then, the smart contract is replicated in all the nodes of the blockchain.

554 Chamber of Digital Commerce (n 104) 15; Durovic, Janssen (n 167) 762;

555 Smits (n 223) 43ff. See also Art. 2.1.2 PICC, 2:201 PECL, II. – 4:201 DFCR, and 11 of the UN Convention on the Use of Electronic Communications in International Contracts.

556 Durovic, Janssen (n 167) 762.

557 Smits (n 223) 44ff. See also Art. 2:201 (2) PECL, and II. – 4:201 (2) DFCR. In Italy, see art. 1336 *cc*.

can interact with the smart contract code.[558] More specifically, and from a technical point of view, if the smart contract operations are restricted to a specific address (or wallet or user's profile) in the blockchain, the offer is directed to a specific participant in the blockchain. In the opposite case, any participant in the blockchain can send transactions, so the offer is open to the general public.

Turning to acceptance, it does not have to meet any specific requirements apart from the offeree's agreement on all the terms of the offer. Therefore, once the offeror has uploaded the smart contract, the offeree could accept it by signing a transaction with a private key.[559]

If the declaration of the offeree does not refer to all the terms of the offer or does not consent to the precise related terms, it is not an acceptance but rather a counter-offer.[560] In the latter case, the counter-offer has to be followed by an acceptance to form a contract. Here, the problem is the immutability of blockchain technology. The code of the smart contract cannot be modified in the blockchain. Consequently, there is no other option than to accept (or not to accept) it.[561] The offeree would need to upload a new smart contract on the blockchain. The upload would correspond to a new offer and the offeree would become the offeror.

Acceptance can also occur in the absence of a specific declaration when the offeree's conduct implies it.[562] More precisely, if the offeree starts performing the contract, her actions can be considered as a valid acceptance of the offer. Uncertain behaviour of the offeree showing an apparent acceptance is required. For example, in a blockchain, ceding the control to the code over a certain amount of money can be considered acceptance.[563]

558 Chamber of Digital Commerce (n 104) 17; J. Madir, 'Smart Contracts: (How) Do They Fit Under Existing Legal Frameworks?' (*SSRN*, 14 December 2018) 7 <https://ssrn.com/abstract=3301463> accessed 1 October 2021.

559 Chamber of Digital Commerce (n 104) 17; Madir (n 558) 7.

560 Smits (n 223) 54.

561 B. Carron, V. Botteron, 'How smart can a contract be' in D. Kraus, T. Obrist, O. Hari (eds), *Blockchains, Smart Contracts, Decentralised Autonomous Organisations and the Law* (Edward Elgar 2019) 124 talk about a 'take it or leave it' offer. Werbach and Cornell (n 181) 343 argue that smart contracts are unilateral because only one party places them on the blockchain.

562 Smits (n 223) 57–58. See Art. 2.1.6 (3) PICC, 2:204 (1) PECL and II. – 4:204(1) DFCR. In Italy, see Art. 1327 *cc*.

563 Raskin (n 229) 322; Carron and Botteron (n 561) 128 take the example of the transfer of cryptocurrencies by an investor in an ICO. Durovic and Janssen (n 167) 762–763 imagine the uploading of a smart contract to transfer the

In scenario 2, similarly to scenario 1, a user holding a node in permissionless blockchain uploads a smart contract on the blockchain. Contrary to scenario 1, the uploading does not correspond to an offer because a contract is already concluded after uploading. The request is made off-chain. In this case, the parties can complete the contract both offline and online, by e-mail or by accessing a website.

Scenario 3 is comparable to scenario 1. Indeed, every user holds a node and interacts on the blockchain. The only difference is that the blockchain is permissioned instead of being permissionless.

Scenario 4 is comparable to scenario 2 because offer and acceptance occur off-chain, even though in scenario 4 the blockchain is permissioned.

### 2.1. Time of conclusion of the contract.

In scenarios 2 and 4, establishing the time of contract conclusion does not add anything to the past because the contract is concluded off-chain. So, if the contract is concluded offline, traditional rules apply. If the contract is concluded online, exsting rules are interpreted to fit the electronic context, as described in section 2.1 of chapter 3.

In scenarios 1 and 3, instead, offer and acceptance are exchanged through the blockchain. This is a new modality of contract conclusion, so it is necessary to verify whether and how existing rules can be interpreted to fit this new context.

In a white paper by R3 and Norton Rose Fulbright,[564] the conclusion of a smart legal contract on the blockchain is compared to the exchange of data messages through e-mails. Offer and acceptance are expressed by data messages sent in the blockchain using public-key infrastructure through an Internet connection. Indeed, according to the MLEC and the UN Convention on the Use of Electronic Communications in International Contracts, a data message is any information generated, sent, received or stored by electronic, magnetic, optical or 'similar means'.[565] This definition was in-

ownership of a car for 10 ethers, and state that the upload of the 10 ethers by an offeree is an acceptance done by conduct.

564 R3, Norton Rose Fulbright, 'Can smart contracts be legally binding contracts?', R3 and Norton Rose Fulbright White Paper (November 2016) 22 <https://sites-nortonrosefulbright.vuturevx.com/596/14051/uploads/r3-and-norton-rose-fulbright-white-paper-full-report-144581.pdf> accessed 1 October 2021.

565 Art. 2(1)(a) of the MLEC and Art. 4(1)(c) of the United Nations Convention on the Use of Electronic Communications in International Contracts.

tended to apply to all existing communication techniques and all types of paperless messages.[566] Moreover, as with e-mails, the offeror and the offeree do not use an instantaneous means of communication (such as the telephone) but they are absent and a specific time passes between offer and acceptance.

Section 2.1 of chapter 3 has given an account of the dispatch rule, the receipt rule, and the actual notice rule. According to the dispatch rule, the contract is concluded when the offeree sends the acceptance; the receipt rule determines that the contract is concluded when the offeror receives the acceptance; lastly, following the actual notice rule, a contract is formed when the offeror acquires notice of the acceptance, i.e. when the acceptance reaches the offeror's address (unless the offeror proves that acquiring knowledge of the acceptance was impossible for reasons non-dependent on her fault). Therefore, it is necessary to interpret such rules to establish the time of contract conclusion when it happens through the blockchain.[567]

As already said, in the blockchain offer and acceptance are expressed by data messages. These data messages are sent and received using electronic addresses, i.e. the accounts or wallets that every user has to create to take part in the blockchain and to send transactions. There is no difference with electronic commerce, where the offer and the acceptance are sent from an electronic address or received by an electronic address in the form of data messages. For this reason, the dispatch, the receipt, and the actual notice rules have to be interpreted in the same way. Namely, according to the dispatch rule, the contract is concluded when the offeree sends the acceptance (in the form of a data message) by her electronic address; according to the receipt rule, the contract is concluded when the offeror's electronic address receives the acceptance (in the form of a data message); according to the actual notice rule, similarly to the receipt rule, the contract is concluded when the offeror's electronic address receives the acceptance unless the offeror proves that she could not access her information system for reasons not dependent on her fault.

566 A. Mukherjiee, 'Smart Contracts – Another Feather in UNCITRAL's Cap' (2018) Cornell International Law Journal Online <http://cornellilj.org/smart-contracts-another-feather-in-uncitrals-cap/> accessed 1 October 2021.

567 Giancaspro (n 197) 830 argues that 'the answer may lie in a broad interpretation of the legal rules discussed above'.

The remaining issue is establishing which acts correspond to the sending and the receipt of the acceptance in the blockchain. It is believed[568] that the offeree sends her acceptance when she sends the acceptance transaction after having signed it with her private key. Indeed, at that moment the offeree sends a data message from her address to the smart contract's address. As concerns the receipt, it is thought[569] that the offeror receives the acceptance when her account can retrieve the acceptance transaction after validation. Indeed, after the validation step, each node in the blockchain updates the state of its copy of smart contract.[570]

In summary, according to the dispatch rule, the contract is concluded when the offeree sends the acceptance transaction after having signed it with her private key. The contract is concluded when the offeror's account can retrieve the acceptance transaction, according to the receipt and the actual notice rule (under the actual notice rule, the offeror can prove that he could not acquire knowledge of it for reasons not dependent on her fault). Applying the dispatch rule, the receipt rule, or the actual notice rule depends on the applicable law.

The contract is concluded through the performance of the contract by the offer in case of acceptance by conduct. [571] This statement does not need further interpretations in the domain of blockchain-based smart legal contracts.

## 2.2. Revocation of offer and acceptance.

As seen in the previous section about the time of contract conclusion, the revocation of offer and acceptance is not of interest in scenarios 2 and 4. The present section considers revocation in scenarios 1 and 3.

If the offeror would like to revoke her proposal,[572] the immutable character of blockchain technology might represent an obstacle. The offeror

---

568 See G. Finocchiaro, C. Bomprezzi, 'A legal analysis of the use of blockchain technology for the formation of smart legal contracts' (2020) 2 MediaLaws 111, 121.

569 *Ibid.*

570 Chapter 1, section 7.

571 Art. 2.1.6(3) PICC, Art. 2.205 (3) PECL, Art. II. – 4:205 (3) DFCR. In Italy, see Art. 1327 *cc.*

572 Indeed, in some legal systems (such as German law), offers are irrevocable, unless the offeror states that she is not bound. Other legal systems (such as French law) adopt an intermediate position between absolute revocation (like

might be prevented from revoking unless a 'revocation of proposal' operation is available from the beginning.[573]

As already explained,[574] the dispatch rule was conceived in common law as a compromise between the free revocability of the offer (until the conclusion of the contract) and the need to protect the offeree. Indeed, with traditional ways of communication for concluding contracts at a distance, acceptance could have taken much time before arriving at its destination. So, the offeree should have been able to accept a contract with the certainty that it would have been binding. With electronic contracts and the exchange of offer and acceptance through electronic forms of communication, the transmission of the acceptance has become instantaneous, so the dispatch rule has lost its function. For this reason, the EDI model framework agreements, the PICC, the PECL, the DFCR, and some common law countries have favoured the receipt rule instead of the dispatch rule.[575] Because of such instantaneity, the literature has expressed some doubts about the possibility to revoke the acceptance.[576] Indeed, the revocation of the acceptance has to reach the offeror before the acceptance.[577] Thus, the capability to discern whether revocation of acceptance was antecedent

---

in English law) and irrevocability. More precisely, any offer is revocable before acceptance unless it is abusive (e.g. the offer contains a ~~time~~ period within which it is to be accepted, or the offeree could reasonably believe that the offer would remain open for a reasonable time). Similarly, the PICC, PECL, and DFCR balance the interest of the offeror with that of the offeree. Indeed, they state that the offeror can revoke her offer until the offeree has sent a statement of acceptance, and there are two exceptions to revocability (Art. 2.1.4 PICC, 2:202 PECL, II. – 4:202 DFCR). See Christandl (n 331) 301ff. In Italy, Art. 1328 *cc* provides that the offeror can revoke her proposal until she has acquired knowledge of the acceptance.

573 The smart contract cannot be modified once uploaded on the blockchain.

574 Chapter 3, Section 2.1, n 339.

575 Chapter 3, Section 2.1.

576 Chapter 3, Section 2.1.

577 Art. 2.1.10 PICC provides that the withdrawal of the acceptance can occur before or at the same time as the acceptance reaches the offeror. Indeed, the revocation of the acceptance must precede the conclusion of the contract. So, under the receipt rule, the revocation must occur before the acceptance reaches the offeror. With the legal notice rule, revocation is equally possible until the offeror is presumed to have acquired knowledge of the acceptance (in Italy, see Art. 1328 *cc*). Also in common law countries that follow the dispatch rule, the revocation becomes effective when it reaches the offeror. See P. Fasciano, 'Internet Electronic Mail: A Last Bastion for the Mailbox Rule' (1997) 25(3) Hofstra Law Review 971, 975. So, while the offeror is bound by the offer and may no longer change her mind once the offeree has dispatched the acceptance (because

to acceptance is questionable. It should be demonstrated that the offeror's server (or the offeror's provider's server) recorded the revocation before the acceptance, which could be left to chance and the unpredictability of computer systems.[578]

The immutability of blockchain also renders problematic the revocation of the acceptance, unless the smart contract code allows a 'revocation of acceptance' operation. In case the revocation of the acceptance is technically possible, the time-sequential order of data in concatenated blocks and the immutable character of the blockchain – that provides incontrovertible evidence of the addition of a specific transaction at a specific time – might help to establish whether the revocation of acceptance came before the acceptance.

Maybe, the time interval between the moment when the offeree signs the transaction of acceptance and when the latter is added to the blockchain (that is necessary to complete the validation step) makes the problem of the revocation of acceptance less relevant. However, researchers are trying to reduce such a time interval to address the scalability problem of blockchain.[579] This problem mainly concerns permissionless blockchain. Indeed, validator nodes make challenging competitions to add a new block; thus, the validation step takes more time. Moreover, the validator nodes should add the transaction that revokes the acceptance before that of acceptance. The latter operation would be under the control of the validator nodes and not of the offeree, especially in permission-

---

the dispatch of the acceptance determines the conclusion of the contract), the offeree looses her freedom to revoke when the acceptance reaches the offeror.

578 For example, due to a malfunction of the computer system, the revocation reaches the server while the acceptance does not.

579 Z. Zheng, S. Xie, H. Dai, X. Chen, H. Wang, 'An Overview of Blockchain Technology: Architecture, Consensus, and Future Trends' (proceedings of the 2017 IEEE 6th International Congress on Big Data, Honolulu, 25–30 June 2017) 557, 561 <https://www.researchgate.net/publication/318131748_An_Overview_of_Blockchain_Technology_Architecture_Consensus_and_Future_Trends> accessed 1 October 2021. The European Union Blockchain Observatory and Forum address the problem of scalability of blockchain technology in the Report 'Scalability, interoperability and sustainability of blockchains' (<https://www.eublockchainforum.eu/sites/default/files/reports/report_scalaibility_06_03_2019.pdf?width=1024&height=800&iframe=true> accessed 1 October 2021) p. 10. The Report rightly points out that this slowness 'is part of the price of securing networks'. It refers to a 'loose trilemma' because blockchain cannot be scalable, decentralised, and secure at the same time. Consequently, 'designers of blockchain-based platforms need to consider the trade-offs between these three parameters that best fit their particular use case'.

less blockchains where identities are unknown.[580] For these reasons, it is thought that the matter does not differ so much from that of the revocation of acceptance in electronic contracts.

### 3. *The language of the code.*

Even though there are no legal obstacles to express a contract in the form of computer code, it seems complex to embed the complexity of a contract into the software. This is preliminarily due to the huge differences between the formal language of the code and natural language. Allen illustrates these differences in syntax, semantics, and pragmatics (the three main aspects of speech).[581] The author affirms that 'the syntax of natural languages is more path-dependent and generally less rigorous than that of formal languages'.[582] As concerns semantics, the natural language is much more ambiguous than the formal one, and 'there are more shades of meaning'.[583] The most significant difference is in pragmatics because computers do not consider the context, which is fundamental to catch what the parties meant with the agreement.[584] Highlighting these differences is important because, despite paper contracts, smart contracts have to perform the underlying contract. The smart contract code has to interpret the contract to perform the contract.

On the one hand, the rigorousness of the language of the code helps avoid divergent interpretations by the contracting parties.[585] On the other hand, legal language needs a certain degree of flexibility. As pointed out by Sklaroff[586] (and also described in the second chapter of this study),[587]

580 For example, some transactions might be delayed in permissionless blockchains because miners prefer to validate the transactions with high transaction fees first.

581 Allen (n 544) 323–324.

582 *Ibid.* 323. Syntax is 'a logic inherent in devices such as pre-, in-, and suffixes, articles, and word order that express logical relations such as subject-object relations, action, transitivity, time, etc.'.

583 *Ibid.* 323. Semantics is 'the meaning that different words and combinations of words have'.

584 *Ibid.* 323 – 324. Pragmatics 'studies what words mean in the context in which they are uttered'.

585 Authors consider lack of ambiguity as a positive characteristic of smart legal contracts because it may significantly reduce disputes. See Chapter 2, Section 5.

586 Sklaroff (n 177).

587 Chapter 2, Section 2.

flexibility creates efficiencies in the realm of contracts. Indeed, such flexibility allows the adaptation of the contract to all future circumstances and continuously changing context. Moreover, contracts do not only represent what parties have laid down in a medium (paper-made or digital). Contracts are by their nature incomplete. Contract terms do not only derive from the express agreement of the parties but also their tacit agreement, the rules of law or practices established between the parties or usages.[588] The party agreement has to be supplemented through gap-filling.[589]

The above aspects prevent contracts from being conceived and included entirely in computer code (at least for now).[590] However, because these limitations are technical, solutions have to be found on a technical level.

Instead, on a legal level, legal experts wonder when it can be said that the party had the intention to conclude a contract, given that the average man is not capable of understanding the language of the code.[591] Others argue that the contract could be voidable because it was concluded by mistake.[592] An attempt to answer this question is made below.

### 3.1. Contractual intention.

As per section 1 of this chapter, both parties agree to be legally linked to the agreement, in addition to the meeting of the minds. According to the prevailing view, the intent has to be objective and not subjective, in the sense that it does not matter the inner intention of the party, her per-

---

588 This is what Art. II.-9:101(1) DFCR provides. See also Art. 5.1.2 PICC, Art. 6:102 PECL.

589 Carron, Botteron (n 561) 120–121. About gap filling in a comparative perspective, see Smits (n 223) 130–135. In Italy, Art. 1374 *cc* disciplines the integration of contracts. See Antoniolli, Veneziano (n 445) 280–282.

590 Advancements in technology could allow the conclusion of contracts entirely in code. On this point, see above Chapter 2, Section 2, in particular n 181.

591 R. H. Weber, 'Smart contracts: Do we need New Legal Rules?' in A. De Franceschi, R. Schulze (eds), M. Graziadei, O. Pollicino, F. Riente, S. Sica, P. Sirena (co-eds), *Digital Revolution – New Challenges for Law. Data Protection, Artificial Intelligence, Smart Products, Blockchain Technology and Virtual Currencies* (Beck, Nomos 2019) 304; Carron, Botteron (n 561) 128 ff; Pinsent Masons, 'Smart insurance Contracts: A discussion paper by Pinsent Masons and Applied Blockchain' (2017) 12 <https://www.the-digital-insurer.com/wp-content/uploads/2017/10/980-FinTech_Smart_Insurance_Contracts_Flyer.pdf> accessed 1 October 2021; O' Schields (n 232) 186.

592 Rikken *et al.* (n 113) 22; Carron, Botteron (n 561) 134–137.

ceptions or understandings. The agreement must be understood from the external perspective of a reasonable observer to protect the other party's expectations and preserve the efficiency and legal certainty of contractual relationships.[593] Moreover, this intention must be directed towards the creation of legally enforceable relations. In commercial agreements, the intention of being legally bound is presumed because of the nature of commercial transactions, unless differently agreed by the parties.[594]

On the latter point, as already described,[595] some authors affirm that smart legal contracts are self-enforcing, i.e., they eliminate the need for legal enforcement. So, smart contracts might be intended to be not legally enforceable, and their contractual nature might be denied.[596] Some legal experts have refused this assumption. Savelyev admits that 'if the result is in fact the same in substance to the one, usually regulated by usual contracts (…) then it may be argued that the nature of the relations in the core of it are also the same'.[597] Moreover, Durovic and Janssen consider that, even if 'the parties do not wish to enforce their contracts in court because they believe that such enforcement will be unnecessary since a smart contract is guaranteed to be performed', however, 'what certainly seems to exist, though with some limited effects in practice, is the intention of a legal relation that justifies the performance of the contract and prohibits claiming restitution of what has been executed as undue payments or unjustified enrichments'.[598] They add that 'the fact that parties do not wish to enforce their smart contracts in court is not the same as wishing that if the smart contracts end up in court, they will not be upheld by the court'.[599]

---

593 Smits (n 223) 64–70. See also Art. 2:102 and II.-4:102 DFCR. In the Italian legal system, the intention to be legally bound to a contract is not an express requisite. However, it is considered an informal requirement. Italian law also adopts an objective standard for determining such intention. So, to protect the other party's reasonable reliance on a binding agreement, a party is bound if another party could reasonably assume the intention despite the absence of a subjective intention. See A. Monti 'Art. 2:101–107' in Antoniolli, Veneziano (n 445) 94–95.

594 Smits (n 223) 70–77.

595 Chapter 2, Section 4.

596 Werbach and Cornell (n 181) 339 state that they may look more like so-called 'gentlemen's agreements'.

597 Savelyev (n 96) 11.

598 Durovic, Janssen (n 167) 767.

599 *Ibid.*

There is agreement with the above statements and it is believed that smart legal contracts can give rise to legally binding contracts. Smart legal contracts are considered self-enforcing because of the characteristics of blockchain technology. The decentralised and tamper-resistant characters of the blockchain determine that no single party is in absolute control of the blockchain and can interrupt or modify the execution of the smart contract code. So, if the code performs the contract, this means that the obliged party cannot but perform because she cannot infringe the rules of the code. As a consequence, it is believed that there is no need for enforcement. In the following chapter, this claim is criticised. It begins by clarifying the meaning of decentralisation, which does not necessarily lead to a lack of control over the performance of the contract. Then, there is an attempt to demonstrate that blockchain does not eliminate the need for contract-enforcement.

The idea that smart contracts live by their own rules and are part of a parallel and independent legal system, which the parties intend to apply in place of traditional contract law, is denied. In Section 6 of Chapter 2, it is affirmed that the coexistence of the law of the code with the law of the countries is unrealistic because it is unlikely that the parties would renounce to go in front of a court or to apply existing legal remedies in the event something goes wrong. Furthermore, it is observed that discussions around blockchain regulation are essentially following the same path of the Internet. Most of the literature concludes that, as was for the Internet, blockchain technology would not replace the current legal framework with the law of the algorithms.

Then the most interesting aspect is the difficulty of ascertaining an actual mutual expression of intent when the contract is expressed in computer code. As outlined at the beginning of this section, according to the principle of legitimate confidence and the party's duty to get informed and understand what she is doing before accepting the offer, it does not matter the party's inner intent. Instead, legal systems usually prefer to carry out an objective evaluation of the party's statements or conduct taking into account the circumstances of the case and the general principle of good faith. Because the meaning of computer code is unintelligible to the average man, it might be difficult to acknowledge the existence of a legally binding agreement.

It is argued that the mere fact that the contract is expressed in computer code does not suffice to exclude the contractual intention.[600]

---

600 Finocchiaro, Bomprezzi (n 568) 123.

There is agreement that, as Carron and Botteron state, smart contracts can be compared to contracts with general terms and conditions.[601] Standard contracts are drafted unilaterally by one party and supplied to the other. For this reason, some rules apply to contracts whose terms have not been individually negotiated that determine when the party not involved in the drafting is considered bound by the contract. Contract terms are not individually negotiated in standard form contracts and in individual contracts whose terms have been imposed by one party. Today, it is generally acknowledged that the drafting party has to take reasonable steps to bring terms to the other party's attention when the contract is made or beforehand.[602] 'To take reasonable steps' means that 'the supplier has to take care that the other party is actually aware of those terms and may easily read them'.[603] Similarly, Annex I(1)(i) of the Unfair Contract Terms Directive (Directive 1993/13/EC) states that the consumer should have a 'real opportunity of becoming acquainted' with the terms 'before the conclusion of the contract', otherwise the term is considered unfair and does not bind the consumer. The Directive only refers to B2C contracts, while general principles do not restrict this obligation to consumer contracts. In Italy, Article 33(2)(l) of the Italian Consumer Code replicates Annex I(1)(i) of the UCTD. Another relevant provision is Article 1341 *cc*, which states that terms in standard contracts are effective only if the party who accepts them had a sufficient chance to know their content.[604]

The existence of consent has been discussed about wrap contracts, which are adhesion contracts concluded online.[605] The most common wrap contracts are click-wrap and browse-wrap agreements. They are presented and concluded in a non-traditional manner. Indeed, in a click-wrap agreement, the terms are offered in a scrollable box or at a hyperlink; then, the other party has to click on an 'I agree' button to accept. In a browse-wrap agreement, the terms are accessible through hyperlinks ('Terms of use' or 'Legal terms'). The user accepts using a website or downloading the digital content, without clicking on the 'I agree' box or taking any other positive action. In both cases, the offeror has to provide the other party with sufficient notice of the existence of the terms before or at the time of contract

601 Carron, Botteron (n 561) 114.

602 See N. Jansen, 'Art. 2:104: Terms not Individually Negotiated' in Jansen, Zimmermann (n 315) 272–280. See Art. 2.1.19 PICC, 2:104 PECL, II.-9:103 DFCR.

603 *Ibid.* 278.

604 See Monti (n 593) 98–101.

605 Chapter 3, Section 2.1.3, n 398.

conclusion according to the caselaw.[606] In this regard, it is not enough to give information about the terms, but the latter have to be conspicuously and clearly presented to the non-drafting party. Therefore, the supplier has to ensure that the other party is (or should reasonably be) aware of entering into a contract. Without these arrangements, it has been argued that it is unlikely that the non-drafting party is aware of the existence of a contract in browse-wrap contracts because she is not required to take any positive assenting action. Similarly, in click-wrap contracts, online users do not give importance to the action of clicking on a box as they do with the physical act of placing a signature. In the latter case, however, a higher level of awareness is presumed because the offeree is asked to do something to enter the agreement.

To summarise, in standard contracts – being them in paper or online – it is necessary to provide the other party with the terms of the contract in a clear and comprehensible version for the average man in ways that allow her to become reasonably aware of being entering a contract. Otherwise, one cannot affirm that the non-drafting party intended to conclude a contract.

In EU law, some rules aim to ensure the awareness and comprehensibility of contract terms for the weakest party in online contracts. In particular, it is referred to the information requirements laid down in the e-Commerce Directive and Consumer Rights Directive described in Section 2.1 of Chapter 3. The latter outlined that the requirements of the e-Commerce Directive are not mandatory in B2B contracts and do not apply to contracts concluded exclusively by an exchange of electronic mail or by equivalent communication. Indeed, because in B2B contracts parties have a similar bargaining power it is presumed that they can express a high-quality level of consent. Besides, on the Internet, businesses usually conclude adhesion contracts with consumers in wrap agreements, instead of exchanging e-mails. The latter modality of contract conclusion is more suitable for parties that already know each other and are both involved in the process of the drafting of the contract. In Article 10(3), the e-Commerce Directive provides that 'contract terms and general conditions provided to the recipient must be made available in a way that allows him to store and reproduce them', but does not specify when such terms must be provided to the recipient. Instead, recital 39 of the Consumer Rights

606 Reference is made to the American case law and the European Court of Justice. On this topic, see R. Momberg, 'Standard terms and transparency in online contracts' in De Franceschi (n 476) 189–207.

Directive states that 'it is important to ensure for distance contracts concluded through websites that the consumer can fully read and understand the main elements of the contract before placing his order'. Finally, both the e-Commerce Directive and the Consumer Rights Directive stress the importance of transparency of such information.[607]

Carron and Botteron argue that 'an offer formulated through a smart contract presents similar features to those of a contract with general terms and conditions. Both are difficult to understand for the vast majority of offerees'.[608] This statement is acceptable. However, it only refers to contracts concluded on-chain.[609] Moreover, it only considers the non-traditional language of presentation of the terms, not the non-traditional way of acceptance of those terms.

As explained in section 2 of this chapter, in on-chain contracts there are 'take it or leave it' offers; because of the immutability of the blockchain, there is not the possibility to make a counter-offer. So, the contract is drafted unilaterally, and the other party has no other option to accept or not accept. For this reason, it is thought that the parallel with standard contracts is appropriate. There are also similarities with wrap contracts because of the non-traditional way of expressing assent.[610] Indeed, once the offeror has uploaded the smart contract code on the blockchain, the offeree can accept it by sending some data to the smart contract's address (e.g. by signing a transaction of acceptance with a private key or by transferring a certain amount of cryptocurrencies). Therefore, it is believed not only that the contract has to be presented in a comprehensible manner – i.e. by accompanying the code with its translation in natural language – before the conclusion, but also that the other party must have the opportunity to understand the moment in which she is going to enter into a contract.[611] For example, O'Shields talks of the possibility to provide an 'I agree' button;[612] McKinney, Landy and Wilka propose a check-box or 'execute' button.[613]

In abstract, the above hypothesis corresponds to scenarios 1 and 3, where the exchange of offer and acceptance occurs on-chain. Then the

---

607 See below, Section 4 of this chapter.

608 Carron and Botteron (n 561) 114.

609 The authors speak of offers made 'by integrating lines of computer code into the blockchain' (p. 113).

610 Finocchiaro, Bomprezzi (n 568) 123.

611 *Ibid.*

612 O' Schields (n 232) 186.

613 McKinney, Landy, Wilka (n 120) 6.

distinction between B2B and B2C contracts is also considered relevant[614] because wrap-agreements are usually concluded between a business and a consumer. The business takes advantage of the open character of the Internet to find potential customers. Having said this, it is thought that the parallel between contracts concluded on-chain and wrap-contracts is more suitable for scenario 1, and only when the permissionless blockchain is used to conclude B2C contracts. In the remaining cases (i.e. B2B contracts in scenario 1, and scenario 3 which is exclusively a B2B scenario), it is thought that businesses can have greater economic possibilities to consult an expert that can understand the language of the code. These contracts may also be concluded based on framework agreements setting the main object of future contracts and the modalities of their conclusion on-chain.[615] In particular, the fact that in scenario 3 the parties build and share a dedicated infrastructure through which they conduct their business gives more value to the above considerations.

In scenarios 2 and 4, the conclusion of the contract takes place off-chain. Both in scenarios 2 and 4 contracts are concluded B2C. In B2C contracts, it is more likely that the business drafts the contract unilaterally and submits it to the consumer. The contract conclusion may occur in the simultaneous presence of parties or by navigation of a website by the consumer. In both cases, however, it is thought that the business has to provide a natural language version of the terms of the contract and take all reasonable steps to guarantee the consumer's awareness.

In conclusion it is believed that a party cannot always prevent that a contract expressed in the language of the code can produce its effects against her because of a lack of her contractual intention, according to the principle of confidence and the party's duty to get informed and to understand what she is doing. Instead, it should be considered the circumstances that preceded the conclusion of the contract, and the qualities of the accepting party.

### 3.2. The mistake.

Even admitting that the offeree intended to conclude the contract, somebody argues that the party might invoke a fundamental mistake as a basis for calling the contract voidable. Indeed, because most parties do not usu-

614 Finocchiaro, Bomprezzi (n 568) 124.
615 *Ibid.*

ally understand the computer code, there might be a discrepancy between the party's perception of the facts and the contract.

Section 2.1.3 of Chapter 3 illustrated that not all mistakes can cause the avoidance of the contract. The interest of the mistaken party has to be balanced with the other party's reliance on the agreement. For this reason, the mistake has to be fundamental, and it has to be recognisable by the non-mistaken party. The mistake is recognisable when a person of average diligence would have detected the mistake. This 'recognisability test' should be applied in objective terms. For example, Article 1431 *cc* refers to the content, the circumstances of the contract, or the quality of the contracting parties. In general, the contract is voidable when the non-mistaken party could not reasonably rely on the validity of the contract. The non-mistaken party's reliance on the validity of the contract is also unreasonable a particular behaviour of the party causes the mistake. For example, the party caused the mistake by giving incorrect information, or her silence caused the mistake. Indeed, the parties have to act in good faith during negotiations and the formation of contracts (Article 1337 *cc*).

In light of the above, it is thought that the offeree cannot always invoke her mistake to repudiate a smart contract. The above considerations are applied to the four scenarios.

In the previous section, it was assumed that the offeror has to submit a natural language version of the contract to the offeree in B2C contracts (concluded both off-chain and on-chain) because of a lack of the other party's involvement in drafting the contract and the consumer's weaker negotiating position. In the other cases, it was claimed that the other party takes the risk of entering a contract of which she is unaware because, taking into account the circumstances preceding the conclusion of the contract and the parties' negotiating power, it is thought that the principle of confidence should prevail.

Having said that, it is assumed that it is more likely that one can consider the mistake reasonably relevant and recognisable in such B2C scenarios. Indeed, the code is drafted and submitted unilaterally by the non-mistaken party; the consumer is the weakest party and almost certainly does not have the opportunity to be advised by an IT expert; the consumer cannot analyse the computer code.[616]

---

616 Section 2.1.3 of Chapter 3 noticed that the familiarity of the mistaken party with a computer system is an important yardstick to recognise the mistake.

## 4. The e-Commerce Directive and the Consumer Rights Directive. Information requirements.

Section 2.1 of Chapter 3 mentioned the Directive 2000/31/CE on electronic commerce and the Directive 2011/83/EU on consumer rights in distance and off-premises contracts. These Directives include some rules that apply before or at the moment of placing an online order. So, it is important to verify whether these rules are also applicable to the conclusion of blockchain-based smart legal contracts.

The e-Commerce Directive approximates certain national provisions on information society services also relating to electronic contracts,[617] i.e. contracts concluded at a distance and by electronic means.[618] 'Electronic means' refer to 'electronic equipment for processing (…) and storage of data'.[619] In scenarios 2 and 4 the Directive is applicable when contracts are concluded online, by e-mail or by access to a website. There are not any novelties because contracts are concluded off-chain. In scenarios 1 and 3, it is thought that there are no obstacles to the application of the Directive. As outlined in Section 2 of this chapter, the offeror and the offeree do not use an instantaneous mean of communication. Still, they are absent and a specific time passes between offer and acceptance. Moreover, the offeror instantiates a smart contract and the offeree accepts the contract by sending a data message to the smart contract code. Both use a public-key infrastructure and an Internet connection. A distributed and decentralised electronic ledger (the blockchain) processes and stores the offeror's uploading, the offeree's data message, and the resulting change of state of the smart contract code.

Similarly, the Consumer Rights Directive apply to distance contracts, that is 'any contract concluded between the trader and the consumer under an organised distance sales or service provision scheme without the simultaneous physical presence of the trader and the consumer, with the exclusive use of one or more means of distance communication up to and including the time at which the contract is concluded'.[620] Recital 20

617 See Art. 1(2) of the Directive.

618 According to Art. 2(1)(a) of the Directive, 'information society services' are 'services within the meaning of Art. 1(2) of Directive 98/34/EC as amended by Directive 98/48/EC, i.e. any services normally provided for remuneration, at a distance and by electronic means at the individual request of a recipient of services.

619 See recital 17 of the Directive.

620 See Art. 2(7) of the Consumer Rights Directive.

also considers mail orders and the Internet as means of distance communication. Other provisions explicitly refer to distance contracts concluded electronically.[621] So, there is no doubt that the Directive applies to scenarios 2 and 4. For scenarios 1 and 3, it is believed that the Directive is also applicable to contracts concluded on-chain for the same reasons expressed above about the distance and electronic nature of such contracts (even though the Directive 2011/83/EU only concerns B2C contracts).

Having clarified that, both Directives set down some information requirements that the service provider or the trader shall provide to the recipient of the service and the consumer.[622] Article 10 of the e-Commerce Directive establishes that the information requirements are not mandatory in B2B contracts. Still, they do not apply to contracts concluded exclusively by exchange of electronic mail or by equivalent individual communications. The information requirements laid down in the Consumer Rights Directive are always mandatory in distance B2C contracts. Article 6(8) of the Consumer Rights Directive states that these information requirements are in addition to information requirements contained in the e-Commerce Directive.

In scenarios 2 and 4, it is already clear when information requirements shall apply. In scenarios 1 and 3, the Consumer Rights Directive is surely not applicable to B2B contracts, in particular in scenario 3 that is exclusively a B2B scenario. Regarding the e-Commerce Directive, whether the on-chain modality of the conclusion of smart legal contracts can be considered an equivalent individual communication like electronic mail could be questioned.

In that regard, in Section 2 of this chapter it has been explained that in blockchain the offeror can direct her offer towards one (or more) specific person(s) or to the public. In the former hypothesis, only authorised blockchain addresses can interact with the smart contract code. In the latter, any participant in the blockchain can send data messages to the smart contract code. When the offeror directs the offer towards one (or more) specific person(s) it is thought that the contract is concluded by a form of individual communication equivalent to electronic mail.[623] Indeed, by indicating one (or more) specific address(es), the offeror identifies the recipient(s) of the offer. In the opposite case, the recipient of the offer is indifferent to the offeror, as is when a business makes available her offer

621 See Art. 8(2) and Art. 11(3).

622 See Section 2.1 of Chapter III, and Section 3.1 of this chapter.

623 Finocchiaro, Bomprezzi (n 568) 125.

on a website. So, it was assumed that when the offeror addresses her offer to one (or more) determined recipient(s), the information requirements laid down in Article 10 of the e-Commerce Directive do not apply.[624]

Maybe, this form of individual communication is more frequent in scenario 3 because the blockchain is permissioned. Permissioned blockchains are closed systems with known participants, thus it is easier for the offeror to identify the recipients. Moreover, as evidenced above,[625] the conclusion of contracts by exchanging e-mails or other forms of individual communication is more common in B2B contracts – as is in scenario 3 – where the offeree usually has more bargaining power. Instead, scenario 1 could be suitable for offers made to indeterminate recipients because the blockchain is permissionless, and participants are unknown. Businesses could use a permissionless blockchain like in scenario 1 to offer their products or services to indeterminate consumers. For example, OpenBazaar[626] is an online marketplace that is also open to businesses and based on a permissionless blockchain.

Another question is whether these information requirements can be expressed in the language of the code. On this point, it is thought that there are two main obstacles, one technical and one legal.[627]

About the former, someone has observed that not all contractual conditions are operational. There are non-operational contractual conditions, such as those that determine the applicable law or jurisdiction.[628] Similarly, information requirements need a descriptive, and non-operational, language.

From a legal point of view, both Directives stress the importance of transparency of information. Article 5(2) of the e-Commerce Directive states that 'where information society services refer to prices, these are to be indicated clearly and unambiguously'; Article 10 of the same Directive dictates that the information is given by the service provider 'clearly, comprehensibly and unambiguously'. Article 6 of the Consumer Rights Directive establishes that the provider shall provide the consumer with the information 'in a clear and comprehensible manner'.

624 *Ibid.*
625 Section 3.1 of this chapter.
626 See Chapter 2, Section 8.
627 Finocchiaro, Bomprezzi (n 568) 125–126.
628 See Chapter 2, Section 2.

As explained above, information requirements help the other party become aware of the conclusion of the contract and its contents.[629] In other words, they aim to enhance trust in electronic and distance contracts, where contracts are often concluded between strangers and the offeree cannot directly test services and products. A higher level of protection is needed in B2C contracts, where the consumer is the weakest party, and in online adhesion contracts, such as wrap agreements. For these reasons, according to the e-Commerce Directive, information requirements are mandatory in B2C contracts and applicable to all contracts not concluded with electronic mail or other equivalent individual forms of communication. According to the assumptions made in Sections 3.1 and 3.2 of this chapter, smart legal contract should be provided in natural language in the same cases where information requirements are mandatory (i.e. in B2C contracts and unilaterally drafted contracts), and for the same reasons (different level of bargaining power, lack of involvement in the draft of the contract, greater difficulty to understand the contract). Therefore, it is believed that also information requirements should be given in natural language to be considered unambiguous, clear, and comprehensible, as requested by the Directive on e-Commerce and the Consumer Rights Directive.[630]

However, Article 3(2)(l) of the Consumer Rights Directive excludes that the Directive can apply to contracts 'concluded by means of automatic vending machines or automated commercial premises'. A study has observed that, because of the analogy between vending machines and smart contracts, 'a smart contract which is itself the legal contract...may not be caught by this legal instrument (whereas legal contracts that merely use a smart contract to execute an element of the contract will likely be caught)'.[631]

It is believed that the above exemption does not cover the conclusion of smart legal contracts in the blockchain. Indeed, contract conclusion

629 Chapter 3, Section 2.1; Section 3.1 of this chapter.

630 Finocchiaro, Bomprezzi (n 568) 126.

631 European Commission (n 11) 69. The study also cites the guidance of the Commission on the Directive, which considers that the exception 'would apply to contracts concluded on automated commercial premises such as automated gas stations without the physical presence of the trader's representative for the conclusion of the contract' thus deducing that the norm should be interpreted broadly. *See* 'DG JUSTICE GUIDANCE DOCUMENT on the Directive 2011/83/EU on consumer rights' 10, available at <https://ec.europa.eu/info/sites/info/files/crd_guidance_en_0_updated_0.pdf> accessed 1 October 2021.

through vending machines is quite different because of the proximity of the device, the visibility of the product contained therein, and their immediate availability for the consumer.[632] On the contrary, excluding the application of the Directive would be discriminatory.

Because information requirements have the purpose of strengthening the offeree's confidence in the other party's performance, De Graaf[633] reflects on the practical need for information requirements for blockchain-based smart legal contracts. He argues that 'Many commercial parties that wish to sell products or services on the Internet gave an interest in complying with those laws. Traditionally, they sell more when buyers trust them. And one way to gain trust is by providing information about themselves and by complying with Internet laws. However, there is no (or less of a) need to do so with smart contracts. Because smart contracts execute themselves, trust in the code is important, not trust in the supplier'.[634] According to this author, the obliged party cannot control the computer system that performs the contract on her behalf. By uploading the smart contract on the blockchain, the party cannot refuse to perform. There is no need to trust in the other party – that cannot avoid execution – but trust is in the code.

De Graaf's considerations are rejected. First, because it is thought that blockchain-based smart contracts are not always out of the control of the obliged party. The idea that trust is no more in the other party is refused. Chapter 5, Part 1, develops these thoughts. Second, information requirements do not only contribute to the enforcement of the contract. De Graaf rightly observes that 'If the supplier feels no need to comply with these laws and (therefore) also does not provide information about himself, enforcements by courts of law becomes difficult, if not impossible. And if the supplier has no physical address and his assets are unknown, it is difficult to litigate against him and execute his assets if he is ordered by a court to pay a sum of money'.[635] Information requirements do not only concern the identity of the obliged party or her geographical address of establishment – which allow the enforcement of the contract – but also the products and services offered, the prices, the technical steps to follow to conclude the contract, the places and the modalities of access

632 M. Maugeri, 'Smart contracts e disciplina dei contratti' (2020) 2 Osservatorio del diritto civile e commerciale 400, 401.

633 De Graaf (n 218) 9.

634 *Ibid.*

635 *Ibid.* 9–10.

to the terms of the contract, the technical means for identifying input errors before placing the order, the languages of the contract, etc. In short, information requirements try to empower the awareness of the weaker party's actions to rebalance the parties' negotiating position and foster e-commerce. Therefore, even though on the one hand parties might be more confident that the contract is performed thanks to the blockchain, on the other hand, the blockchain does not remove the risk of unaware and disadvantaged parties.[636] For these reasons, it is thought that information requirements are still useful legal instruments.

### 4.1. Acknowledgement of receipt.

Article 11 of the e-Commerce Directive states that if the recipient of the service places his order, the service provider has to acknowledge the receipt of the recipient's order without undue delay and by electronic means. As explained above,[637] this duty does not introduce a new way for the exchange of offer and acceptance, but is intended to give certainty about the conclusion of the contract because the recipient is distant and cannot know if the order arrived at its destination. The acknowledgment of receipt is not mandatory in B2B contracts and shall not apply to contracts concluded exclusively by exchange of electronic mail or by equivalent individual communication. The reasons for these derogations are the same as those concerning information requirements. In B2B contracts, the parties have similar bargaining power. In contracts concluded by the exchange of e-mails, parties are already known. In short, in these situations, the conclusion of the contract is less risky for the recipient, and the latter can more easily understand whether and when a contract was concluded. Therefore, Article 11 of the e-Commerce Directive is applicable and not applicable in the same cases information requirements apply or do not apply. More specifically, in scenarios 2 and 4, the acknowledgement of receipt is usually helpful because contract conclusion occurs outside of the blockchain (when the contract is concluded at a distance and by electronic means). In scenarios 1 and 3, acknowledging receipt is not mandatory in B2B contracts, especially in scenario 3, which is exclusively a B2B scenario. Then, it was argued that, when the offeror directs the offer towards one (or more) specific address(es) in the blockchain, the contract might be

636 Finocchiaro, Bomprezzi (n 568) 127.
637 Chapter 3, Section 2.1.

considered concluded by a form of individual communication equivalent to electronic mail. Thus, in that event, Article 11 of the e-Commerce Directive does not apply. It was estimated that this form of individual communication is more frequent in scenario 3.

Maybe, the distributed character of blockchain might help fulfil the function of the acknowledgment of receipt, i.e., detecting the receipt of the order by the service provider. Indeed, the transaction is replicated in the network nodes after the validator nodes have validated the acceptance transaction and have added it to the blockchain; then, the transaction is replicated in the network nodes. So, that transaction is potentially visible by the recipient.[638]

Nevertheless, the acknowledgment of receipt aims to give certainty to the recipient about the arrival of her order, according to the principles of transparency and good faith, especially if the contract is concluded with a weaker party. Therefore, it is believed that the service provider still has to acknowledge the receipt of the recipient's order, especially when the acknowledgment of receipt has the additional function of making the summary of the order, like in the Italian legal system.[639] The blockchain might be useful to give evidence of the receipt of the order.

## *5. Form.*

Section 1 of this chapter claimed that a contract could also be expressed in the language of the code according to the informality and non-discrimination principles. Smart contracts fall under the definition of 'electronic document' laid down in the e-IDAS Regulation, which states that an electronic document is 'any content stored in electronic form, in particular text or sound, visual or audiovisual recording'.[640] Indeed, smart contracts

---

638 This depends on the right to read transactions. As seen above in Section 5 of Chapter 1, in permissionless blockchains everyone can usually read transactions, while in permissioned blockchains this is usually only possible for authorised addresses.

639 Article 13(2) of the Italian Legislative Decree no. 70 of 9 April 2003 implementing the e-Commerce Directive states that the acknowledgment of receipt has to provide a summary of both general and particular contractual conditions, information about the essential characteristics of the provided goods or services, and indicate in details the prices, the means of payment, the means of transport, the withdrawal, the delivery costs, and the applicable taxes.

640 Art. 3(35).

are computer programs stored on a decentralised ledger.[641] In its Report 'Blockchain and digital identity', the European Union Blockchain Observatory and Forum affirm that 'as fully digital ledgers, blockchains are by definition electronic documents under eIDAS. That means, among other things, that blockchains, or more properly the data, included smart contracts, contained therein, cannot be denied legal force solely because of their electronic nature'.[642]

When the law requires the written form, one wonders whether blockchain signatures can be considered electronic signatures; in case of a positive answer, whether they can be considered equivalent to handwritten signatures.

According to Article 2(a) of the UNCITRAL Model Law on Electronic Signatures, electronic signatures are 'data in electronic form in, affixed to or logically associated with, a data message, which may be used to identify the signatory in relation to the data message and to indicate the signatory's approval of the information contained in the data message'. According to Article 3(10) of the e-IDAS Regulation, electronic signatures are 'data in electronic form which is attached to or logically associated with other data in electronic form and which is used by the signatory to sign'.

In the blockchain, users sign transactions with their private key. Transactions are data messages that are exchanged between the accounts.[643] The first transaction concerning a smart contract is uploading a new smart contract code on the blockchain. A user signs a 'deploy' transaction. The smart contract code is added to the blockchain and associated with an address. Then, the smart contract code changes its state according to the transactions it receives.[644]

When the parties use blockchain-based smart contracts to conclude legally binding contracts – that is, in scenarios 1 and 3 – the offeror makes

---

641 In the USA, some countries (Arizona, California, Nevada, Tennessee, Ohio) have introduced *ad hoc* rules that recognise all records in the blockchain as electronic records under the Uniform Electronic Transaction Act (UETA). See 2017 Ariz. HB 2417 (n 259); 2018 Cal. AB 2658 (n 259); Nev. Rev. Stat. Ann. § 719.090; 2018 Ohio. SB 220 1306.01; 2018 Tenn. SB 1662 47–10–202 (n 259). See A. J. Bosco, 'Blockchain and the Uniform Electronic Transactions Act' (2018/2019) 74 The Business Lawyer 243.

642 See page 21. The report was published on 2 May 2019 and is accessible at the link <https://www.eublockchainforum.eu/sites/default/files/report_identity_v0.9.4.pdf> accessed 1 October 2021.

643 Chapter 1, Section 1.

644 Chapter 1, Section 7.

her offer through the upload of the smart contract on the blockchain, and the acceptance occurs by sending a transaction to the address of the smart contract.[645] Both the offeror and the offeree link some data (the private key) to other data (the transactions) and approve the information included in the latter data (offer and acceptance). So, such signatures can be considered electronic signatures.[646]

As explained in Chapter 3, not all electronic signatures can be considered equivalent to handwritten signatures.[647] In particular, the e-IDAS Regulation adopts a two-tier approach: it establishes that qualified signatures are equivalent to handwritten signatures; the principle of non-discrimination applies to the other kinds of electronic signatures. Therefore, in the latter case, it is up to the courts to evaluate the effects of an electronic signature. In the Italian legal system, digital, qualified, and advanced electronic signatures are considered equivalent to handwritten signatures. In addition, the same legal value is recognised to a document formed following the requirements set by the AGID under Article 71 of the CAD, upon prior IT identification of its author, in such a way as to guarantee its security, integrity, and immutability and the fact that it is ascribable to the author, in a clear and unequivocal manner. In all other cases, the suitability of the document to satisfy the requirement of the written form can be freely assessed in court, concerning its characteristics of security, integrity, and immutability.

The digital signature is peculiar to the Italian legal system and makes use of asymmetric cryptography. The latter technology is also present in the blockchain, as described in the first chapter.[648] Each user is provided with a pair of keys, one public and one private. The private key is secret and is used to sign transactions. Instead, anyone knows the public key. Asymmetric cryptography guarantees the provenance and authenticity of the message.

The Italian digital signature is a qualified signature. Therefore, it has to be created by a qualified electronic signature creation device and based on a qualified certificate for electronic signatures.[649] A qualified signature cre-

645 See Section 2 of this Chapter.

646 Finocchiaro, Bomprezzi (n 568) 130. Also the Arizona House Bill 2417, the Tennessee Senate Bill No. 1662 and the California Assembly Bill 2658 provide that cryptographic signatures in the blockchain can be considered electronic signatures (n 259).

647 Section 2.1.4.

648 Sections 1 and 2.

649 Art. 3(12) of the e-IDAS Regulation.

ation device is configured software or hardware used to create an electronic signature[650] that meets the requirements laid down in Annex II of the Regulation.[651] The definition of electronic signature creation data is more abstract than the former definition of Directive 1999/93/EC[652] that referred to codes or private cryptographic keys.[653] This is due to the principle of technology neutrality, so the Regulation implicitly also mentions cryptographic private keys when it refers to electronic signature creation data.[654] Cryptographic private keys are also used to sign blockchain transactions. The requirements of Annex II essentially concern the confidentiality and security of the data to create the electronic signature.[655] According to Article 29(2) of the Regulation, the Commission can establish reference numbers of standards for qualified electronic signature creation devices. If the device meets those standards, compliance with the requirements of Annex II is presumed. The Commission has not established reference numbers of standards under Article 29(2). However, it has adopted Implementing Decision (EU) 2016/650[656] under Article 30(3). Indeed, Article 30 of the Regulation provides that the conformity of the devices with the requirements of Annex II shall be certified by appropriate public or private bodies[657] that have to carry out a security evaluation process according to the standards established by the Commission. So, the standards of Implementing Decision (EU) 2016/650 may give indications for interpreting the requirements of Annex II.[658]

---

650 Art. 3(22).

651 Art. 29(1).

652 The e-IDAS Regulation has repealed the above Directive.

653 Art. 2(4) of the Directive 1999/93/EC.

654 K. Erler, 'Article 29 Requirements for Qualified Electronic Signatures Creation Devices' in Zaccaria *et al.* (n 385), 246.

655 M. C. Meneghetti, 'Articolo 3' in Delfini, Finocchiaro (n 385) 43.

656 Commission Implementing Decision (EU) 2016/650 of 25 April 2016 laying down standards for the security assessment of qualified signature and seal creation devices pursuant to Articles 30(3) and 39(2) of Regulation (EU) No 914/2014 of the European Parliament and of the Council on electronic identification and trust services for electronic transactions in the internal market [2016] OJ L 109/40.

657 In Italy, according to Art. 35(5) CAD, this task is assigned to the *Organismo di certificazione della sicurezza informatica (OCSI)*; Art. 4 of the Italian d.p.c.m. 30 Ottobre 2003 provides that the OCSI is the *Istituto Superiore delle Comunicazioni e delle Tecnologie dell'Informazione* under the Italian Ministry of Economic Development.

658 K. Erler (n 654) 251. Art. 1(1) of the Decision specifies that the standards apply where the electronic signature creation data is held in an entirely but non-neces-

A qualified certificate for electronic signature is a certificate, i.e. an attestation which links electronic signature validation data to a natural person and confirms at least the name or the pseudonym of that person,[659] issued by a qualified trust service provider that meets the requirements laid down in Annex I of the Regulation.[660] The certificate has the function to link the signature to an identified subject. If the certificate is qualified, there is a higher level of security between a signatory and a signature.[661] A qualified trust service provider is a natural or legal person that provides qualified trust services and is granted the qualified status by the supervisory body.[662]

It has been noticed that despite the principle of technology neutrality and the elaboration of a list of generic requirements, an essential element of a certificate is a particular system of electronic signature, i.e. the PKI Infrastructure,[663]which is also used to validate signatures in the blockchain.

In light of the above, despite transactions in the blockchain are signed through cryptographic private keys, and a PKI infrastructure is used to guarantee the provenance and integrity of data messages, electronic signatures can be considered qualified only in the presence of a qualified signature creation device and a qualified certificate.[664] Therefore, the wallet containing the keys should meet some requirements that guarantee confidentiality and security of the electronic signature creation data. Moreover, a certificate issued by a qualified trust service provider should attest the link between the keys and a precise identity.[665]

---

sarily exclusively user-managed environment. Otherwise, in the case a qualified trust service provider manages the device, the certification shall be based on a process that, pursuant to Art. 30(3)(b) of the Regulation, uses comparable security levels (Art. 1(2)). Art. 30(3)(b) of the Regulation provides that such comparable security levels shall apply when there are no available standards.

659 Art. 3(14) of the Regulation.

660 Art. 3(15).

661 Meneghetti (n 655) 44.

662 Art. 3(20) of the Regulation. In Italy, the supervisory body is the AGID.

663 G. Finocchiaro, 'Article 3 Definitions' in Zaccaria *et al.* (n 385) 58–59.

664 Finocchiaro, Bomprezzi (n 568) 131.

665 The Report 'Blockchain and digital identity' of the EU Blockchain Observatory and Forum, at page 23, assumes that 'it is possible that blockchain (...) signatures could be considered eIDAS-conform, including potentially up to the highest level, by recognising blockchains within solutions managed by trust service providers'. Similarly, Giuliano concludes that blockchain technology makes use of the technological components of the digital signature. However, there is no equivalence with handwritten signatures in the lack of a trust service provider that certifies underlying identities. See M. Giuliano, 'La blockchain

An electronic signature can be considered advanced if it meets the following requirements: (a) it is uniquely linked to the signatory; (b) it is capable of identifying the signatory; (c) it is created using electronic signature creation data that the signatory can, with a high level of confidence, use under his sole control; (d) it is linked to the data signed therewith in such a way that any subsequent change in the data is detectable.

It is thought that the use of PKI in the blockchain satisfies the requirement (a).[666] Asymmetric cryptography – i.e. the private and the public key that every user holds to transact – is resistant to unauthorised data access, so it preserves data confidentiality. Indeed, in asymmetric cryptography, the key used to encrypt the data differs from the key used to decrypt it. For this reason, asymmetric cryptography is more secure than symmetric cryptography, because it is not necessary to share a key to decrypt a message.[667] Asymmetric cryptography allows the verification by the receiver of the provenance and integrity of the received message. The sender encrypts the data with her private key and sends both the encrypted message and its hash. The receiver decrypts the message with the sender's public key. If the result is identical to the hash, the recipient can be sure that the message originated from the sender and was not modified by third parties.[668]

Nicotra and Sarzana di S. Ippolito[669] argue that such signatures might be adopted in permissioned blockchains because they are closed networks with pre-identified participants (unlike in permissionless blockchains). The possibility to identify the signatory could determine the satisfaction of the requisite (b). It is thought that this is plausible in B2B scenarios[670] (scenario 3) because businesses can have the economic capacity to equip themselves with such instruments.[671] Moreover, it is more likely that the

---

e gli smart contracts nell'innovazione del diritto del terzo millennio' (2018) 6 Diritto dell'Informazione e dell'Informatica 989, 1021.

666 Finocchiaro, Bomprezzi (n 568) 132.

667 In symmetric cryptography, the encryption key coincides with the decryption key. In asymmetric cryptography, the sender encrypts the message with the recipient's public key. The recipient decrypts the message with her private key that is kept secret by the receiver.

668 See Chapter 1, Section 2.

669 M. Nicotra, F. Sarzana di Sant'Ippolito (eds), *Diritto della blockchain, intelligenza artificiale e IoT* (Ipsoa 2018), 64.

670 Finocchiaro, Bomprezzi (n 568) 132.

671 Art. 55 of the Italian *d.p.c.m. 22 febbraio 2013 Regole tecniche in materia di generazione, apposizione e verifica delle firme elettroniche avanzate, qualificate e digitali, ai sensi degli articoli 20, comma 3, 24, comma 4, 28, comma 3, 32, comma 3, lettera b), 35, comma 2, 36, comma 2, e 71* establishes that providers of advanced

economic value of their transactions is higher than that of B2C transactions, so there is a greater need to adopt the written form in contracts.[672] The authors claim these solutions could also meet the requirement (c), e.g. through OTP tokens or biometric authentication.[673]

Lastly, requirement (d) requires controls over the integrity of signed data even after the subscription.[674] It is thought that the immutable nature of blockchain (thanks to distribution and concatenated hashes) combined with the use of asymmetric cryptography can ensure the detectability of any changes over time.[675] Indeed, data are linked to hashes that uniquely represent such data. Every attempt of tampering would cause the change of the hash and the subsequent hashes in the chain.[676]

The Italian CAD recognises the same legal value of handwritten signatures to documents formed in accordance to the requirements set by the AGID pursuant to Article 71 of the CAD, which refers to the 'signature with the SPID'. The guidelines of the AGID[677] state that signatories can only be natural persons[678] with a SPID digital identity level two or high-

---

electronic signatures can be subjects that use them with third parties for institutional, corporate or commercial reasons. They can produce them in house or through third service providers.

672 Szczerbowski observes that 'parties usually prefer written form in contract of substantial economic value'. See J. J. Szczerbowski, 'Place of smart contracts in civil law. A few comments on form and interpretation', Proceedings of the 12th Annual International Scientific Conference NEW TRENDS 2017, 335 (*SSRN*, 9 November 2017) <https://ssrn.com/abstract=3095933> accessed 1 October 2021.

673 Nicotra, Sarzana di Sant'Ippolito (n 669) 64–65.

674 S. Troiano, 'Article 26 Requirements for advanced electronic signatures' in Zaccaria *et al.* (n 385) 228.

675 Finocchiaro, Bomprezzi (n 568) 133.

676 In its report 'Legal and Regulatory Framework of Blockchains and Smart Contracts' (n 25), 12 the UE Blockchain Observatory and Forum writes that blockchains would appear to meet the technical criteria of simple and advanced electronic signatures.

677 See Chapter 3, Section 2.1.4, n 439.

678 Both for non-professional and professional use (also representing a legal person).

er.[679] The service provider affixes its qualified electronic seal[680] to the document and sends it to the signatory's identity provider. After the signature with the SPID, the identity provider affixes its qualified electronic seal.

Article 8-*ter*(2) of the Italian *Decreto Semplificazioni* – which has introduced a specific discipline for distributed ledger technologies and smart contracts[681] – states that smart contracts satisfy the requirement of the written form, upon prior IT identification of the interested parties, meeting the *Agenzia per l'Italia Digitale* (AGID) requirements, following its guidelines. The Article is very similar to Article 20(1-*bis*) of the CAD because it recognises the same legal value of handwritten signatures to documents formed in accordance with the requirements set by the AGID under Article 71 of the CAD. Indeed, the Determination of the General Director of the AGID no.116/2019 of 10 May 2019 – that has established a Working Group for the preparation of such guidelines and technical standards – provides that the guidelines have to be formed by the procedure set out in Article 71 of the CAD and the Regulation for the adoption of Guidelines for the implementation of the CAD.[682] However, unlike Article 20 of the CAD, the Simplification Decree generically refers to a process upon prior identification of the parties without setting any requirements (whose determination is left to the AGID).[683] Moreover, because the article does not consider electronic signatures, Manente[684] wonders whether the

679 They are assurance levels. The first level is for transactions with low risk and requires a single-factor authentication system (e.g. a password). The second level is for transactions with a substantial degree of risk and requires a double-factor authentication system (e.g. a password and an OTP). The third level is for transactions with a high degree of risk. It requires double-factor authentication systems based on digital certificates and stored on devices that meet some security requirements set by Annex III of the Directive 1999/93/EC (now Annex II of the e-IDAS Regulation).

680 Like qualified electronic signatures, qualified electronic seals are created by a qualified electronic seal creation device. They are based on a qualified certificate for electronic seals (Art. 3(27) of the e-IDAS Regulation).

681 See Chapter 2, Section 6, n 259.

682 The Determination can be accessed at the following link <https://trasparenza.agid.gov.it/archivio28_provvedimenti-amministrativi_0_121975_725_1.html> accessed 1 October 2021.

683 To date the Agid has not issued any specific guidelines.

684 M. Manente, 'L. 12/2019 – Smart contract e tecnologie basate su registri distribuiti – prime note', Studio 1_2019, March 2019, 6 <https://www.notariato.it/it/content/studio-12019-di-legge-122019-%E2%80%93-smart-contract-e-tecnologie-basate-su-registri-distribuiti-%E2%80%93> accessed 1 October 2021. Article

AGID can also provide the use of digital, qualified, or advanced signatures in blockchain-based smart contracts.

The signature with the SPID and the process of the *Decreto Semplificazioni* are only applicable in Italy. Nevertheless, according to the principle of non-discrimination (Article 25 of the e-IDAS Regulation), the other Member States can evaluate the equivalence with the written form. The e-IDAS Regulation does not set any evaluation parameters, which are left to national legislation.

In Italy, the CAD establishes that judges shall evaluate the security, integrity, and immutability of the document. Maybe, judges might consider that asymmetric cryptography, hash function, and decentralised databases guarantee the integrity and the immutability of the document. The greatest difficulty seems the fact that in permissionless blockchains the keys are not ascribable to precise identities. However, sometimes it could be possible to reconnect an account to an identified person.[685] In this regard, the explanatory note of the 2017 UNCITRAL Model Law on Electronic Transferable Records (MLETR) states that 'the possibility of linking pseudonyms and real name, including based on factual elements to be found outside distributed ledger systems, could satisfy the requirement to identify the signatory'.[686]The model law does not concern contracts but electronic transferable records. However, it addresses the problem of the written form and the equivalence between handwritten and electronic signatures.[687]

---

8-*ter* has been much criticised. See G. Finocchiaro, 'Intelligenza artificiale e protezione dei dati personali' (2019) Giurisprudenza Italiana 1670–1671.

685 For instance, when the address appears on a personal webpage, blog, or forum. About the pseudonymous character of public keys in permissionless blockchain, and the techniques used to trace back to underlying identities, see P. De Filippi, 'The interplay between decentralization and privacy: the case of blockchain technologies' (September 14, 2016) Journal of Peer Production, Issue n. 7: Alternative Internets, 11–13 (available at SSRN <https://ssrn.com/abstract=2852 689> accessed 1 October 2021); M. Finck, 'Blockchains and Data Protection in the European Union' (2018) 1 European Data Protection Law Review 17, 22; J. Barcelo, 'User Privacy in the Public Bitcoin Blockchain' (2007) 6 Journal of Latex Class Files 1; A. Gambino, C. Bomprezzi, 'Blockchain e protezione dei dati personali' (2019) 3 Diritto dell'Informazione e dell'Informatica 619, 633.

686 UNCITRAL Model Law on Electronic Transferable Records (n 162) 37. See G. Finocchiaro, 'La Legge Modello dell'UNCITRAL sui Titoli di Credito Elettronici' (2021) 1 Contratto e Impresa 38.

687 The explanatory note cites distributed ledger technology more than once.

## 6. *Smart contracts concluded 'smart'.*

The previous sections explored the formation of blockchain-based smart legal contracts. The exchange of offer and acceptance between the parties was taken into consideration. They investigated the existence of the parties' contractual intention when contracts are expressed in the language of the code. In these cases, contracts are concluded by humans. Durovic and Janssen affirm that such smart contracts are only executed 'smart' because they are performed automatically.[688] They are concluded 'unsmart' because algorithms are not employed to conclude contracts. As seen from the analysis of scenarios 1 and 3, blockchain and smart contracts are mere tools for contract formation.

Smart contracts can also be concluded 'smart'. In Chapter 3,[689] it was given an account of the conclusion of contracts through so-called 'software agents', deterministic computer programs that can conclude contracts on behalf of humans according to predetermined instructions. Smart contracts are also deterministic computer programs. So, they may include pre-set parameters for the conclusion of contracts. In other terms, smart contracts might act as agents in charge of concluding contracts. When predetermined conditions occur, the smart contract/agent self-concludes the contract. The main difference between only self-executing smart legal contracts and self-concluding smart legal contracts is that algorithms replace humans in contract conclusion in the latter. For example, Slock.It[690] is a German company for renting everything connected to a lock, such as a bike or even a house. The lock is smart because software can unlock it when the person who wants to rent the bike or the house makes the payment. The software is an Ethereum-based smart contract. The payment is sent to the address of the smart contract, and the smart contract allows the unlocking of the bike or the house. So, the blockchain-based smart contract concludes (and executes) a contract on behalf of the lessor.

In the previous example, there is an interaction between the algorithm and a human. But, as evidenced by De Filippi and Wright,[691] because smart contracts are machine-readable, they can be used to conclude agreements through machine-to-machine transactions. Blockchains are supporting new applications for the Internet of Things. For instance, IBM and

688 Durovic, Janssen (n 167) 760.

689 Section 2.1.1.

690 <https://blog.slock.it/> accessed 1 October 2021.

691 De Filippi, Wright (n 17) 82.

Samsung have built A.D.E.P.T., a blockchain-powered Internet of Things platform based on Ethereum where machines are assigned blockchain addresses and digital currencies, and smart contracts are programmed to send or receive payments. An intelligent device that makes use of A.D.E.P.T. is a washing machine released by Samsung that can buy new detergent online.[692]

Suppose a blockchain-based smart contract is concluded smart. In that case, one wonders whether the contractual will has to be attributed to the party or the machine, given that the latter automatically concludes contracts.

The matter is identical to that illustrated in Section 2.1.1 of Chapter 3 about the debate on the qualification of software agents as agents or as mere tools for expressing the party's will. It was explained that the majority agreed on the latter. The 'smart' conclusion of the contract is the execution of a pre-set intention of the party. Even when the program does not match with the party's intent because of an error, the contract bounds the party according to the principle of legitimate confidence in the validity of the contract.[693] The party that used the computer program may resort to the producer or the provider of the software. The contract is voidable only when the non-mistaken party could not reasonably rely on the validity of the contract because the mistake was recognisable by a person of average diligence.

If the software agent is considered an agent in the legal sense, contracts concluded by the software agent would be treated as concluded by the principal.[694] Therefore, the outcome is the same as qualifying the software agent as a passive conduit for a human actor.

In the hypothesis of an error of the program, the contract does not bind the principal because the program acted outside the boundaries of the authority conferred to it by the principal.[695] Conversely, the contract binds the principal when the third party was led to believe by the principal that such authorisation took place[696] and could reasonably believe that

692 *Ibid.* 158–159.

693 See Chapter 3, Section 2.1.3.

694 According to the rules on direct representation. See Art. 2.2.3(1) PICC, 3:102(1) PECL, II.-6:105(a) DFCR. In Italy, see Art. 1388 *cc*.

695 See Art. 2.2.6(1) PICC, 3:204(1) PECL, II.-6:107(1) DFCR. In Italy, see Art. 1398 *cc*.

696 See Art. 2.2.5(2) PICC, 3:201(3) PECL, II.-6:103(3) DFCR. The Italian *Codice civile* does not contain a specific provision on apparent authority, developed by

the agent did act within the boundaries of the conferred authority.[697] For example, Loos talks about an intelligent refrigerator that orders 100 bottles of fresh milk to the supermarket. Here, the author assumes that no valid contract is concluded because 100 bottles of milk is not a normal order for a consumer, thus the supermarket could not reasonably believe that the refrigerator acted following the principal's intention. On the contrary, he considers that if the refrigerator orders 300 grams of shrimps (that the consumer hates) instead of 300 grams of lamb (that the consumer loves) the lack of authority is not apparent. So, the principal is bound to the contract.[698]

Blockchain-based smart contracts can also work in conjunction with artificial intelligence.[699] Autonomous devices can conclude blockchain-based smart contracts independently from their owners. As outlined in Chapter 3,[700] when contracts are concluded through non-deterministic computer programs, it is more difficult to consider such programs as mere tools at the parties' disposal and attribute contractual intention to the parties. However, some think that the party that equipped herself with an autonomous agent and enabled it to act on her behalf intended to enter into the contracts concluded by the autonomous agent. Similarly, in the case of an error of the software, they claim that the party assumed the risk of wrong orders. So, the party will be bound by the contract unless there are preconditions for avoiding the contract.

Even if the autonomous agent is treated as a representative, the party is equally bound to the contract according to the rules on direct representa-

---

juridical cases and academic writings. See M. Graziadei, 'Chapter III. Authority of agents' in Antoniolli, Veneziano (n 445) 156–157.

697 And the agent would not have to pay damages to the third party. See Art. 2.2.6 (2) PICC, 3:204(2) PECL, II.-6:107(3) DFCR. Likewise, Art. 1398 *cc* states that the third party can obtain the payment of the damages if she relied on the validity of the contract without fault.

698 These examples are taken from M. Loos, 'Machine-to-Machine Contracting in the Age of the Internet of Things' in Schulze *et al.* (n 458) 71–72.

699 The European Union Blockchain Observatory and Forum has published a report about the conjunction of blockchain with the most important today emerging technologies, i.e. IoT and AI. In particular, the report envisions that 'blockchain can also facilitate autonomous machine-to-machine transactions' (p. 22). The report was published on 21 April 2020 and is entitled 'Convergence of blockchain, AI and IoT'. It can be found at the following link: <https://www.eublockchainforum.eu/sites/default/files/report_convergence_v1.0.pdf> accessed 1 October 2021.

700 Section 2.1.1.

tion. The agent would act under a general authorisation to conclude some kinds of agreements. The contract does not bind the party if the program makes an error caused by a wrong prediction unless the third party was led to believe by the principal that such general authorisation took place and the third party could reasonably believe that the agent did act within the boundaries of the conferred authority.[701]

## 7. *Smart contract code as a mean to express contracts or to perform already existing contracts?*

Section 3 of this chapter has given an account of the technical problems that prevent encoding entire contracts in the language of the code. Indeed, as illustrated in Section 7 of Chapter 2, at present smart contracts are only being used to automate the performance of some conditions of a broader contract.

Even though technical advancements would make it possible to express contracts in the form of lines of code direclty, the average party cannot read and understand their contents. There would be the risk of a non-binding contract because of the absence of contractual intention,[702] or the contract could be considered voidable because of fundamental and recognisable mistakes.[703]. Whether the code merely executes the contract or represents contractual conditions, there is a programming and a natural language version of the contract. So, one wonders which one should govern the legal relationship between the parties.

In the former hypothesis, the smart contract merely automates some of the terms of a pre-existing agreement. For this reason, it is thought that the natural language version prevails because the parties expressed their will through a traditional contract and rely on it.

In the latter hypothesis, it is considered that because the other party does not understand the programming language, the agreement is reached

---

701 Loos (n 698) 72–73 makes an example of an autonomous refrigerator that orders two crates of beer to the supermarket based on a wrong prediction. He assumes that 'since the order of two crates of beer is nothing out of the ordinary, there is no reason why the supermarket could not reasonably believe that the refrigerator would not be authorised to conclude this contract'.

702 See Section 3.1 of this chapter.

703 See Section 3.2 of this chapter.

using human-intelligible language, and the contracting party puts such language as the basis of the agreement.[704]

Suppose the natural language version of the contract governs the legal relationship between the parties. In that case, the smart contract code is not meant to express contracts but to perform existing contracts. Of course, the code has to coincide with what the parties agreed in the contract. Maybe the code does not perform as intended by the parties and causes the breach of the contract. The issue deals with liability, which is deepened in the following chapter.

It follows from the above that smart contracts (codes) can express contracts only when there is no simultaneous translation in natural language. It could occur when the parties can understand the agreement even in the language of the code and rely on that version of the contract. It is believed that this may occur in four circumstances. The first might be the conclusion of B2B contracts where IT specialists can support the contracting parties;[705] in the second, the contract might be concluded by parties that know the language of the code. Concerning the third, technological developments might allow the conclusion of contracts in a language that is machine and human-readable simultaneously;[706] the fourth is contract conclusion by machines.[707]

The first two scenarios are theoretically possible, but it is thought that it is unlikely that they could happen in practice. There would be no practical or legal reasons why businesses or programmers should conclude their contracts in such kind of language, given that the contract would be incomprehensible to the vast majority of people.[708] The third option is

---

704 'For example, assume party A sets up a crypto-asset exchange contract on Ethereum. (...) In order to attract human counter-parties to this offer, A will have to explain it to them in a language they can understand, for instance through a website (...) or other user interface. (...) Even though the underlying smart contract code may technically be visible, many users will likely *de facto* rely on A's other communications.' See Bacon *et al.* (n 15) 31.

705 In Section 3.1 of this chapter it was argued that businesses might have greater economic possibilities to consult an expert who can understand the code's language.

706 Section 2 of Chapter 2 (n 168) cited some projects that express and implement legal contracts in software, such as Common Accord, Legalese, and the Ricardian Contract. Mik (n 97) 291 talks about contracts drafted in natural language 'with encoding in mind'.

707 See the previous Section.

708 Section 3.1 of this chapter shows that businesses likely transact based on pre-existing natural language framework agreements.

more conceivable than the other. The parties could rely on the automated performance of their contract without having to provide two separate versions of the contract. However, the fourth situation is considered the most desirable. The automatic conclusion of the contract would add to the automatic performance of the contract, thus taking advantage of the benefits of automation. In particular, as contract conclusion and performance become increasingly reliant on artificial intelligence, smart contracts could become autonomous. They could represent the 'true' smart contracts.

## *8. Findings and conclusions.*

This chapter investigates the intersection between blockchain-based smart contracts and the rules on contract formation. To this end, the preliminary question was whether smart contracts could be considered legally binding contracts.

It started from the definition of contract, and clarified that contracts could be expressed – at least in theory – in the form of computer code. However, the mere fact that some lines of code represent contractual obligations does not mean that a contract is formed. Indeed, the very basis of a contract is the agreement between two (or more) parties.

Having clarified that, it was found out that the agreement can occur off-chain or on-chain. In the former hypothesis, blockchain technology is irrelevant to contract formation. At the moment of uploading the smart contract on the blockchain, the parties have already met their minds.. Blockchain technology is only a database. Consequently, there is no need to analyse how to interpret contract law rules to make blockchain-based smart contracts fit into contract law. If the contract is concluded off-line, traditional contract law rules apply. If the contract is concluded online, existing rules are interpreted to fit the electronic context, thanks to the international principles of non-discrimination and functional equivalence. Moreover, specific rules included in the e-Commerce Directive and Consumer Rights Directive apply before or when placing online orders.

In the case of on-chain agreements, blockchain becomes a mean of communication between the parties. In other terms, blockchain technology is a new modality of contract formation. Therefore, as done with vending machines, electronic means such as EDI or e-mails, and the Internet, it has been verified whether and how this new technology affects contract formation.

The chapter puts in correlation contract law requirements to blockchain-based smart contracts. It investigated the exchange of offer and acceptance, and their revocation, and the time of conclusion of the contract. It resulted that the smart contracts formed on-chain can be considered contracts concluded at a distance and by electronic means through the exchange of data messages. Smart contracts and all other records in the blockchain are electronic records and blockchain signatures are electronic signatures. It follows that the rules on the (electronic) form of the contract are also suitable for these kinds of applications, even though the majority of existing solutions are currently not equipped to comply with the requirement of the written form. It also follows that the rules set by the e-Commerce Directive and the Consumer Rights Directive are generally applicable (with some doubts about the applicability of the Consumer Rights Directive when the contract is solely expressed in lines of code, because of Article 3(2)(l) of the Directive).

Much attention was paid to contractual intent, because of the particular language used to express contracts. The first assumption was that, because computer code is unintelligible to the average man, it might be difficult to acknowledge the existence of a legally binding agreement. According to the principle of legitimate confidence and the party's duty to get informed and understand what she is doing before accepting the offer, the only fact that the contract is expressed in computer code would not suffice to exclude contractual intention. The interpreter should evaluate whether the party is aware of the contract by considering the case circumstances and parties' quality. The analysis of the scenarios has been useful in this regard. In particular, in blockchain the contract is drafted unilaterally, and the other party has no other option to accept or not accept it. A parallel with adhesion contracts has been found.

Moreover, similarities were found with wrap contracts because of the non-traditional way of expressing assent. Lastly, it was made a distinction between B2B and B2C contracts, because of the different bargaining power of consumers. It was claimed that in those events the contract should also be provided in natural language and some expedients should be adopted so that the accepting party could understand that she is going to conclude a contract.

Even though a natural language version of the contract accompany the code and there are the preconditions to admit that the offeree intended to conclude a contract, it was expressed the opinion that, when the contract is drafted unilaterally and presented to the weakest party, it is more likely that the non-drafting party can invoke a fundamental mistake as a basis for calling the contract voidable. The mistake has to be considered recognisable by the non-mistaken party. According to the principle of transparency, the clarity level and comprehensibility of the contract constitutes an important criterion of evaluating the apparent importance of the mistake. For the same reasons, it was assumed that the information requirements set by the e-Commerce and the Consumer Rights Directive should be provided in natural language (putting aside the technical obstacles to translate non-operational clauses into the language of the code).

Following the above, it was observed that the parties consider the natural language version of the contract as the very basis of their agreement. The latter is the 'contract' that has to govern parties' relationships, while the smart contract code is not the 'contract', but a translation of it in the language of the code to automatically perform already existing contracts. Hence, smart contracts can be 'contracts' when the agreement is directly translated into a machine-readable form. In that situation, smart contracts can be both means of expressing and automatically performing the same contract. It is viewed that this could be feasible with the increasing use and development of negotiations by machines. Indeed, convergent platforms that merge blockchain, IoT, and AI are emerging. As clarified in Chapter 2, software agents' smart contracts and contract conclusions can also exist without the blockchain. However, Nick Szabo envisioned that computer software could substitute humans in contractual activities. Despite the invention of Surden computable contracts, the code remains under the control of the party. Instead, with the blockchain, it is asserted that Nick Szabo's dream has become implementable. No one can control the system except for the code itself, thanks to blockchain characteristics of decentralisation and immutability. That is why when talking about smart contracts one usually refers to blockchain-based smart contracts. This issue is deepened in the following chapter.

In a nutshell, it seems from the above analysis that blockchain-based smart contracts are nothing more than electronic contracts. They do not pose further juridical problems than those with electronic commerce and Surden's 'computable' contracts development (at least as concerns contract formation).

# CHAPTER 5: CONTRACT PERFORMANCE

## *PART 1: BREACH OF CONTRACT*

### *1. Introduction.*

The contracting party must trust that the other party performs the obligations that she has undertaken in the contract. Contracting parties do not usually trust each other because the obliged party could breach the contract. The goal of contractual liability is to steer the behaviour of the obliged party towards the performance of the contract and provide the other with a certain level of certainty that she will obtain the execution of the contract.[709] The creditor may obtain damages for non-performance, ask for specific performance, or terminate the contract. The possibility of exercising remedies for non-performance of the contract compensates for the trust absence in the contracting party.[710]

With smart contracts, the obliged party performs her obligations through the code.[711] Smart contracts are computable contracts because

---

709 European Union Blockchain Observatory and Forum (n 25) 17.

710 C. Poncibò, L. A. Di Matteo, 'Smart contracts, Contractual and Noncontractual Remedies' in Matteo, Cannarsa, Poncibò (n 106) 122; Weber (n 591) 308; Cuccuru (n 225) 186–187;

711 Blockchain-based smart contracts are deterministic computer programs; they do not include artificial intelligence. The software is a simple tool that a party uses to perform the contract, and of which she is liable. See McKinney, Landy, Wilka (n 120) 321; L. W. Cong, Z. He, 'Blockchain Disruption and Smart Contracts', 27 December 2017, 11, available at SSRN <https://ssrn.com/abstract=2985764> accessed 1 October 2021; K. Lauslahti, J. Mattila, T. Seppälaä, ' Smart Contracts – How will Blockchain Technology Affect Contractual Practices?' ETLA Reports No 68, 2017, 3, <https://www.etla.fi/wp-content/uploads/ETLA-Raportit-Reports-68.pdf> accessed 1 October 2021.
As discussed in Section 2 of Chapter 2 and Section 3 of Chapter 4, artificial intelligence might be used to fill the gaps in the contract by interpreting contractual conditions. The machine might fill contract gaps by interpreting vague terms through the information fed into predictive analytics, and sending the necessary inputs to execute the smart contract code. According to Casey and A. Niblett, these would be 'Self-Driving Contracts' (A. J. Casey, A. Niblett, 'Self-Driving Contracts' (2017) 43 Journal of Corporation Law 1. Malfunctions of such software might cause a breach of the contract. However, these kinds

they can substitute the contracting party once the program is instantiated. The code not only makes actions instead of a human but can also understand whether and how it has to act.

Blockchain adds something to smart contracts. Thanks to blockchain decentralisation and tamper-resistance, the party that is bound by the contract cannot prevent the execution of the contract. Therefore, the breach of the contract should be eliminated in such contracts, and contract remedies should become unnecessary. Blockchain-based smart contracts are considered self-enforcing and the blockchain has been named 'trustless trust' system.

In reality, it has been pointed out that blockchain technology cannot give rise to breach-less contracts.[712] There can be several situations in which the self-execution of a smart contract leads to the breach of that contract. There has been an attempt to catalogue these hypotheses into three groups: a) the code content does not match with the will of the parties, thus determining that the execution of the contract does not satisfy the creditor; b) technological problems that impact on the performance of the contract; c) other problems due to the closed nature of the blockchain, when there is the need to link the smart contract with the off-chain world to perform the contract.

Given that blockchain-based smart contracts cannot avoid the breach of contracts, someone wonders about the suitability of existing remedies for non-performance.[713] Indeed, as seen at the beginning, their function is to induce the other party to perform the contract under the threat of law enforcement. Instead, in blockchain-based smart contracts, the creditor does not trust that the other party performs the contract. The obliged party cannot exercise control over the execution of the code. The creditor has to trust that the code executes correctly. There is a shift from trust in the other party to trust in the code.

This chapter aims to verify whether existing rules on contract performance are tailored to apply to blockchain-based smart contracts.

---

of technologies are still in their infancy. They raise the same questions on the applicability of existing liability rules discussed in Section 2.2 of Chapter 3.

712 Poncibò, Di Matteo (n 710) 124; McKinney, Landy, Wilka (n 120) 329.

713 De Graaf (n 218) 9.

## 2. *Potential cases of violation of the contract.*

As observed in the previous section, there can be several situations of breach of the contract even in presence of self-executing smart contracts, that could be catalogued into three groups: a) the code content does not match with the will of the parties, thus determining that the execution of the contract does not satisfy the creditor; b) technological problems that impact on the performance of the contract; c) other problems due to the closed nature of blockchain, when there is the need to link the smart contract with the off-chain world to perform the contract.

Regarding the first, the code has to coincide with what the parties that use a blockchain-based smart contract agreed in the contract. The code could not perform as intended by the parties and causes the breach of the contract.

Technological problems that can negatively affect contract execution can vary and damage different components of a blockchain-based application. First of all, the code of the smart contract can be subject to bugs, like any computer program.[714] Problems may also derive from the underlying blockchain.[715] The latter can give room for manipulation of the execution

714 Savelyev (n 96) 14; for example, in 2016 Peter Vessenes (co-founder of the Bitcoin Foundation) estimated that Ethereum smart contracts contained 100 errors every 1000 lines of software code. See P. Vessenes, 'Ethereum Contracts are Going to be Candy for Hackers' (*Vessenes*, 18 May 2016) <http://vessenes.com/ethereum-contracts-are-going-to-be-candy-for-hackers/> accessed 1 October 2021.

715 E. Mik, 'Blockchains. A Technology for Decentralized Marketplaces' in Di Matteo, Cannarsa, Poncibò (n 106) 175. They predominantly have regard to the selection and order of transactions. On this point, see L. Luu *et al.*, 'Making Smart Contracts Smarter' in Proceedings of the 2016 ACM SIGSAC Conference on Computer and Communications Security, Vienna, October 2016, 254–269 <https://eprint.iacr.org/2016/633.pdf> accessed 1 October 2021. For example, transaction-ordering dependency occurs when two transactions that invoke the same contract are included in one block. Users have uncertain knowledge of which state the contract is at when their individual invocation is executed. Thus, there is a discrepancy between the state of the contract that users may intend to invoke and the actual state when their corresponding execution happens. Decisions about the order of transactions are up to the miner, so the final state of the contract depends on how the miner orders the transactions. This can give unexpected results to a user invoking a smart contract when there are concurring transactions. For instance, in a sale agreement, the seller updates the price of the item. The buyer may have to pay a higher price than what she agreed to pay when she sent the buy request.

of a smart contract that exploits the security flaw and makes smart contracts susceptible to abuse.[716] Moreover, oracles can be compromised.[717] As seen in Chapter 1,[718] oracles connect the blockchain with the outside, both inbound and outbound. So, not trustworthy oracles can negatively influence the performance of the contract.[719] Lastly, because oracles do not create the information to send to smart contracts themselves but obtain it from external data sources, it is necessary to select a trustworthy data source. Indeed, the external data source may malfunction or become inactive.[720]

Turning to group c), this encompasses the situations when contract execution is only possible by linking the smart contract to the off-chain world.

As already explained, the blockchain cannot directly retrieve information except for those dictated by the protocol (e.g. the transfer of cryptotokens).[721] In this regard, oracles and data sources were mentioned. Therefore, if such information is not given at all or is incorrect, the contract is not executed or not executed properly. This cannot only happen for technical malfunctions (group b)) but also for human errors or actions. For example, the courier signals to have delivered the package to the specified

716 To take the example of transaction-ordering dependency, Luu (n 715) 257 describes a Puzzle contract in Ethereum that rewards users who solve a computational puzzle. A malicious owner of the contract could exploit transaction-ordering. Namely, the owner could wait until a user sends a correct solution of the puzzle and immediately send a transaction that reduces the reward of the contract to zero. If the miner executes the latter transaction before the user's transaction, the user does not get any reward. Another example is the notorious TheDao hack (n 257), where an attacker could steal over three million ethers by utilising so-called reentrancy vulnerability. See Luu (n 715) 259.

717 Mik (n 97) 297. To avoid oracle failures, someone suggests making use of multiple oracles and data sources. However, Gatteschi, Lamberti and Demartini (n 106) 56 observe that 'this approach is still prone to errors, as an ill-intentioned person could still perform a coordinated attack on multiple platforms inspected by the oracles'.

718 Section 7.

719 Oracles might send wrong data to the smart contract (inbound) or the external source (outbound).

720 Giancaspro (n 197) 833. For instance, a smart insurance contract has been programmed to pay the policyholder in the event of a flight delay of two hours. One could imagine that the software of the airport timetable does not operate for a few hours that correspond to the time when a flight delay should be recorded. The example is taken from M. Clément, 'Smart Contracts and the Courts' in Di Matteo, Cannarsa, Poncibò (n 106) 280.

721 See Chapter 1, Section 7.

address while it has not been sent, or the package content differs from what the parties agreed. The inclusion of input data in the blockchain is under the direct control of someone and does not benefit from the decentralised character of the blockchain.

Furthermore, when the execution of the contract has to produce its effects off the chain, the execution of the smart contract code does not guarantee the performance of the contract. Due to the closed character of the blockchain, further operations outside the database have to follow the outputs of the smart contract code. For example, a smart insurance contract for flight delays detects the policyholder's right to payment. The output of the smart contract code is not sufficient to make the payment, because the insurance company has to activate the payment.[722]

### 3. *Clarifications on the meaning of 'decentralisation'.*

As already said, blockchain is a decentralised database. There is much confusion on the meaning of the term 'decentralisation'. It is often associated with a lack of a governing authority that is liable for its technical functioning.[723] Instead, 'decentralisation' has a precise technological meaning.[724]

From a technical point of view, blockchain is decentralised because a consensus protocol – i.e. a software run by all network nodes – pre-establishes the rules to update the ledger. There is not a central 'master database' that unilaterally decides the updating. Nodes are not dependent on a single master node. On the other hand, governance is related to the concept of control, i.e. the ability to decide and amend the rules that govern a system.

Having clarified that, decentralised technology does not automatically mean an absence of control. It is evident in permissioned blockchains. They are built to fit a specific purpose of a single company or a consortium

---

722 The alternative is that the insurance company makes the payment in cryptocurrencies. Indeed, smart contracts can directly transfer crypto-currencies because they are native tokens of the blockchain.

723 For example, Open Bazar's terms of use state that OB is a network 'without any central organization controlling the platform' (the terms of use can be only read during the download of the application).

724 In Chapter 1, Section 6, it was affirmed that this is a false myth surrounding blockchains.

of companies that invest in setting up the entire hardware and software infrastructure. So, they decide the rules of the protocol.[725]

In permissionless blockchains, Mik notices that each node in the system follows the same protocol. Decisions on such algorithms are not up to network participants.[726] Once they enter the system, their nodes download the software and execute that software. Therefore, there is a kind of control at the software governance level.

Decentralisation of the technology does not aim to exclude any form of governing authority. Maybe, this misunderstanding is due to the political ideas that surrounded blockchain invention. As above mentioned, blockchain originated from a group of crypto-anarchists that wanted to free people from institutions control.[727] Decentralisation of blockchain technology has the purpose of making the system more resilient. Indeed, data storage is distributed, and there is no need to rely on a single point of failure, which is more exposed to attacks and tampering. Decentralisation allows every node to independently verify and validate transactions that update the database and independently recreate the entire history of transactions. In other terms, decentralisation is intended to have safe systems.

Similarly, blockchain decentralisation is combined with unilateral immutability for security reasons. Misbehaviours are discouraged both in permissionless and permissioned blockchains. In permissionless blockchains, there are systems of economic incentives.[728] In permissioned blockchains, participants are incentivised to behave honestly via the threat of legal prosecution.[729] However, this immutability hinders any changes in the

---

725 Finck (n 21) 19 argues that 'even when DLT is highly decentralized at hardware level, it can still be centralized at the software governance level. When protocol maintenance is managed by a single party or small group, decentralization is hardly a given'.

726 Mik (n 715) 166 considers that 'it is frequently forgotten that in public blockchains the decentralized peer-to-peer decision-making refers to the automated and deterministic execution of a consensus algorithm. There is no room for discretion; there are no individual choices beyond what is prescribed or permitted by the algorithm. Each node in the system follows the same protocol – the choices are binary: accept blocks that fulfil the prescribed criteria and reject those that do not'.

727 See Chapter 1, Section 3.

728 As seen in Chapter 1, Section 5, a 51 % attack is complicated in permissionless blockchains. In any case, miners are not interested in altering the system because the ones that might influence it are also those who most financially benefit from it.

729 Participants in permissioned blockchains predetermine their rights and duties on the blockchain.

underlying consensus algorithm. For this reason, the system could be considered uncontrollable.

Actually, in permissioned blockchains, changes are possible because they are closed systems with known participants. Agreements between the involved participants define potential updates.[730] Consequently, updates are governed and controlled. In permissionless blockchains, software changes are only possible through so-called forks, i.e. creating an alternative blockchain. But, since in permissionless blockchains nobody can control the infrastructure (hardware) because everybody can contribute to maintaining it by holding a node, some authors evidenced that 'each fork will need to attract miners, nodes, and users to their version of the software'.[731] In essence, who creates and controls the algorithm cannot impose amendments. However, it is thought that governing authority can be held liable in case of malfunctions. Indeed, network participants can only choose to keep the old version or move to the new one.[732] In both cases, they do not decide the rules of the system. At most, they can determine what system of rules they want to follow.

### *4. Clarifications on the meaning of 'validation' and 'execution'.*

Further misinterpretations have regard to the concept of 'validation' of a new block through a mechanism of shared consensus. The term 'validation' can also have various meanings depending on different contexts (technical or legal).

From a technical point of view, the validation process is the set of rules provided by the code to update the ledger. If most nodes agree that such rules are respected, then the consensus on the 'validity' of the new block is reached. Finally, the block is added to the chain. This is the mechanism of shared consensus, through which the network converges on the version of the truth. The system refuses different potential portions of the chain. In the legal context, the term validation recalls the respect of the law.

---

730 Bacon *et al.* (n 15) 24.

731 *Ibid.* 22.

732 Bashir (n 18) 274 introduces the distinction between 'soft' and 'hard' forks. In the case of a soft fork, only miners are required to upgrade to the new client software to make use of the new protocol rules, while a client that chooses not to upgrade to the latest version will still be able to operate normally. In the case of a hard fork, all users have to upgrade.

Blockchains contain a sequence of smart contract transactions. The first transaction concerning a smart contract is the uploading of a new smart contract on the blockchain, where it is associated with an address. Then, the smart contract can execute itself according to receiving inputs. Every time the smart contract runs an operation, it moves from the current state to the next one. Thus, the subsequent smart contract transactions represent smart contract changes of state. Every transaction is submitted to the network and is validated through the blockchain consensus protocol. Namely, every node re-executes the same operation to verify that it gets to the same state. In case of a positive answer, the transaction is validated and is added to the chain (i.e. all the copies of the smart contract change their state).

The validation process guarantees that the smart contract code cannot avoid execution and/or execute itself incorrectly. The term 'execution' has a technical meaning that differs from the legal one. Execution in computer engineering is the process by which a computer executes the instructions of a computer program. Execution of the smart contract means that the code returns corresponding outputs to given inputs. From a legal point of view, executing the contract means performing the contract. The parties perform the duties of the contractual agreement. Blockchain has not the authority to guarantee that a transaction matches with the real world, i.e., it corresponds to an event with a legal significance.[733] So, while the blockchain validation step can ensure that the smart contract properly executes from a technical side, it cannot certify that its execution corresponds to the operations needed to perform the legal contract. In other terms, blockchain technology cannot guarantee the performance of the contract.

In light of the above, assuming that blockchain-based smart contracts determine a shift from trust in the other contracting party to trust in the code in contract performance is inaccurate. The creditor has to trust that the code has been instructed to operate according to what agreed.

## 5. *Analysis of the scenarios.*

To verify whether existing rules on contract performance are tailored to apply to blockchain-based smart contracts, the four scenarios depicted in

733 In Chapter 1, Section 6, it was affirmed that this is another false myth surrounding blockchains.

Chapter 2 are axamined, starting from the situations where a party uses a blockchain as back-end.

In scenario 4, a business concludes a contract with a consumer and uploads a smart contract on the blockchain. The smart contract is the mean to perform the duties of the business. The consumer does not hold a node of the underlying blockchain, which the business uses as back-end. The blockchain is permissioned.

Section 2 of this Chapter catalogues the possible cases of non-performance of the contract. Maybe the code does not perform as agreed by the parties because of an incorrect contract translation in the code language. In this scenario, the code has been provided by the business to the consumer.[734] So, the consumer has to trust that the business provides a proper translation of the agreement. For the same reason, if malfunctions of the code have a negative impact on the performance of the contract, the consumer has to trust that the business provides a correct code.

If problems derive from the underlying blockchain, one has to verify the subject that exercises control over the blockchain and in which the party has to trust. Indeed, in Section 3 of this Chapter, it was argued that blockchain decentralisation does not mean an absence of control.

In scenario 4, blockchain is permissioned. As outlined above,[735] permissioned blockchains are built to fit a specific purpose of a single company or a consortium of companies that invest in setting up the entire infrastructure, both hardware, and software, that they can control. Thus, again, trust is in the business. The same is true for not trustworthy oracles or data sources.

When contract execution is only possible by linking the smart contract to the off-chain world, both in input and in output, the performance of the contract comes back under the control of the obliged party (the business), in which the aggrieved party has to trust (the consumer). Therefore, the consumer has to trust that the business feeds the smart contract with correct inputs and puts in place the necessary operations that have to follow the outputs of the smart contract.

Scenario 2 is similar to scenario 4, but the blockchain is permissionless. Like in scenario 4, the consumer has to trust that the business provides a correct code and a trustworthy blockchain-based application. The business

734 In Chapter 4, Section 3.1, it was stated that it is more likely that in B2C contracts the business unilaterally drafts the contract and submit it to the consumer.

735 See Section 3 of this chapter.

also has to be reliable when the smart contract interacts with the off-chain world to perform the contract. Unlike scenario 4, the business cannot control the underlying infrastructure (hardware and software). It did not invest in setting up its blockchain, but it adopted a blockchain-based application that leverages a pre-existing blockchain infrastructure. Because the blockchain is permissionless, the business participates in mantaining the blockchain infrastructure by holding a node. To enter a permissionless blockchain, the business has to download the software and install it in its device/node. Nonetheless, malfunctions of the blockchain that may prejudice the contract performance between the business and the consumer are at the own risk of the business.[736] The blockchain-based smart contract is the mean through which the business performs the contract. It was the business that selected the blockchain platform. The consumer concludes the contract with the business and trusts that the business will perform the contract.[737]

In the remaining scenarios, both parties take part in the blockchain. In scenario 3, the parties agreed to build a permissioned blockchain for their purposes. The blockchain is under their control, so trust is not in the code but in the parties themselves. The parties have to trust each other. For example, they have to trust that the other party provides a correct translation of the agreement. In particular, if the performance of the contract can occur by linking the smart contract with the off-chain world, the other party has again to trust the obliged party.

Lastly, in scenario 1, the underlying blockchain platform is permissionless. The parties do not own the blockchain, but each contributes to building and maintaining the hardware by running a node. Each party joins the blockchain on the software side by downloading the corresponding software and installing it in the device/node. The blockchain is not under their control. However, they chose to perform through a smart contract whose execution is carried out on a permissionless blockchain that they

736 For instance, Art. 6.2.1 of the general conditions of the insurance contract Fizzy (<https://fizzy.axa/fr/static/media/conditions-generales.38af84e2.pdf> accessed 1 October 2020) allows the consumer to address a claim to a Mediator or to start litigation against the insurance company in case the automatic payment by Axa does not occur, without specifying the cause of the non-payment. Therefore, the general conditions admit the contractual liability of the insurance company, which the consumer has to trust.

737 Consumers could be even not aware that the smart contract is executed on top of a blockchain.

decided to download. So, non-performance of the contract is at the own risk of the obliged party due to problems with the protocol.

All four scenarios showed that it is still possible to affirm that trust is in the other party. Considering the resulst of the above analysis, existing rules for non-performance are still applicable to blockchain-based smart contracts.

## *6. Application of existing rules on breach of contract.*

The debtor has to perform the obligations undertaken in the contract; otherwise, she is held liable and the creditor can exercise some remedies to enforce the contract. The risk of non-performance is on the debtor, independently of the cause that determined the breach of the contract. Indeed, in blockchain-based smart contracts, the debtor assumes the risk of using non-trustworthy code, blockchain application, blockchain protocol, oracle, or data source. When contract execution is only possible by linking the smart contract to the off-chain world, both in input and in output, the performance of the contract comes back under the control of the obliged party. So, the risk of non-performance is again on her.

However, the debtor's liability can be excluded in the case of *force majeure*. The PICC, the PECL, and the DFCR excuse the debtor when impediments to performance are beyond the debtor's control and could not have reasonably been avoided or overcome.[738] Article 1218 of the Italian Civil Code states that the debtor is liable for non-performance unless non-performance is due to a cause non-imputable to him. The debtor has to prove such impediment; otherwise, she is held liable.[739]

It is thought that malfunctions of the different components of a blockchain-based application (being it the code of the smart contract, the blockchain protocol, the oracle, or the data source) are not unforeseeable. In particular, this is even more valid when technical errors affect the smart contract code or the underlying blockchain, given the immaturity of blockchain technology.[740] Equally, it is thought that errors in the trans-

738 Art. 7.1.7 PICC, 8:108 PECL, III.-3:104 DFCR.

739 Chapter 3, Section 2.2, gave an account of the differences between Civil and Common law. Common law generally allows remedies for non-performance on the sole basis of non-performance, while civil law requires that non-performance is also attributable to the debtor. However, such differences become less strict in practice.

740 Giancaspro (n 197) 833 expresses the same opinion.

lation of the code are not unforeseeable, especially if one considers the complexity and the infancy of such activities. In general, especially when the performance of the contract needs to put in action some operations in the off-chain world, *force majeure* is evaluated on a case-by-case basis.[741]

General principles also state that the creditor cannot resort to the remedies for non-performance if the creditor herself has caused wholly (or partially) the breach of the contract.[742] In Italy, Article 1227 *cc* provides that the creditor's behaviour can limit or exclude the right to damages if it determines the partial or total impediment to contract performance. As regards this research, it may be the case that malfunctions of the blockchain-based application provided by the creditor cause the breach of the contract by the debtor and consequent damages to the creditor. Problems with the creditor's blockchain-based application are the cause of the non-performance of the debtor.[743]

Parties may also exclude or limit the debtor's liability. Article 7.1.6 of the PICC, Article 8:109 of the PECL, and Article III.-3:105 of the DFCR establish the principle of good faith and fair dealing as a general limit for the invocation of exemption clauses. In Italy, Article 1229 *cc* declares that exoneration of liability clauses for fraud or gross negligence is void. These rules have to be read together with the rules on unfair contract terms[744] when exemption clauses are not individually negotiated, particularly if the creditor is a consumer. In the Italian legal system, it has been already recalled Article 1341 cc, which requires that such clauses have to be specifically approved in writing. In B2C contracts, Directive 93/13/EEC on Unfair Contract Terms in Consumer Contracts contains a list of terms that may be regarded as unfair, including exclusion or limitation of the business' liability.[745] The Italian Consumer Code that implemented the

---

741 For example, the courier that has to signal to have delivered a package to a specified address has an accident and the package is not delivered.

742 See Art. 7.1.2 PICC, 8:101 PECL, and III.-3:101 DFCR.

743 The example of note 715, in this chapter, is taken into consideration. The buyer has to pay a higher price to the seller due to transaction-ordering dependency. The buyer pays a lower price and is considered in breach of the contract with the seller. The buyer can damage the seller because the seller could have concluded a contract with another buyer willing to pay the higher price. However, the cause of the buyer's breach of the contract is a bug in the underlying blockchain. If the latter has been provided by the seller (e.g. in a B2C scenario, where the business makes use of a blockchain as back-end) the seller's behaviour may be relevant to exclude the seller's right to damages.

744 About unfair contract terms, see Chapter 3, Section 2.2, n 457.

745 See Annex (1)(a), (b) of the Directive.

Directive includes similar clauses, considered void unless proven otherwise.[746] Therefore, due attention has to be paid to the distinctions between standard and unilaterally negotiated contracts and B2B or B2C contracts, evidenced in the four scenarios, to evaluate the inclusion of exemption clauses.

The creditor may entrust the performance of the contract to a third party. According to Article 9.2.6 of the PICC, Article 8:107 of the PECL, and Article III.-2:106 of the DFCR about performance entrusted to another, the only person responsible for performance is the contractual party. In Italy, the applicable rule is Article 1228 *cc*.[747] The debtor is excused only when the non-performance of the third person can be excused, i.e. when the impediments were beyond the third person's control and could not be reasonably be expected to have been avoided or overcome. Similarly, the Italian legal system establishes that the debtor is liable for the auxiliary's malicious, fraudulent, or negligent acts. The debtor is excused if non-performance of the contract is not attributable to the auxiliary.

The liable contracting party may then turn to the third party. The following section focuses on third-party service providers.

## 7. *Third-party service providers.*

As affirmed in Section 2 of this chapter, blockchain-based applications comprise multiple components. To simplify, Hileman and Rauchs[748] group such components into three 'layers': protocol, network, and application. The protocol layer is the core software infrastructure upon which the other two layers reside. The network layer is the network that connects the blockchain participants, and it brings the protocol layer to life. The application layer is built on top of the blockchain infrastructure.[749] These layers are powered by software.

---

746 Art. 33(2)(a),(b) of the Italian Consumer Code.

747 See Chapter 3, Section 2.2.

748 Hileman, Rauchs (n 23) 26.

749 As an example it is taken the one provided by Rauchs *et al* in the 2nd Global Enterprise Blockchain Benchmarking Study (n 99) 23 using J.P. Morgan's Interbank Information Network (IIN). IIN is built using Quorum protocol layer; more than 200 international banks compose the network layer; IIN Resolve is the first application deployed on the IIN enabling users to streamline compliance processes.

The contracting parties can build these layers with internal staff or through the engagement of third parties. Third parties are software providers that can develop the core protocol layer, the network layer, or the application layer.[750] They can also provide more than one service. For example, application developers can also build networks for their clients; protocol developers can also support their customers to develop their networks, and so on.[751] Singh and Michels[752] talk about 'Blockchain-as-a-Service' (BaaS) offerings, i.e. service providers that offer and manage various components of a DLT infrastructure.[753]

Contracting parties can conclude contracts with these BaaS providers. The obliged party may turn to the BaaS provider if she is held liable for the non-performance of the contract. For instance, a technological problem with one of the components of the blockchain-based application can negatively impact the performance of the contract. The technical malfunction determines the breach of the contract between the obliged party/user of the blockchain-based application and the BaaS provider by the BaaS provider.

To establish the applicable rules, these contracts need a classification.[754] On this point, because they provide software, reference is made to the considerations of Section 2.2 of Chapter 3 about contracts for the supply of software. It was explained that national legal systems apply existing contract law rules designed for other contracts and that legal experts sometimes have characterised them as hybrid or *sui generis* contracts. In the Italian legal system, computer contracts whose object is software divide into software license agreements and software development agreements. The former is a standardised contract, which allows the use of the software. Thus, it is treated as a contract for rent (*contratto di locazione*).[755] With the latter, the software is specially written to meet the requirements of the

750 Hileman, Rauchs (n 23) 28.

751 *Ibid.*

752 J. Singh, J. D. Michels, 'Blockchain as a Service', Queen Mary University of London, School of Law, Legal Studies Research Paper No. 269/2017, 4, available at <https://ssrn.com/abstract=3091223> accessed 1 October 2021.

753 For instance, in the Spunta project (see Chapter 2, Section 8), the protocol layer is Corda by R3; Italian banks compose the network that is managed by SIA (it is called 'SIAchain'); NTT Data has developed the application SPUNTA.

754 A. Davola, 'Blockchain e Smart Contract as a Service: Prospettive di mercato a criticità normative delle prestazioni BaaS e SCaaS alla luce di un'incerta qualificazione giuridica' (2020) 2 Il Diritto Industriale 147.

755 Artt. 1571 ff *cc*.

customer. It is considered more similar to a project contract (*contratto d'appalto*),[756] a service agreement (*contratto d'opera*),[757] or a professional service agreement (*contratto d'opera professionale*),[758] depending on the internal organisation of the provider.[759]

It is thought that it is more likely that businesses conclude tailored contracts, specifically developed to fit their specific needs because they have the economic power to do so and stronger bargaining power.[760] On the contrary, it might be that consumers opt to download free standard software.[761]

These kinds of contracts provide that the obliged party assumes the risk of defects unless the creditor knew them or should have known them with due diligence.[762] These rules apply in case of software errors or malfunctions. The supplier is held liable unless the creditor knew the possibility of software errors or malfunctions or should have known it with due diligence. In this regard, the supplier can inform the customer about possible errors or malfunctions in the contract,[763] or the customer itself should have foreseen such possibility according to the case circumstances. For instance, it is reasonable that a beta version of the software is not as

756 Artt. 1655 ff *cc*.

757 Artt. 2222 ff *cc*.

758 Artt. 2229 ff *cc*.

759 The rules of the first kind of contract apply if the provider is a big enterprise, ~~of~~ the second if it is a small enterprise, and the third if it is a professional. The first two types of contracts contain obligations to achieve a particular result, while the third contains obligations to use reasonable care. For more details about these contracts, see F. Galgano (ed), *Le obbligazioni in generale, il contratto in generale, i singoli contratti* in F. Galgano (ed), *Trattato di diritto civile*, vol. 2 (Cedam 2014) 721–764. About the application of such contract rules to software contracts, see A. Stazi, A. Baldi, 'Contratti di utilizzazione del software' in D. Valentino (ed), *Dei singoli contratti*, in E. Gabrielli, *Commentario del codice civile*, vol. 2 (Utet 2016) 117–141; G. Finocchiaro, 'I contratti ad oggetto informatico' in Finocchiaro, Delfini (n 344) 618–630.

760 Returning to the suggested four scenarios, this might be the case of numbers 2 and 4, where a business develops its application to attract customers. Scenario number 3 might also be suitable, which is typically a B2B one.

761 For example, Open Bazaar is open source and free. Customers only have to download the software and start to buy and sell.

762 See Artt. 1578, 1667, and 2226 *cc*.

763 Stazi, Baldi (n 759) 138.

reliable as the final version.[764] Moreover, if the customer is a business, a higher level of awareness should be expected.[765]

Blockchain technology is young. In 2017 the majority of networks still were in the proof-of-concept, experimentation phase. Only between 2018 and 2019 did most of them enter production.[766] Blockchain technology has several technical problems to overcome yet, and multiple security concerns. Therefore, it is believed that a diligent person could reasonably foresee the danger of defects of blockchain platforms, implicitly accepting the possibility of malfunctions. It is believed that these assumptions can apply both to businesses and consumers. In fact, malicious attacks on blockchain platforms are not a novelty, some of them being very notorious.[767] Every person that would like to get some information before downloading the software of a blockchain platform could easily become conscious of blockchain shortcomings, simply through research on the Internet. Moreover, the same official websites of blockchain applications sometimes warn the customer about the safety of their products.[768] On the other hand, average consumers do not have a high level of computer literacy. So, the business must act in good faith and make consumers aware of the risks, ensuring that they understand the legal implications of their choices. Otherwise, it is unlikely that they could exclude their liabilities.[769]

Contracts usually describe in details the features and functionalities of the supplied software. This is necessary to set the object of the contract and to objectively verify the performance (or non-performance) of the contract. The law itself might establish conformity requirements. In this respect, to ensure better protection for consumers and avoid that the contract sets very low standards, the Directive (EU) 2019/770 establishes that supplied digital content not only comply with subjective requirements for conformity laid down in the contract, but also with objective require-

764 A. Colombi Ciacchi, E. von Schagen, 'Conformity under the Draft Digital Content Directive: Regulatory Challenges and Gaps' in Schulze, Staudenmayer, Lohsse (n 458) 114.

765 Finocchiaro (n 759) 613.

766 Rauchs *et al* (n 99) 30.

767 It has already been mentioned the 2016 TheDao Hack.

768 As an example, the FAQs of the OpenBazaar website warn about, for instance, the possibility to lose virtual currencies or the unsafety of hot wallets.

769 Furthermore, in Chapter 4 (Sections 3.2 and 4) it was explained that lack of clear information by the business can lead to the violation of the information requirements laid down in the Consumer Rights Directive or allow the consumer to invoke a fundamental mistake to call the contract voidable.

ments[770] (unless otherwise agreed by the parties, provided that the consumer expressly and separately accepts the deviation when concluding the contract).[771] These requirements have in common the standard of reasonableness regarding the contract nature and purpose, the circumstances of the case and the parties usages and practices involved.[772]

Moreover, the law might provide audit procedures[773] or the presence of certification bodies,[774] especially to face the danger of bugs in the smart contract code or the non-correspondence of the translation in the language of the code to the natural language version of the contract.

Compliance with conformity requirements can be presumed if the technology meets specific standards. Given the immaturity of the technology, standardisation organisations have recently started to work on the development of blockchain standards.[775] In September 2017, the International Organization for Standardization (ISO) established the ISO technical committee (TC) 307.[776] The work of ISO/TC 307 is subdivided into three working groups (WG). The third group is on smart contracts and their applications (WG3).[777] The European Commission is one of the five li-

---

770 Artt. 7,8.

771 Art. 8(5). Recital 49 specifies that the consumer could, for instance, tick a box or press a button.

772 See recitals 45 and 46 of the Directive.

773 The report of the European Union Blockchain Observatory and Forum (n 25) 24–25 declares: 'There can also be serious issues if a smart contract has a flaw: a bug in an agreement that deals with asset transfers can be very damaging indeed. Yet it need not necessarily be a bug. Depending on the complexity of the agreement, it can be extremely difficult to correctly or adequately encode contract terms. A smart contract might execute as written and yet still behave in ways not foreseen by its writers. For this reason, smart contract "audits" – often complex, highly technical processes to check for the validity and viability of smart contract code – become important. That raises the question of whether such audits have to become requirements, or also need legal recognition of some kind to make a smart contract valid? This has yet to be decided'.

774 Borgogno (n 263) 304.

775 On this topic, see P. Delimatsis, 'When disruptive meets streamline: international standardization in blockchain' in Kraus, Obrist, Hari (n 561) 83.

776 <https://www.iso.org/committee/6266604.html> accessed 1 October 2021.

777 The first is on foundations, taxonomy and terminology (WG 1); the second on security, privacy and identity (WG 2). There are also three study groups: financial services, government services and supply chain management; governance of blockchain and DLT systems; interoperability and compatibility of blockchain and DLT systems.

aison organisations.[778] Up to now, the ISO/TC 307 has published four standards.[779]

The Smart Contract Working Group of the Dutch Blockchain Coalition[780] considers desirable that such standards (ontology) are also developed for the translation of natural language in the language of the code, which would express rights and obligations independently of any platform. Allen[781] imagines creating a 'private dictionary' for drafting purposes with predictable interpretations under national law.[782]

As discussed in Section 2.2 of Chapter 3, it is common to include contractual provisions to exclude or limit the supplier's liability.[783] Section 6 of this chapter described the corresponding general principles and the Italian discipline, connected them with the rules on unfair contract terms. In particular, suppliers include so-called 'as is' clauses in free licenses, such as

778 The other liaison organisations are: the International Federation for Surveyors; the International Telecommunication Union (ITU); the Society for Worldwide Interbank Financial Telecommunication (SWIFT); the United Nations Economic Commission for Europe (UNECE). The European Commission also takes an active role, working closely with all relevant bodies around the world (<https://digital-strategy.ec.europa.eu/en/policies/blockchain-standards> accessed 1 October 2021).

779 ISO 22739:2020 (Vocabulary), ISO/TR 23244:2020 (Privacy and personally identifiable information protection considerations), ISO/TR 23455:2019 (Overview of and interactions between smart contracts in blockchain and distributed ledger technology systems) and ISO/TR 23576:2020 (Security management of digital asset custodians).

780 Rikken *et al.* (n 113) 23.

781 Allen (n 544) 336.

782 Some projects such as Common Accord or Legalese are building software libraries to draft smart legal contracts. See J. Goldenfein, A. Leiter, 'Legal Engineering on the Blockchain: 'Smart contracts' as Legal Conduct', 24 May 2018, available at SSRN: <https://ssrn.com/abstract=3176363> accessed 1 October 2021.

783 Particularly for consequential or indirect damages.

open source licenses.[784] Considering that many permissionless blockchain platforms are open source,[785] the above rules appear relevant.[786]

Collateral services usually accompany the supply of software (such as support and maintenance), which implies the conclusion of further agreements. Similarly to what affirmed about software agreements, it is necessary to classify such contracts according to the applicable law. Moreover, the object of the contract and rights and duties of the parties have to be identified to allocate the parties' risks and liabilities, also taking into account eventual clauses of exclusion or limitation of liability.

Third-party service providers may also provide oracles and data sources, the connections between the blockchain and the outside world. Oracles are links between on-chain and off-chain data. Oracles are external layers of a blockchain-based application that can transmit information from external data sources to smart contracts, and vice versa. The obliged party can conclude a contract with providers of oracle services.[787] Depending on the data source, there can be hardware, software, or human oracles. Hardware oracles extract information from the physical world thanks to information reading devices, such as electronic sensors or barcode scanners. Software oracles retrieve data from online sources, like a website. They are hardware and software components that can be supplied through specific contracts.[788] Finally, humans can directly feed the oracle with the required information by signing them using cryptography. These humans

---

784 About the validity of 'as is' clauses in relationship with the rules on exclusion of liability and unfair contract terms in the Italian legal system, see A. RICCI, 'I contratti di licenza d'uso di software in particolare: la licenza a strappo, licenze freeware, shareware e open source' in Finocchiaro, Delfini (n 344) 636–639; Stazi, Baldi (n 759) 137–139.

785 The study of Rauchs *et al* (n 99) 54 revealed that half of covered platforms are open source, with the majority licensed under Apache 2.0 license.

786 For instance, the license for the various software components of the Ethereum wallet states: 'Except when otherwise stated in writing the copyright holders and/or other parties provide the program 'as is' without warranty of any kind, either expressed or implied, including, but not limited to, the implied warranties of merchantability and fitness for a particular purpose. The entire risk as to the quality and performance of the program is with you'. The license can be read when downloading the software.

787 E.g. Provable <https://provable.xyz> accessed 1 October 2021 or Realitio <https://realit.io> accessed 1 October 2021.

788 For example, Art. 1 of the general conditions of the contract Fizzy (see n 736) reports that Axa has a partnership with the American company Flightstats that gives the information on flight arrivals.

may act under a contract.[789] The obliged party may thus turn to the parties with which she concluded such contracts. Again, it is important to determine the rules governing the contract and carefully analyse the contractual conditions to allocate liabilities properly.

The present work does not intend to analyse in detail these contracts, which is not the aim of the study. Instead, it would like to demonstrate that saying that trust is in the code is not accurate. It is not the code that governs the execution of the smart contract. Instead, multiple components (or layers) can influence the performance of the contract, of which the obliged party is directly liable (except when the breach of the contract is excused due to *force majeure* or the creditor's behaviour). Indeed, the latter assumed the risk to perform through a blockchain-based smart contract. The layers can be under the direct responsibility of the obliged party, or other third-party service providers, to which the former may turn.

Finally, tort liabilities or defective product liabilities may arise for damages caused to third parties external to the contract or the parties themselves.[790] In that regard, it seems that there are not further peculiarities or problems than the ones described in Chapter 3.[791]

## 8. *Identification of the liable party.*

Having assumed that the contracting party can be held liable, researchers have raised the issue of unknown identities of blockchain users.[792] This might be problematic because it would hinder the identification of the subject against which to start a dispute.

Some clarifications on blockchain participants' anonymity (better, pseudonymity)[793] are first needed to address this matter.

---

789 For example, a contract that obliges a courier to send a package to an address.

790 For instance, the obliged party can also resort not directly to the supplier, but the producer or the developer of a digital good or content. Indeed, as seen in Section 2.2 of Chapter 3, suppliers are often the prime contractor of a chain of connected subcontracts with other persons, such as the producer or the developer, with whom the final customer does not have a contractual relationship. E.g., in the SPUNTA project, the business network operator (SIA) provides the CORDA protocol to the banks through an agreement with R3.

791 See Section 2.2.

792 See Chapter 2, Section 5.

793 Chapter 4, Section 5 (n 685) discussed the possibility of reconnecting blockchain accounts to specific identities. Regulation (EU) 2016/679 (GDPR) gives a definition of pseudonymisation: ''Pseudonymisation' means the process-

The Cypherpunks were strongly fascinated by asymmetric cryptography to prevent governments and corporations from monitoring people. Their scope was the development of an anonymous digital system to hide identities. In fact, in asymmetric encryption, every user holds two keys, one public and one private. The public key is just a string of random letters and numbers representing the user and that everybody can see without knowing who owns it. The private key is like a password that must never be shared with others.

In reality, the advantage of using public-private key cryptography is to verify the provenance of data and data integrity. It is the most secure technology to electronically sign and avoid accessing data in plain text without authorisation.

Anonymity is not an essential blockchain functioning characteristic. In permissioned blockchains, the identification of nodes is a prerequisite for granting access. For the inventors and supporters of the first blockchain prototypes, asymmetric cryptography had the primary political scope to anonymise transactions with unknown recipients to escape from any form of control. In conclusion, anonymity is not a prerequisite without which it is impossible to benefit from blockchain potentials.

Besides political reasons, in permissionless blockchains there is an interest to keep identities secret. Indeed, permissionless blockchains are usually public, which means that anyone can view transactions. Hence, external parties mustn't trace back to underlying identities to protect users' data.[794]

---

ing of personal data in such a manner that the personal data can no longer be attributed to a specific data subject without the use of additional information, provided that such additional information is kept separately and is subject to technical and organisational measures to ensure that the personal data are not attributed to an identified or identifiable natural person' (Art. 4(1)(5)).

794 About the relationship between blockchain technology and the GDPR, see: De Filippi (n 685); Finck (n 685); L. D. Ibáñez, K. O'Hara, E. Simperl, 'On Blockchains and the General Data Protection Regulation' (2018) <https://eprints.soton.ac.uk/422879/1/BLockchains_GDPR_4.pdf> accessed 1 October 2021; M. Finck, 'Blockchain and the General Data Protection Regulation – Can distributed ledgers be squared with European data protection law?', Study of the Panel for the Future of Science and Technology (STOA), European Parliamentary Research Service, July 2019, <https://www.europarl.europa.eu/RegData/etudes/STUD/2019/634445/EPRS_STU(2019)634445_EN.pdf> accessed 1 October 2021; Gambino, Bomprezzi (n 685).

However, the contracting party needs to identify the other party.[795] Section 2.1.2 of Chapter 3 evidenced the legal relevance of identity in contracts, particularly in electronic commerce. It was also given an account of the problem of digital identity in electronic commerce, and the instruments set by the law to allow digital identification and foster trust of users to contract online with strangers.[796] Similarly, in blockchain users exchange messages at a distance through an Internet connection. So, existing rules are also suitable to the blockchain realm.

In addition to that, it is believed that the matter of digital identification of the counterparty is not strictly linked to blockchain technology. It depends on how the technology is used. The analysis of the four scenarios might help to express this concept more clearly.

In scenarios 2 and 4, one contracting party uses the blockchain as back-end. The smart contract is the mean to perform a contract concluded outside of the blockchain. If the contract is concluded off-line, the contracting parties have been previously identified. If the contract is concluded on-line, identification is fostered through the above existing methods.

Scenario 3 is a permissioned scenario, and the parties have built a-permissioned blockchain for their purposes. There is a higher level of trust between the parties because they already know each other.

Scenario 1 seems to be the only one where contracting parties might not know each other. In this regard, there are no differences with the past and no obstacles in applying existing rules.[797]

A similar identification problem regards the entity against which the liable contracting party can turn in case malfunctions of a permissionless blockchain protocol cause the breach of the contract. Permissionless

795 For instance, to balance the need to indentify the other contracting party and the right to protection of personal data towards external parties, identities can be confirmed off-chain.

796 Mainly, the information requirements laid down in the e-Commerce Directive and Consumer Rights Directive, and the electronic signatures and electronic identification means of the e-IDAS Regulation.

797 The European Union Observatory and Forum has prepared a thematic report about blockchain and digital identity (n 665). The report expresses the possibility to link blockchain credentials to identity information in a decentralised manner. The aim is to set up a system in which the user controls the credentials and the data associated with them. Indeed, nowadays user identity information is centralised on the servers of issuing entities. The report also considers the compliance of blockchain-based digital identities with the GDPR and the e-IDAS Regulation.

blockchains are usually open source,[798] meaning anyone can see the source code and propose improvements. For this reason, terms of use often declare that the system is decentralised and that nobody is in control of it.[799] Consequently, one wonders who can be held liable.

Section 3 of this chapter clarified the meaning of 'decentralisation' and it was argued that even in permissionless blockchains there is a kind of control at the software governance level. Moreover, as Mik notes,[800] saying that a protocol is open source does not mean that everyone can change the code already in operation. Every suggested modification has to be accepted and adopted by the ones having access to the code. Despite what was declared behind permissionless blockchains, there are generally companies, foundations, or other similar entities that identify as the founders of blockchain projects and are entitled to make software upgrades.[801]

Here too, it is considered that the issue does not diverge from that of digital identity in electronic commerce. Namely, if someone wishes to enter a permissionless blockchain, it has to download the software and install it in the device/node. By downloading the software, every participant concludes a license agreement with the licensor and acquires the open source license. The contract is concluded at a distance through the Internet with a previously unknown party, like someone downloads software in the hardware from the web. Consequently, existing rules are applicable.[802]

---

798 Bacon *et al.* (n 15) 24.

799 E.g. OpenBazaar's terms of use state that it is a network 'without any central organisation controlling the platform. This means you are responsible for your own activity on the network'.

800 Mik (n 715) 177, n 61.

801 Bacon *et al* (n 15) 21–22; For example, in Ethereum there is the Ethereum Foundation, whose Ethereum's founder Vitalik Buterin is one of the members (<https://ethereum.org/en/foundation/> accessed 1 October 2021); in OpenBazaar, there is the OB1 company (<https://ob1.io/about.html> accessed 1 October 2021). Mik (n 715) talks about hidden and informal governance structures.

802 According to Art. 6 of the Consumer Rights Directive, the trader shall provide some information to the consumer before distance contract binds the latter. Some information, such as the trading name of the trader or the geographical number at which the trader is established, is useful to identify the contracting party.

## *9. Findings and conclusions.*

The above analysis showed that blockchain technology could give rise to breach-less contracts. It tried to catalogue the situations where there could be a breach of the contract despite the self-executing nature of smart contracts. It clarified the different meanings of 'validation' and 'execution' in the technical and legal domains. It explained that the execution of the smart contract code and the validation step that characterises blockchain technology do not guarantee the right performance of the contract.

Having ascertained this, it examined the applicability of existing rules for non-performance of contracts. Indeed, once uploaded on the blockchain, the smart contract cannot be stopped or modified by the obliged party, which cannot control it. It is said that there is a shift from trust in the other party to trust in the code.

This conviction stems from the decentralised character of blockchain technology. One section was dedicated to the explanation of the term 'decentralisation' in the blockchain realm. The latter differentiates from the concept of decentralised governance, i.e. the ability to decide and amend the rules that govern a system. The fact that blockchain is decentralised does not necessarily mean an absence of control. This misunderstanding is probably due to the political ideas that surround-blockchain invention.

The chapter proceeded with the analysis of the four scenarios. It was found out that the creditor has still to trust the obliged party. The obliged party assumes the risk to provide a trustworthy blockchain-based application to perform the contract. The debtor is excused in case of *force majeure*. Moreover, the obliged party is excused when the non-performance of the contract is caused (wholly or partially) by the creditor's behaviour. The obliged party is also responsible if she involves hird parties, according to the rules on performance entrusted to another. The liable contracting party may then turn to such third parties.

These are the general rules. Alongside these rules, it is important to classify the contract, carefully analyse the contractual conditions, and verify the validity of clauses that limit or exclude liability. Of course, tort liabilities or defective product liabilities may arise for damages caused to third parties external to the contract or the parties themselves.

Lastly, it deepened the aspect of (pseudo)anonymity of blockchain participants, which could prevent identifying the liable party. Also here, some common beliefs related to blockchain technology were denied. It was explained that the anonymity of users is not fundamental to take advantage of blockchain features. It was demonstrated that the other party is not always unknown and that the problem is not different from the issue of digital identity in electronic commerce. Once again, existing rules are applicable.

# PART 2: EX-POST INTERVENTIONS ON THE CONTRACT

## 1. *Introduction.*

One of the most discussed characteristics of blockchain is immutability. Blockchain is an 'append-only' ledger, which eliminates every kind of *ex-post* intervention on registered data.

In contract law, several legal protection mechanisms prevent parties from being bound by detrimental contracts. The agreement might be invalid for various reasons. The critical cases might concern the illegality or immorality of the contract. Moreover, the law does not enforce contracts in the absence of a genuine meeting of the minds. One of the parties might lack legal capacity. Unenforceability might also affect contracts for supervening circumstances, such as non-performance. Unforeseeable events can make performance impossible for the obliged party. The same situations might also lead to the adaptation of the contract instead of its total invalidity or termination. Furthermore, the party might have the right to withdraw from the contract, like in consumer contracts. Finally, the parties might decide to renegotiate the contracts.

In the above hypotheses, smart contracts used to execute contractual conditions should be stopped or modified. Nonetheless, as they reside on a blockchain, any stopping or modification would be problematic.[803] For this reason, one might argue that traditional contract law cannot apply unless it is possible to intervene with technical solutions. Alternatively, one might wonder whether the parties can implicitly exclude post-conclusion corrections by accepting that the contract will perform through an incontrollable technological architecture.[804]

---

803 On this issue, see Cuccuru (n 225) 190–192; Perugini, Dal Checco (n 54) 25; Savelyev (n 96) 19–23; Eenmaa-Dimitrieva, Schmidt-Kessen (n 83) 19–26; Werbach, Cornell (n 181) 367–381; Raskin (n 229) 326–328; Bacon *et al* (n 15) 33–34; P. Cuccuru, 'Blockchain ed automazione contrattuale. Riflessioni sugli smart contract' (2017) 1 Nuova Giurisprudenza Civile 107; A. Stazi (ed), *Automazione contrattuale e "contratti intelligenti". Gli smart contracts nel diritto comparato* (Giappichelli 2019) 176–187; D. Di Sabato, 'Gli *smart contracts*: *robot* che gestiscono il rischio contrattuale' (2017) 2 Contratto e Impresa 378.

804 Cuccuru (n 225) 191 affirms: 'The main question is, therefore, whether blockchains for relationships management should be allowed to have a com-

This part first criticises the idea that blockchain technology is immutable, and tries to make some clarifications on that point. Secondly, it takes into consideration some forms of legal intervention on the contract. To this end, it starts from Italian contract law and makes some parallels with the general principles. Thirdly, it verifies the applicability of the above remedies and rights of the parties in the blockchain-based smart legal contracts, and gives an account of the primary technical solutions suggested by the scholars to stop or modify the execution of smart contracts. Lastly, it examines the possibility for the parties to make *ex-ante* renounces to such remedies and rights.

## 2. *Immutability of blockchain.*

As explained in Section 2 of Chapter 1, blockchain data are hashed. A hash is a string of random letters and numbers of a fixed length that is unique. Every modification in the underlying data causes an alteration of the corresponding hash. The hashes of the single transactions and the various blocks are linked together to form a chain of blocks. Through this mechanism, any unauthorised change to the underlying data would be immediately visible, because it would determine a modification of the hash and the linked ones. That is why descriptions of blockchain technology usually depict it as 'immutable'.

In reality, blockchain data can be subject to modifications. But any modifications would produce a different hash. So, the only way to change the chain should be that the most of nodes agree to recalculate the hashes of the new data. This operation can have a different difficulty according to the kind of blockchain and the consensus protocol.

In permissionless blockchains, this operation is much more difficult. Permissionless blockchains are always open to new nodes, whose corresponding identities are unknown. For this reason, collusions are practically impossible. Besides, in permissionless blockchains, reaching a consensus

---

pletely self-referential and self-standing architecture. Can they exclude by default the possibility to trigger the limits and protections provided by offline legal orders? Can efficiency and automation justify a private ordering which may radically jeopardize public policy enforcement and contractual and third-parties protection? Can private parties opt to drastically reduce the possibility of post-conclusion corrections, preferring the ex ante efficiency of automated assessments?'.

is rendered very hard and costly to avoid malicious nodes and because miners receive rewards as an incentive to maintain the network.

Instead, in permissioned blockchains, the same activity is easier because they are closed systems, and validators know each other. Moreover, because an interested party manages the system, that sets it up for its purposes, there are no reasons to adopt a costly and challenging consensus protocol.

In light of the above, someone puts in evidence that blockchain is not technically immutable. For instance, the Smart Contract Working Group of the Dutch Blockchain Coalition talks about non-unilateral reversibility,[805] while Finck prefers to refer to blockchain as being 'tamper-evident'.[806]

Blockchain-based smart contracts are data registered in a blockchain. Thus, the same reasoning can be applied to the so-called immutability of smart contracts. So, in permissionless blockchains, it is substantially impracticable to stop or alter smart contracts, despite it it is technically possible. Alterations and interruptions are more conceivable in permissioned blockchains.

## 3. *Ex-post interventions on contracts. Invalidity.*

The following subsections briefly address the primary kinds of *ex-post* intervention on contracts. Concerning invalidity, Italian law makes a distinction between nullity and voidability.[807] According to Article 1418 *cc*, contracts contrary to mandatory rules are void. Nullity may derive from a lack of the requisites of the contract provided in Article 1325 *cc*,[808] or their unlawfulness. In particular, the *causa*, the motives,[809] and the object of the contract are unlawful when they are contrary to mandatory rules, public policy, or morals. Instead, a contract is voidable for defects in consent (mistake, fraud, threats) and a lack of capacity (both legal capacity and incapability of understanding and intending). The judgement declaring that the contract is void or voidable is retroactive. As a result, the contract

805 Rikken *et al.* (n 113) 16.

806 Finck (n 21) 30.

807 See Bianca (n 400) 565 ff.

808 The requisites are the agreement, the *causa*, the object, and the form when the law requires a specific one. See Bianca (n 400).

809 The *causa* is the social and economic function of the contract, while the motives are the aims pursued by the parties in undertaking their obligations.

never existed. But, if the contract is voidable, the judgment does not affect third parties' rights if they acquired them under remuneration, and voidability is not due to legal capacity unless they are in bad faith (Article 1445 *cc*).

Parties may claim for restitution of what is supplied under a void or voidable contract. If the party makes a payment, it is entitled to return what was paid (Article 2033 *cc*). If the party supplied determined goods, she has the right to ask for restitution of those goods (Article 2037 *cc*). If the performance of the contract is different from a sum of money or delivery of determined goods (e.g. delivery of services), Article 2041 *cc* applies concerning unjustified enrichment. The latter is a subsidiary rule that restricts restitution of the detriment suffered by the claimant to the extent of the value of the benefits received by the other party. Article 1443 *cc* limits restitution to the benefits the party has received in case of a lack of capacity, and the claimant has to prove such benefits. If the nullity or avoidance is partial, i.e. they only affect single clauses of the contract, the effects of such nullity and avoidance are limited to those clauses, unless the parties prove that they would not have entered into the contract without that part (Article 1419 *cc*).

The general principles of contract law consider defects of consent on the one hand,[810] and illegality and immorality on the other hand. They do not cover lack of capacity because it concerns persons. In particular, Article 15:101 PECL and Article II.-7:301 DFCR deny effects to contracts contrary to fundamental principles, such as public policy or morals. Article 15:102 PECL, Article II.-7:302 DFCR and Article 3.3.1 PICC provide that contract is invalid if it infringes mandatory rules. About defects of consent, separate rules concern mistake,[811] fraud,[812] and threats.[813] As concerns the remedy, the PECL, the DFCR, and the PICC state that the party may claim restitution of what supplied under the contract.[814] They generally establish that monetary value has to be paid if the refund cannot be made in kind for any reason. Lastly, they contain almost identical rules on partial avoidance.

810 For comments to corresponding articles, see Jansen, Zimmermann (n 315) 649 ff (defects of consent) and 1887 ff (illegality and immorality). For a comparison with Italian law, see Antoniolli, Veneziano (n 445) 187 ff.

811 Art. 4:103 PECL, II.-7:201 DFCR, 3.2.2 PICC.

812 Art. 4:107 PECL, II.-7:205 DFCR, 3.2.5 PICC.

813 Art. 4:108 PECL, II.-7:206 DFCR, 3.2.6 PICC.

814 Art. 4:115 PECL, II.-7:212 DFCR, 3.2.14 PICC.

The avoidance effect is limited and does not extend to the entire contract unless it is unreasonable to uphold the remaining contract.[815]

## 3.1. Termination.

Termination can eliminate the effects of a valid contract.[816] In the Italian legal system, termination can occur for fundamental non-performance (Article 1453 *cc*), supervening impossibility (Article 1463 *cc*), or excessive onerousness (Article 1467 *cc*). Termination has regard to contracts where performance and counter-performance are mutually related,[817] so that if one party does not perform, non-performance affects the performance of the other. Because termination determines the ineffectiveness of the contract, only serious reasons can activate it. Indeed, non-performance must be fundamental. The impossibility to perform must be objective and not attributable to the debtor. Excessive onerousness refers to the occurrence of extraordinary and unpredictable events that make performance excessively burdensome.

Termination has retroactive effects for the parties (Article 1458 *cc*), so it is as if the contract had never come into existence. However, when the contract involves a continuous or periodic performance,[818] termination does not affect already rendered performances. The parties can ask for the restitution of what has already been performed. If refund in kind is impossible, they can ask for an equivalent sum of money according to the rules on unjust enrichment. Article 1464 *cc* states that if performance has become partially impossible, the aggrieved party can reduce her performance proportionally. From the latter rule, one may infer the availability of partial termination, and the aggrieved party may ask for partial termination of the contract.[819]

---

815 Art. 4:116 PECL, II.-7:213 DFCR, 3.2.13 PICC.

816 For more details on termination according to the Italian Civil Code, see Bianca (n 400) 690 ff.

817 *Contratti sinallagmatici*, or *a prestazioni corrispettive*.

818 *Contratti ad esecuzione continuata o periodica*.

819 The aggrieved party may also terminate the entire contract if she lacks the interest to perform it in part, but the decision cannot be based on subjective factors according to the principle of good faith.

The general principles[820] recognise termination for fundamental non-performance.[821] Instead, Italian supervening impossibility corresponds to excuse due to an impediment.[822] In case of impossibility, specific performance cannot be obtained,[823] and the contract is terminated automatically. Similarly, the parties can end the contract[824] when performance becomes excessively onerous.[825] Unlike Italian contract law, termination is forward-looking.[826] In the event of termination, the party can ask for restitution, or an equivalent sum of money if a refund in kind is impossible.[827] They also recognise partial termination,[828] and a corresponding right for the other party to reduce her performance.[829]

### 3.2. Rescission.

Rescission of the contract refers to two situations of contract conclusion under unfair conditions described in Articles 1447 and 1448 of the Italian Civil Code.[830] In particular, rescission occurs when a party concludes a contract because of the necessity, known to the other party, of saving himself or others from a present danger of serious personal injury (Article 1447 *cc*), or as a result of his need, of which the other has availed himself for his advantage (Article 1448 *cc*).[831] These cases are similar to the avoidability of the contract for defects of consent, but the Italian Civil Code treats them as causes of termination of the contract.

Instead, the general principles consider that if a party exploits the other party's necessity to conclude a disproportionate contract, the contract is

---

820 For a commentary of the Articles of the PECL, the DFCR, and the PICC on termination, see Jansen, Zimmermann (n 315).

821 Art. 9:301 PECL, III.-3:502 DFCR, 7.3.1 PICC.

822 Art. 8:108 PECL, III.-3:104 DFCR, 7.1.7 PICC.

823 Art. 9:102(2)(a) PECL, III.-3:302(3)(a) DFCR, 7.2.2(a) PICC.

824 According to Art. 9:102(2) PECL, III.-3:302(3)(b) DFCR, and 7.2.2 (b) PICC, specific performance cannot be obtained if performance causes the obligor unreasonable effort or expense.

825 Art. 6:111 PECL, III.-1:110 DFCR.

826 See Art. 9:305 PECL, III.-3:509 DFCR, and 7.3.5 PICC. For a comparison between Italian law and the PECL, see Antoniolli, Veneziano (n 445).

827 Artt, 9:306 – 9:307 – 9:308 – 9:309 PECL, III.-3:510 DFCR, 7.3.6 PICC.

828 Art. 9:302 PECL, III.-3:506(2) DFCR.

829 Art. 9:401 PECL, III.-3:601 DFCR.

830 See Bianca (n 400) 637 ff.

831 The imbalance must amount to more than half of the value of the performance.

voidable.[832] The consequences are the same as invalidity for defects of consent.

## 3.3. Withdrawal.

Once the parties have entered a contract, they can agree to terminate (whole or in part) their contractual relationship.[833] However, they are not free to release themselves from the contract unilaterally, according to the principle *pacta sunt servanda* (Article 1372 *cc*), unless they have prescribed this possibility in the contract. Only the law may allow exceptions to the above principle (Article 1373 *cc*).[834] For example, the consumer's right to withdraw in the distance and off-premises contracts provided in the Italian Consumer Code is an exception.[835] According to Article 1373 of the Italian Civil Code, the party cannot exercise her right of withdrawal when the contract has started its performance unless it involves a continuous or periodic performance. In the latter case, the withdrawal is proactive.

Moving to the general principles, the PECL and the PICC do not include any withdrawal right. Only the DFCR includes general provisions on the exercise and effect of this right.[836] Withdrawal terminates the contractual relationship and the obligations of both parties under the contract. Restituion is governed by the rules provided in Book II, Chapter 3, Section 5, Sub-section 4 on contract termination. The DFCR also has a second section that covers particular rights of withdrawal, including the withdrawal rights for consumers in contracts negotiated away from business premises.[837]

---

832 See Art. 4:109 PECL, II.-7:207 DFCR, 3.2.7 PICC.

833 The agreement is directed to extinguish the preceding contract (*mutuo dissenso*).

834 About withdrawal in the Italian legal system, see Bianca (n 400) 693 ff.

835 Artt. 52 ff. of the Legislative Decree No. 206/2005 implementing Directive 2011/83/EU. The consumer can exercise her right within a specified period of time without having to give any reason and incur any costs. See V. Cuffaro, 'Profili di tutela del consumatore nei contratti *online*' in G. Finocchiaro, F. Delfini (n 344) 389–393.

836 See Artt. II.-5:101 ff. DFCR.

837 The discipline is very similar to that contained in the Consumer Rights Directive.

3.4. Renegotiation.

Changes in the underlying circumstances may lead the parties to renegotiate their contract. Renegotiation determines the modification of the contractual conditions.

The parties may agree to modify their contract according to the principle of contractual freedom. Moreover, the parties may be obliged to renegotiate the contract. In particular, Article 1467 *cc* provides that the party against whom the other demands the dissolution of the contract for excessive onerousness can avoid it by offering an equitable modification of the contractual conditions. Therefore, the claimant is obliged to renegotiate the contract. The party's refusal to renegotiate would be contrary to good faith and fair dealing.[838] Similarly, Article 1450 *cc* on rescission recognises the party against whom the other demands the rescission to avoid it by offering to modify the contract and restore its equity. Apart from these general rules, others have regard to particular kinds of contracts. For instance, Article 1664 cc establishes, in case of unforeseeable circumstances during the performance of building contracts, there have occurred such increases or reductions in the cost of the materials or labor as to cause an increase or reduction by more than one-tenth of the total price agreed upon, the independent contractor or the customer can request that the price be revised.[839]

According to some legal scholars, the above rules imply a general duty to renegotiate the contract. Every time supervening circumstances make the performance of the contract contrary to good faith and fair dealing, the party is obliged to renegotiate it. The principle of *pacta sunt servanda* has to be balanced with the principle *rebus sic stantibus*.[840]

Regarding the general principles, Article 6:111 PECL dictates that parties are bound to enter into negotiations to adapt the contract if it becomes excessively onerous because of a change of circumstances. Articles III.-1:110 DFCR and 6.2.3 PICC contain similar provisions. Furthermore,

---

838 See F. Macario (ed), *Adeguamento e rinegoziazione nei contratti a lungo termine* (Jovene 1996) 293 ff.

839 Other rules are Article 1668 *cc*, always for building contracts; Art. 1492 *cc* for sale contracts; Art. 1578 *cc* for lease agreements; Art. 1623 *cc* for rental agreements.

840 On the duty to renegotiate the contract, see Macario (n 838); R. Sacco, G. De Nova (eds), *Il contratto* (Utet 2004) 722 ff; V. Roppo (ed), *Il contratto* (Giuffrè 2001) 972 ff; F. Gambino, 'Obbligo di rinegoziare e atto dovuto' (2006) XII Studium Juris 1374.

Article 4:109 PECL on excessive benefit and unfair advantage recognises the party entitled to avoid the contract the right to modify it to restore the balances between performances; the same is under Article II.-7:207 DFCR and 3.2.7 PICC.

## *4. The proposed technical solutions.*

The proposed technical solutions to intervene on a smart contract after the uploading on a blockchain can be divided into two main groups: operations on the smart contract code, and interventions on the blockchain.

The first group has regard to all the ways to undo or alter the smart contract code by pre-programming them from the outset.[841] Sklaroff calls them 'dormant alternatives'[842] because they can activate if an *ex-post* intervention on the contract is needed. They have to be inserted in the code from the beginning because of the unilateral immutability of blockchain technology. In other terms, the smart contract code has to cover the entire lifecycle of contracts, including the events that can cause the dissolution or modification after its conclusion. The most immediate technique is to insert a function that deletes the smart contract when activated.[843] This solution might be suitable when the contract has to be eliminated from a legal point of view, e.g. in the event of invalidity, termination, rescission, or withdrawal. Others do not cancel the entire smart contract but allow some kinds of modifications.[844] The latter ones are more apt to modify the initial contract, e.g. when the parties renegotiate the contractual terms.

Despite these possibilities, there are critical aspects. Mainly, it has to consider the costs of drafting a smart contract code incorporating all possible future changes.[845] Indeed, at the moment of contract conclusion, the parties cannot foresee the circumstances that will affect the contract, so

841 On this issue, see A. Juels, B. Marino, 'Setting Standards for Altering and Undoing Smart Contracts' in J. J. Alferes *et al.* (eds), *Rule Technologies: Research, Tools, and Applications*, Proceedings of the 10th International Symposium RuleML (Springer 2016) 151, 163.

842 Sklaroff (n 177) 291.

843 The 'self-destruct' or 'kill' function.

844 For example, the inclusion of functions in an 'off' state, which can be turned on; or the creation of 'satellite' contracts that the central contract can call through pointers.

845 Sklaroff (n 177) 292–293.

they have to consider them all. Moreover, it might often be very complex to imagine all supervening events.[846]

As concerns the second group, Section 2 of this part clarified that the reversibility of blockchain is easier in permissioned blockchains. Instead, in permissionless blockchains, it is very costly and arduous, even though not impossible. For example, in the case the DAO hack,[847] there was a hard fork to nullify the effects of the attack on the blockchain. The blockchain was reversed, and the users could get their virtual currencies back. But, in the absence of an administrator or authorised third party, as Meyer observes, 'with the DAO, many users themselves were affected and thus had an economic incentive to act accordingly. In a dispute between only two contracting parties, however, it will prove virtually impossible to persuade the majority of the other network participants to accept modifications to the blockchain'.[848]

Another suggested method to nullify the effects of a transaction is to enter a 'correcting transaction'[849] to add to the blockchain. It allows changes in the blockchain without having to change it.

Lastly, researchers and companies are studying methods to develop 'editable'[850] blockchains.[851] For instance, chameleon hashes have a digital 'trapdoor' that enables those who can open it to modify the hash without

---

846 E. Tjong Tjin Tai, 'Force Majeure and Excuses in Smart Contracts' available at <https://research.tilburguniversity.edu/en/publications/force-majeure-and-excuses-in-smart-contracts> accessed 1 October 2021, p. 12; also available at: E. Tjong Tjin Tai, 'Force Majeure and Excuses in Smart Contracts' (2018) 26(6) European Review of Private Law 787.

847 See n 257.

848 See O. Meyer, 'Stopping the Unstoppable. Termination and Unwinding of Smart Contracts' (*SSRN*, 29 October 2019) 15 <https://ssrn.com/abstract=3537477> accessed 1 October 2021 (the final version of the paper appeared in Journal of European Consumer and Market Law, 2020, 17 ff). In permissioned blockchains too, it is thought that reversing the blockchain might be inconvenient. All hashes of the blockchain should be changed to modify a transaction. It is thought that it would be as to use 'a sledge-hammer to crack a nut'. Furthermore, considering that every blockchain can record a multitude of smart contracts, it might be inconceivable to intervene on the entire blockchain every time a single contract presents some problems.

849 Bacon *et al.* (n 15) 24.

850 Bacon *et al.* (n 15) 34.

851 R. Lumb, D. Treat, O. Jelf, 'Editing the uneditable blockchain – Why distributed ledger technology must adapt to an imperfect world' (*Accenture*, 2016) <https://www.accenture.com/_acnmedia/pdf-33/accenture-editing-uneditable-blockchain.pdf> accessed 1 October 2021.

any chain modifications.[852] However, someone has criticised such kinds of blockchains because they lack their peculiarity, i.e. to be append-only ledgers.[853] They also might jeopardise the safety of the system.[854]

## *5. Applicability of existing rules. The subject matter of the contractual obligation.*

This work clarified several times that blockchain technology is 'deaf and blind'; in other terms, blockchain technology has a closed nature and cannot control what happens outside of it. Moreover, it was explained that interacting with the off-chain world makes use of oracles, both inbound and outbound.[855]

These aspects acquire relevance in the performance of contracts through smart contracts recorded on a blockchain. In particular, as previously observed,[856] when contract execution has to produce its effects off the chain, smart contract execution does not guarantee contract performance. Further operations outside the database have to follow the outputs of the smart contract code, and it depends on the subject-matter of the contractual obligation.

The Italian legal system distinguishes between obligations to give something, do something, or not do something.[857] Starting from the last, blockchain-based smart contracts cannot be used to perform obligations

---

852 Ibáñez, O'Hara, Simperl (n 794) 8. The authors note that 'despite the fact that a party could try to redact a blockchain in its favour, it is still needed that all others accept the redacted version'. Moreover, '(…) to be redactable a blockchain needs to include chameleon hashes since its inception making impossible to add redactability to existing Blockchains'.

853 J. J. Roberts, 'Why Accenture's Plan to 'Edit' the Blockchain is a Big Deal' (*Fortune*, 20 September 2016) <https://fortune.com/2016/09/20/accenture-blockchain/> accessed 1 October 2021; H. Chang, 'Blockchain: Disrupting Data Protection', University of Hong Kong Falculty of Law Research Paper No. 2017/041, 3 <http://ssrn.com/abstract=3093166> accessed 1 October 2021.

854 For example, as reported by M. L. Perugini (ed), *Distributed Ledger Technologies e sistemi di Blockchain* (Key 2018) 48 there might be a danger of 'Key Exposure', i.e. the possibility of violating the confidentiality of private keys.

855 Chapter 1, Section 7.

856 See Part 1 of this chapter.

857 For further details, see Bianca (n 450) 107 ff. Art. III.-1:102 DFCR talks about the debtor's doing or not doing of what is to be or is not to be done under the obligation.

not to do something. On the contrary, the execution of a smart contract implies positive actions. Concerning obligations to do something, as Perugini and Dal Checco argue, 'the smart paradigm will be applicable in case of direct e-commerce, as it happens in the majority of online services'.[858] Automatic performance cannot occur in indirect e-commerce, at least until the Internet of Things would seize the mass market.[859] The same reasoning applies to obligations to give something.

Within the obligations where a 'smart' performance is possible, it is thought that one should distinguish between goods and services that are native blockchain, from those that are not. An appropriate example of native blockchain is virtual currencies, as opposed to electronic money.[860] Blockchain-based smart contracts can directly execute the obligations that have to do with native blockchain assets because they are included in the database. For instance, if an insurance company has to pay the policyholder in virtual currencies, it can perform its obligation to give virtual currencies entirely through the smart contract. Indeed, the code verifies the fulfilment of the condition that justifies the payment and moves the currencies from its account to the policyholder's blockchain account. Conversely, if the contract provides the payment in electronic money, the smart contract code can only give the output of making the payment, but it cannot make the payment. The bank of the insurance company has to transfer the money from the bank account of the insurance company to the policyholder's bank account.

---

858 Perugini, Dal Checco (n 54) 10. In its Communication to the Council, the European Parliament, the Economic and Social Committee and the Committee of the Regions of 16 April 1997 ('A European Initiative in Electronic Commerce'), the Commission of the European Communities stated that electronic commerce 'includes indirect electronic commerce (electronic ordering of tangible goods) as well as direct electronic commerce (online delivery of intangibles)'.

859 De Filippi and Wright (n 17) 156 talk about the 'Blockchain of Things'. Chapter 4 has also given an account of the Report of the European Union Blockchain Observatory and Forum about the conjunction between blockchain and other emerging technologies, such as the IoT (n 699).

860 About legal characterisation and regulatory initiatives concerning virtual currencies, see F. Barrière, 'The Payment with Bitcoins and other Virtual Currencies – Risks, liabilities, and regulatory responses' in De Franceschi *et al.* (n 591) 327; in Italy, see A. Gambino, C. Bomprezzi, 'Blockchain e criptovalute' in G. Finocchiaro, V. Falce (eds), *Fintech: diritti, concorrenza, regole – Le operazioni di finanziamento tecnologico* (Zanichelli 2019) 267. Central banks and regulators are also contemplating the potential of Central Bank Digital Currencies (such as a digital euro, in Europe). See European Union Observatory and Forum (n 138) 1–3.

Contract performance is not under the control of the blockchain, as noticed in Part 1 of this chapter. It also derives that even admitting that the smart contract code cannot be stopped or modified because of the characteristics of blockchain technology, the execution of the smart contract code does not necessarily reflect on the outside world. Thus, despite the unilateral immutability of the blockchain, it could be possible to *ex-post* intervene on the contract. The following example illustrates these considerations more effectively.

Suppose that a party concludes a contract to rent a house. The contract provides that the tenant pays a certain amount of money on a specified day every month. A smart contract automates the payment on the agreed day. Imagine that the tenant withdraws from the contract before the end of the rental period. In the abstract, the immutability of blockchain should impede the smart contract to stop making the payment for the remaining months. In reality, if the payment is not due in virtual currencies, even though the smart contract code gives the output of paying, the bank of the tenant could stop the payments.

### 5.1. The false myth of decentralisation.

Blockchain is considered an immutable database. As specified above,[861] it should be more appropriate to talk about "tamper-evidence" because it can be modified despite great difficulties. Resistance to modifications is due not only to concatenated blocks and hashes but also to the decentralised character of the system. The more the latter is decentralised, the more it is unilaterally immutable. Indeed, it was pointed out that in permissioned blockchains it is easier to reach collusion between the nodes because of a higher level of centralisation.

However, as argued in the preceding part of the chapter, blockchain decentralisation is a false myth.[862] Decentralisation has a technical meaning that does not necessarily correspond to an absence of control over the infrastructure.

As done before, these arguments are applied to the four scenarios starting from permissioned blockchains.

In scenario 3, the parties hold the infrastructure and exercise control over it. Therefore, from a technical point of view, they could reach the

861 Section 2.
862 Section 3.

required majority to change the chain. In scenario 4, one party of the contract entirely manages a permissioned blockchain, and uses it as backend. Similarly, the party may intervene on the smart contract code.

In the two remaining scenarios, instead, the presence of a permissionless blockchain makes difficult any change. In these cases, one might assume that traditional contract law cannot be applied when it is not possible to intervene with technical solutions. Blockchain decentralisation would deprive the parties of the possibility of activating those contractual institutions that require an *ex-post* intervention on existing contracts. This view is denied.

Indeed, all the examined disciplines have in common the restitution of any rendered performance that was not due by virtue of invalidity, termination, rescission, withdrawal, or renegotiation of the contract. Restitution is necessary because such performance occurred *sine causa*. The unjustified performance gives rise to an obligation for the recipient to return it, and the performing party has a corresponding right to ask for the restitution of what performed. In the examined scenarios, the contracting party that received unjustified performance because it was impossible to halt the execution of the smart contract has an obligation of restitution towards the other. Even though the obliged party does not manage the blockchain, the latter can honour the duty to return because it can perform it independently from the smart contract code. One may affirm another time that blockchain decentralisation does not determine a lack of control by the parties on the performance of their obligations. Existing rules are still applicable.

### 5.2. Identification of the obliged party.

As considered in the preceding section, the party still could perform her obligation of restitution of what executed *sine causa*, the immutable and decentralised character of the blockchain not representing an obstacle in this sense. However, someone affirms that the fact that parties act under pseudonyms impedes identifying the party obliged to return and to whom the other party can address a claim for restitution.[863]

On this point, as already explained,[864] the pseudo-anonymity of users is not a prerequisite without which it is impossible to benefit from

863 Meyer (n 848) 7.

864 Chapter 5, Part 1, Section 8.

blockchain potentials. The preservation of the anonymity of blockchain participants was a must for the Crypto-anarchists for political reasons. Moreover, the transparency of permissionless blockchains requires keeping underlying identities secret for privacy reasons. It does not exclude that the contract parties identify each other or that they already know each other. The matter is the same addressed in Section 8, Part 1, of this chapter. Namely, in scenario 3, the parties already know the other party's identity. When a party uses the blockchain as backend (scenarios 2 and 4), the contract is not concluded on-chain. So, the parties are pre-identified: offline, or through the existing legal instruments of identification of the parties in electronic commerce. The latter is also applicable in scenario 1, which does not differ from the conclusion of contracts online. Indeed, users conclude contracts in the blockchain by communicating at a distance thanks to an Internet connection.

In summary, sometimes the problem of the identification of the obliged party is a false problem; other times, it does not differ from the problem of electronic identification in electronic commerce. So, one can face it with the same legal instruments.

## 6. *Ex-ante renounce to ex-post interventions. Invalidity.*

Acknowledged that existing rules are applicable, the only way that parties have to escape from *ex-post* interventions on the contract is to exclude *ex-ante* from the exercise of the above remedies and rights in the contract.[865] The following subsections verify this possibility by focusing on each of such remedies and rights.

Nullity concerns the protection of super-individual interests and values. As such, the latter are non-derogable and non-negotiable. For this reason, contract terms excluding nullity have no effect. The parties' contractual autonomy is limited in these cases.

In the Italian legal system, one can infer it from Article 1423 *cc* that excludes that the other party can confirm the validity of the contract. Moreover, Article 1462 *cc* on exchange contracts establishes that a clause providing that one of the parties cannot set up defences to avoid or delay performance due by her does not affect defences based on nullity. From

865 Cuccuru (n 225) 191 wonders whether private parties can opt to drastically reduce the possibility of post-conclusion corrections, preferring the *ex-ante* efficiency of automated assessments.

these provisions, legal scholars hold that parties cannot validly depart from nullity of the contract.[866]

Recently, the Italian Supreme Court dealt with *ex-ante* renounce to the nullity of a contract.[867] It recalled both Article 1423 and 1462 *cc*. It also reminded the superiority of those interests and values behind the grounds for invalidity of contracts. Furthermore, the Supreme Court considered that a contractual renounce to the nullity of a contract hinders the possibility for the court to raise it (or an objection to it) of its motion.

As concerns contract voidability, similarly Article 1462 *cc* on exchange contracts states that a clause providing that one of the parties cannot set up defences for avoiding or delaying performance due by her also has no effects on defences based on voidability.[868] In contrast to nullity, voidability admits confirmation (Article 1444 *cc*). However, the confirmation cannot occur before the party entitled to sue for annulment knows of the voidability.[869] It follows that parties cannot contractually exclude voidability from the beginning.

Article 3.1.4 PICC states that the provisions on fraud, threat, and illegality are mandatory.[870] Article 4:118 PECL and Article II.-7:215 DFCR explicitly deny the validity of anticipatory exclusion or restriction to remedies for fraud and threats.[871] The same Articles of PECL and DFCR recognise such exclusions or restrictions in cases of mistake, unless the exclusion or restriction is contrary to good faith or fair dealing.[872]

---

866 G. D'Amico (ed), *"Regole di validità" e principio di correttezza nella formazione del contratto* (Jovene 1996) 24 ff; R. Tomassini, 'Invalidità (dir priv.)' in *Encicl. Diritto*, XXII, 1972, 586.

867 Cass. Civ. (II), 18 October 2018, no. 26618. For a comment to this decision, see S. Calvetti, 'Si può rinunciare a far valere una nullità contrattuale?' (2018) 184 Diritto & Giustizia 9.

868 D'amico (n 866) 24 ff; Tomassini (n 866) 586.

869 A. Maniaci, 'Le clausole di incontestabilità nei contratti di assicurazione' in G. De Nova (ed), *Le clausole a rischio di nullità* (Cedam 2009) 83.

870 The comment to this article of the PICC explains that 'it would be contrary to good faith for the parties to exclude or modify these provisions when concluding their contract'.

871 These restrictions or exclusions would be contrary to good faith or fair dealing. See P.Iamiceli, 'Art. 4:111–119'in Antoniolli, Veneziano (n 445) 247.

872 Iamiceli (n 871) 247 affirms that 'in this case, it seems that these are minor violations which do not entail any intention to alter the equilibrium of the negotiation between the parties; within these limits, exclusions or restrictions of remedies can be allowed, in line with the general duty of good faith and fair dealing'.

## 6.1. Termination.

There has been a debate among Italian scholars about the admissibility of an *ex-ante* contractual exclusion of the party's right to terminate the contract for fundamental non-performance. In summary, the ones who denied the possibility to renounce ~~to~~ the termination of the contract argued that the contract would betray its reciprocal nature and become more similar to gratuitous contracts or gambling.[873] Therefore, these contracts would be suspicious, and one might wonder whether to consider these clauses unlawful.[874] Moreover, such clauses would introduce an element of risk like in speculative contracts[875] that is not suitable to contracts where performance and counter-performance are mutually related.[876]

On the other hand, others have observed that the performing party would have further remedies for non-performance in addition to termination, i.e. the right to claim for the other party's specific performance or obtain the payment of damages.[877] They have also highlighted that the party might be interested in avoiding the termination of the contract.[878] Then, Article 1462 *cc* establishes that a clause providing that one of the parties cannot set up defences for the purpose of avoiding or delaying performance due by her has no effects on defences based on nullity, voidability, and rescission of the contract, not on termination; so, even admitting the contractual exclusion of the right to terminate contracts, a defence based on termination would always be possible.[879]

---

873 R. Sacco (ed), *Il contratto* in F. Vassalli (ed), *Trattato di diritto civile italiano* (Utet 1975) 936.

874 R. Sacco, 'I rimedi sinallagmatici' in R. Sacco, G. De Nova (eds), *Il contratto* in *Trattato Sacco* (Utet 2004) 616.

875 G. Scalfi, 'Risoluzione del contratto, I), Diritto civile' in *Enc. Giur. Treccani* (1991) 4.

876 U. Carnevali, 'Della risoluzione per inadempimento, Artt. 1453–1454' in *Comm. Scialoja-Branca* (Zanichelli 1990) 110.

877 G. De Nova (ed), *Il contratto ha forza di legge* (LED Edizioni Universitarie 1993) 38. The author considers that only in the absence of the remaining remedies, the exclusion of termination would be invalid.

878 G. Sicchiero, 'Comm. All'art. 1453 cod.civ., La risoluzione per inadempimento' in P. Schlesinger (ed), *Il Codice civile. Commentario* (Giuffrè 2007) 393. For example, in project financing operations, the investors are interested in maintaining the contracts for the supply of goods or services to guarantee those incomes necessary to repay the investment. See F. Delfini (ed), *I patti sulla risoluzione per inadempimento* (Ipsoa 1998) 11.

879 G. Amadio (ed), *Lezioni di diritto civile* (Giappichelli 2018) 10.

The latter position is recent. In particular, renounce would be valid under the following conditions: – the performing party can rely on the other remedies for non-performance (specific performance, damages); – the clause cannot exclude termination for non-performance attributable to intent or gross negligence, according to Article 1229 *cc*.[880]

Instead, legal experts admit an *ex-ante* renounce to terminate the contract for supervening impossibility or excessive onerousness.[881]

Article 8:109 PECL establishes that the parties may exclude the remedies for non-performance unless it would be contrary to good faith and fair dealing to invoke the exclusion. The PICC and DFCR contain similar provisions.[882] It means that the general principles allow an *ex-ante* renounce to the termination of the contract for non-performance unless it is contrary to good faith and fair dealing.[883]

The above general principles can also be applied when the performing party terminates the contract for supervening impossibility. Indeed, supervening impossibility determines the non-performance of the contract by the other party, even though non-performance is excused. Thus, termination for supervening impossibility is a remedy for non-performance. Equally, termination for excessive onerousness is a remedy for non-performance of the contract given that performance is considered contrary to good faith in such situations.

---

880 Art. 1229 *cc* states that clauses limiting liability for fraud or gross negligence on the part of the debtor are void. Some authors have put in connection clauses of exclusion of termination of the contract for non-performance and Article 1229 *cc*. See C. Menichino (ed), *Le clausole di irresponsabilità contrattuale* (Giuffrè 2008) 17; Sicchiero (n 878) 413. The jurisprudence also seems to accept the validity of such clauses within the same limits, despite there are few pronunciations. The more recent decision is Cass., 18 June 1980, no. 3866.

881 The discipline on termination of contracts for supervening impossibility and excessive onerousness is derogable. See Sacco (n 873) 978–979; 988–989; G. De Nova (ed), *Recesso e risoluzione nei contratti* (Giuffrè 1994) 8; De Nova (n 877) 40.

882 Art. III.-3:105(2) DFCR, Art. 7.1.6 PICC.

883 Delfini observes that these principles aim to avoid the non-performing party maliciously preventing the other party from remedying for non-performance. Italian scholars apply the same reasoning when they determine the limits within whom the clause of exclusion of termination for non-performance is valid. See F. Delfini, 'Autonomia privata e risoluzione del contratto per inadempimento' (2014) 3 Nuove Leggi Civili Commentate 577.

## 6.2. Rescission.

The right to rescind the contract is considered unavailable.[884] As is for nullity, this is inferred from the prohibition to validate the contract (Article 1451 *cc*).[885] Likewise, Article 1462 *cc* on exchange contracts establishes that a clause providing that one of the parties cannot set up defences to avoid or delay performance due by her does not affect defences based on rescission.[886]

Article 3.1.4 PICC states that the provisions on gross disparity are mandatory.[887] Article 4:118 PECL and Article II.-7:215 DFCR explicitly deny the validity of anticipatory exclusion or restriction to remedies for excessive benefit or unfair advantage-taking.[888]

## 6.3. Withdrawal.

The party can renounce her right to withdraw from the contract unless the rule that recognises the right is mandatory,[889] or explicitly excludes this possibility. For example, the Italian law on lease agreements provides that they are null if they advantage the owner unfairly.[890] Of course, the lessee's renounce to the exercise of her right of withdrawal would determine an unfair advantage for the lessor. So, an exemption clause would be null.[891] The consumer's right to withdraw the contract is also mandatory. Indeed, mandatory rules protect superior interests. However, the law also might make some exceptions. For instance, Article 59, let. o), of the Italian Consumer Code[892] recognises that the consumer can accept to *ex-ante* renounce to her right of withdrawal from a contract to supply digital

884 M. De Poli, 'Rescissione' in *Enc. Giur. Treccani Online* (2015).

885 F. Gazzoni (ed), *Obbligazioni e contratti* (Edizioni Scientifiche Italiane 2009) 1012.

886 D'amico (n 866) 24 ff; Tomassini (n 866) 586.

887 The comment to this article of the PICC explains that 'it would be contrary to good faith for the parties to exclude or modify these provisions when concluding their contract'.

888 These restrictions or exclusions would be contrary to good faith or fair dealing. See P.Iamiceli, 'Art. 4:111–119' in Antoniolli, Veneziano (n 445) 247.

889 G. Gabrielli, F. Padovini, 'Recesso (dir.priv.)' in *Enc. Diritto* (1988) XXXIX.

890 Art. 79 Law 392/1978.

891 See Cass. Civ. (III), 13 February 2015, no. 2868.

892 Art. 59 includes a list of exemptions to consumers' right of withdrawal.

content through an immaterial medium if the performance has already begun.

The DFCR prescribes that the parties may not, to the detriment of the entitled party, exclude applying the rules concerning the right of withdrawal or derogate from or vary their effects.[893]

## 6.4. Renegotiation.

As seen above,[894] the Italian civil code contains some rules that give the right to the contractual party to ask for the renegotiation of the contract, and that oblige the other party to review the contractual conditions. According to the general principle of good faith and fair dealing, someone consider that there is a general duty to renegotiate when supervening circumstances alter the contract equilibrium

Given that the contracting party has a right to renegotiate the contract, one wonders whether the parties can *ex-ante* renounce exercising that right. Indeed, it is true that the principle of good faith and fair dealing (Article 1375 *cc*) is mandatory because it is apt to protect superior values. On the other hand, it might be that the parties are willing to bear the risk of remaining bound to the original contract. For example, in building contracts, the independent contractor has the right to ask that the price be revised if unforeseeable circumstances determine an increase in the materials or labour costs (Article 1664 cc). The parties may agree to derogate such right. Derogation is possible because the parties are free to adapt the contract and differently spread the contractual risk. Therefore, there is a belief that the party can renounce the right to renegotiate the contract.[895]

The same one can infer from the general principles on change of circumstances. The duty to adapt the contract derives from the principle of good faith and fair dealing, which is mandatory. However, Article 6:111(2)(c) PECL excludes this right if the risk of the change of circumstances is one that, according to the contract, the party affected should be required to bear. Likewise, Article III.-1:110(3)(c) DFCR prescribes that the right of variation apply only if the debtor did not assume the risk of that change of circumstances. Finally, Article 6.2.2(1)(d) PICC denies hardship when the disadvantaged party has assumed the risks of the events.

893 Art. II.- 5:101(2) DFCR.

894 Section 3.4.

895 P. Gallo (ed), *Trattato del contratto, 3* (Utet 2010) 2363.

## 6.5. Limitations to contractual autonomy.

The above subsections demonstrated that the principle of freedom of contract does not permanently exclude *ex-post* interventions on contracts. Other overriding values can curtail the parties' autonomy.[896] Even when the law admits derogation, it has not to be contrary to the principle of good faith and fair dealing.

In particular, the party that is negatively affected by the derogation has to express informed consent. To this end, reference is made to Chapter 4 on contractual intention.[897] The importance of providing a clear and understandable contract was underlined, especially in unilaterally drafted contracts and consumer contracts. In particular, the study recalled some important Italian and European rules. Namely, Article 1341 *cc* for the contracts with general terms and conditions, the Articles of the Italian Consumer Code, the 1993 Unfair Contract Terms Directive, and the information requirements laid down in the e-Commerce Directive and the Consumer Rights Directive.

Indeed, suppose the contracting parties ex-ante agree that one of them renounce to activate some remedies (such as termination, withdrawal, or renegotiation). In that case, a result is an unbalanced contract in favour of the other party. The Italian legal system considers that some clauses are more likely to be unfair, so the contracting parties must approve them in writing.[898] In consumer contracts, it enlists those clauses presumed to be unfair unless the other party proves that such clause result from individual negotiations.[899] Morevoer, some contractual clauses are directly void,[900] such as liability exoneration clauses described in Part 1 of this chapter.[901] As far as it concerns here, the exclusion of the right to ask for the termina-

896 Eenmaa-Dimitrieva, Schmidt-Kessen (n 83) 23.
897 Section 3.1.
898 Art. 1341(2) *cc*.
899 Art. 33(2) of the Italian Consumer Code.
900 Art. 36(2) of the Italian Consumer Code.
901 Section 6. Art. 1341(2) provides that clauses that establish limitations of the drafting party's liability have to be specifically approved in writing. The Directive 93/13/EEC and the Italian Consumer Code state that liability limitation clauses are unfair.

tion of the contract for non-performance is a limitation of the other party's liability.[902]

In brief, parties that use a smart contract for contract performance may agree to renounce *ex-post* interventions on the contract unless there are some limitations to the principle of contractual autonomy. According to the principle of good faith and fair dealing, they also have to ensure that the disadvantaged party understood or ought to have understood the terms of the exclusion.

## 7. *Findings and conclusions.*

The present analysis showed that the so-called immutability of blockchain technology does not pose substantial obstacles to applying existing rules regarding *ex-post* interventions on the contract.

Investigations were conducted by considering the major contractual institutes that determine the elimination or modification of the contract: invalidity, termination, rescission, withdrawal, renegotiation. In these events, authors have highlighted that smart contracts could not be stopped or modified.

The starting point was the subject matter of the contractual obligation. It was noticed that when contract performance occurs off the chain, blockchain immutability is irrelevant because blockchain is a closed database. It cannot influence the outside world. The difference between smart contract execution and contract performance was recalled. Even though the parties cannot act on the smart contract after having uploaded it on the blockchain, they may stop the performance of the contract or modify its terms when other operations have to follow the operations of the smart contract code.

The only hypothesis of direct execution of the obligations by the blockchain-based smart contract is when contracts exchange native blockchain assets, such as virtual currencies. Indeed, the smart contract has direct control over those assets. But control by the blockchain does not always mean an absence of control by the parties. As seen by focusing on the four scenarios, blockchain decentralisation is a technical feature of the technology and is not related to an impossibility to govern the system.

902 As already reported in subsection 6.1, both legal scholars and jurisprudence have put in connection liability limitation clauses of Art. 1229 *cc* and the clauses of exclusion of the right to terminate the contract for non-performance.

Even if the smart contract continues its execution, the other party must return what received *sine causa* under existing rules. If restitution in kind is impossible, the law provides the payment of a sum of money. However, scholars have pointed out that the pseudonymous character of blockchain would hinder the identification of the obliged party. It is believed that this problem does not differ from that of digital identity in electronic commerce. Furthermore, blockchain participants are not always unknown.

Alternatively, the parties may agree to renounce an *ex-post* intervention on the contract when concluding the contract. In this regard, it was given an account of the limits of the principle of contractual autonomy.

From a technical point of view, modifications of the database are not totally excluded. It is not so accurate to affirm that blockchain is immutable. More precisely, blockchain is unilaterally immutable, or tamper-evident. However, changes are very costly or might weaken the safety of the system. Instead, it could be more desirable to program the smart contract code as to foresee these supervening circumstances. As Meyer argues, 'it would be closer to the spirit of the fully automated contracts'.[903] Unfortunately, as asserted in Chapter 2,[904] such programming activities are still technically impracticable for most kinds of contracts.

903 Meyer (n 848) 7.
904 Section 7.

# CHAPTER 6: JURISDICTION AND APPLICABLE LAW

## *1. Introduction.*

As illustrated in Chapter 2, one of the supposed characteristics of smart legal contracts on the blockchain is self-enforcement.[905] The decentralisation and the tamper evidence of blockchain technology determine that no single party is in absolute control of it and can interrupt or modify the execution of the smart contract code. No party can refuse the results of the execution of the code. No party can infringe the rules of the code. Suppose such code is used to perform contractual obligations automatically. In that case, there is no room for manoeuvre for the obliged party, so there is no need for the other party's intervention to enforce her rights. For this reason, one talks about self-enforcement.

In reality, Chapter 5, Part 1 pointed out that blockchain technology cannot give rise to breach-less contracts. There can be several situations in which the self-execution of a smart contract leads to a breach of that contract. There has been an attempt to catalogue these hypotheses: a) the code content does not match with the will of the parties, thus determining that the execution of the contract does not satisfy the creditor; b) technological problems that impact on the performance of the contract; c) other problems due to the closed nature of blockchain, when there is the need to link the smart contract with the off-chain world to perform the contract.

Moreover, the meaning of 'decentralisation' was explained from a technical point of view, and distinguished from decentralised forms of technology control. Thus, it was clarified that using a decentralised database does not necessarily mean excluding any possibility of control or management. It was demonstrated that sometimes the obliged party has the material control of the technology, or she assumes the risk of non-performance independently of the cause determining the breach of the contract. In summary, it was denied that trust is in the code. Instead, trust is still in the other party. The aggrieved party may claim for enforcement of her rights, and traditional rules are still applicable.

If the contracting party seeks to enforce the contract in front of a court, someone has outlined some difficulties in identifying the jurisdiction and

905 Section 4.

the applicable law.[906] Indeed, blockchain-based smart contracts are a global phenomenon. Contracting parties might belong to different countries. In this hypothesis, the anonymity of blockchain users and the location of the nodes might hinder the application of the necessary parameters set by private international law rules. The matter is similar to that of the Internet, which is both intangible and transnational. When commerce is carried out through the Internet, usually negotiations involve parties coming from different countries. The difficulty in establishing the digital identities of the parties and the location of transactions made on the Internet causes some problems in the choice of the jurisdiction and the applicable law.[907]

The chapter considers existing criteria of determination of jurisdiction and applicable law in cross-border contracts considering blockchain characteristics. The ultimate goal of this analysis is to verify whether and to what extent blockchain technology is (or is not) suitable to existing rules.

## 2. *Blockchain and the Internet.*

Someone compares blockchain technology to the Internet.[908] They are considered both without space borders and immaterial. Moreover, they can connect unknown people that act under unverified identities.

The Internet is an open network. Anyone having an Internet connection and an electronic device can enter the net. For this reason, the Internet is intrinsically transnational.[909] IP addresses identify the devices but not the underlying identities. The cartoon of the New Yorker with the famous sentence "On the Internet nobody knows you are a dog" is very representative in this sense.[910] Similarly, blockchain technology is made up of nodes, electronic devices that compose its infrastructure. Everyone willing to participate in a blockchain has to download the necessary software in her machine. Blockchain accounts – random letters and numbers that do

906 See Chapter 2, Section 5.

907 See Chapter 3, Section 2.3.

908 F. Guillaume, 'Aspects of private international law related to blockchain transactions' in Kraus, Obrist, Hari (n 561) 59.

909 In Section 1 of Chapter 3 the characteristics of the Internet and electronic commerce on the Internet were discussed.

910 In 1993, the New Yorker published a cartoon showing a dog sitting behind a computer screen with the sentence 'On the Internet, nobody knows you are a dog'. This cartoon is very famous because it represents anonymity on the Internet.

not reveal anything about the participant to the blockchain – identify the users.

However, these characteristics are lost in permissioned blockchains. Unlike the Internet, access is not open. Permissioned blockchains usually were born to fit a specific purpose, so they are only available to authorised and known participants. Therefore, the international location of the nodes is not taken for granted. Permissioned blockchains resemble more to described EDI,[911] closed electronic networks used by commercial entities.

Another aspect is that blockchain is not an alternative to the Internet. Instead, the blockchain sits on top of it. More specifically, it collocates over the transport layer.[912] So, it is believed that equalling blockchain technology to the Internet might be quite misleading. In particular, the Internet is a communication system, while blockchain is a database. Sometimes people may make use of blockchain technology also to exchange information.[913] But they may limit themselves to store information that they exchanged outside the database. For example, if two parties make an exchange of virtual currencies on the blockchain, they do not only record a transfer of assets but also utilise it to effectuate that transfer. Instead, if they conclude a contract they agree to perform (totally or in part) through a blockchain-based smart contract, the blockchain is merely a mean to record the smart contract and its state changes.

In summary, it results that blockchain sometimes has some common characteristics with the Internet, sometimes not. Commonalities depend on the kind of blockchain adopted, and also on the different use of the technology. From the above one could derive that in case of similarity, existing rules are applicable. In the event of divergence, one should wonder whether blockchain technology causes new problems that need new legal solutions or if there are no obstacles in identifying the criteria necessary to determine the jurisdiction and the applicable law.

---

911 On EDI, see Section 1 of Chapter 3.

912 See section 1 of Chapter 1.

913 Mik (n 715) 170 affirms that 'It is rarely appreciated that, at a technical level, blockchains are databases or, as commonly stated, cryptographically secured ledgers. (…)'unlike traditional ledgers that only record assets or events, some blockchains are capable of generating and transferring a limited range of crypto-tokens'.

### 3. *Criteria of determination of jurisdiction and applicable law. Location of contract formation.*

Current criteria of determination of jurisdiction and applicable law are based on territoriality. In Chapter 3, they were subdivided into contract formation location, contract performance location, residence location, domicile, place of business or administration.[914] In the following sections, each of them is applied to disputes regarding contracts concluded and/or performed through blockchain-based smart contracts.

Concerning the location of contract formation, the Italian legal system states that to identify the jurisdiction *ratione loci* for cases related to obligation rights, the court may also be where the obligation was born.[915] This application has revealed quite problematic in electronic commerce because of the difficulties in identifying the server and because e-mail addresses are not physical but logical addresses. It is thought that in blockchain there are the same obstacles.

As reported in Chapter 3,[916] the location of contract formation typically corresponds to the place where the last act necessary to make the contract binding occurs. So, one could infer it from the rules determining the time of conclusion of distance contracts. When parties conclude their contracts using the blockchain, it was affirmed that one could compare such a conclusion to the exchange of data messages through e-mails. Indeed, every contracting party sends messages using a system of double-keys and after having opened a blockchain account. It was argued that, according to the applicable rule, the contract is concluded when the offeree sends the transaction of acceptance (dispatch rule) or when the transaction of acceptance can be retrieved by the offeree's account (receipt and actual notice rule).[917] Therefore, the place of contract formation should be that of the sending or receiving electronic address.

Similarly to the conclusion of contracts through the Internet, blockchain accounts are logical, and not physical. The location of blockchain nodes that record blockchain transactions may be everywhere. However, the answer may vary depending on the use of the blockchain and the way of contract conclusion.

---

914 Section 2.3.
915 Art. 20 of the Italian Code of Civil Procedure.
916 Section 2.1.
917 Chapter 4, Section 2.1.

As observed In Chapter 4, contract conclusion does not always take place on the chain.[918] Taking into account the four scenarios, this is the case of scenario 1 and 3. Instead, in scenarios 2 and 4, the conclusion of the contract is outside the blockchain. Namely, contracts conclusion can be online or offline. In the former case, the issue has regard to electronic commerce on the Internet. In the latter hypothesis, addresses are physical.

From the above, one could derive that blockchain technology does not represent further problems when contracting parties use it as a means to perform previously concluded contracts. When parties conclude contracts on the chain, the issue does not diverge from those concluded online.

On this point, some rules establish that the place of dispatch or receipt of electronic messages is deemed to be that of the party's business or administration.[919] Also, here, as is for Internet contracts, this location may be unknown because the parties are unknown. Section 3.2 focuses on the place of business and administration.

### 3.1. Location of contract performance.

According to the Bruxelles I-bis Regulation for civil and commercial matters, contract performance location may be a criterion to establish competent jurisdiction in matters relating to a contract. In the case of sale of goods, the place of performance of the obligation is where under the contract the goods were delivered or should have been delivered. In the case of provision of services, the place is where the services were provided under the contract or should have been provided. Moreover, Article 20 of the Italian Code of Civil Procedure on jurisdiction *ratione loci* states that for cases related to obligation rights, the court may also be that of the place where the obligation has to be performed.

Establishing the place of contract performance in blockchain might be a difficult task because it is dematerialised. Equally to the Internet, blockchain technology is a medium, not a place.

However, it is thought that one should pay attention to the subject matter of the obligation. The previous chapter[920] talked about native-blockchain assets. The latter are supplied on-chain, through transactions that move those assets from an account to another. Because they are sup-

918 Section 2.

919 See Chapter 3, Section 2.3.

920 Chapter 5, Part 2, Section 5.

plied in a virtual context, performance is not an adequate connecting factor. When the execution of the contract needs a link between the blockchain and the outside, it is further distinguished between goods and services that have to be supplied online or off-line. The former case falls within direct e-commerce on the Internet. In the second, the execution of the contract takes place in the physical world. Therefore, in the latter case, there are no impediments applying a parameter based on territoriality, like in indirect e-commerce.

In light of this, one can assume that blockchain technology does not raise further juridical issues than those related to the advent of the Internet.

The location of contract performance is a special jurisdiction under the Bruxelles I-*bis* Regulation. According to the general provisions, one shall look at the domicile of the defendant. Similarly, Article 20 of the Italian Code of Civil Procedure provides an alternative jurisdiction. The general rule is set down in Article 18 and 19. It states that the jurisdiction is that of the defendant's residence or domicile (for natural persons) or that of the place where the defendant has its registered office, establishment or an authorised representative for legal proceedings (for legal persons).

### 3.2. Place of residence, domicile, business, and administration.

European Regulations, International Conventions, and the Italian legal system usually adopt the place of residence, domicile, business, or administration as a basis for determining the jurisdiction or applicable law.[921] All these have in common the fact that they imply party's identification, being it a business, a consumer, a natural or a legal person. For this reason, someone considers that blockchain technology hinders the application of the present rules because of the pseudo-anonymous character of blockchain participants.

About the combination blockchain/anonymity, it has been already clarified that the latter is not essential to the functioning of the former.[922] Indeed, in permissioned blockchains, access is based on pre-authentication. Moreover, as demonstrated through the analysis of the four scenarios,

921 Chapter 3, Section 2.3.
922 Chapter 5, Part 1, Section 8.

contracting parties are not necessarily unknown.[923] The results of such analysis are also illustrated hereinafter.

In scenarios 2 and 4, one contracting party uses the blockchain as backend. The smart contract is the mean to perform a contract concluded outside of the blockchain. In particular, parties may conclude off-line or online contracts. As regards the first modality, the contracting parties likely know each other. If the contract is concluded on-line, for instance, by access to a website, the other party's location is unknown. The issue is not connected to blockchain technology but digital identities in electronic commerce on the Internet. As already seen, there are legal instruments that allow or favour identification, both at the international and European levels.[924]

Scenario 3 is a permissioned scenario. The parties built a permissioned blockchain for their purposes. There is a higher level of trust between the parties because they already know each other. In scenario 1, it is most probable that parties do not know each other. Indeed, they enter a blockchain platform anonymously to conclude contracts with other anonymous blockchain participants. It is believed that the situation is comparable to contract conclusion on the Internet through online platforms or websites. Therefore, present rules about information requirements or the use of other methods of identification are applicable.

Again, the problem of jurisdiction and applicable law is sometimes false, while other times it is analogous to that of online commerce.

## *4. Online Dispute Resolution.*

Alternative Dispute Resolutions (ADRs) have been developed to solve disputes without going to court. Online Dispute Resolutions (ODRs), instead, are ADRs that take place online. Like ADRs, ODRs are efficient, fast, and low-cost ways of resolving disputes. Moreover, they are particularly apt to e-commerce because of the particular mean used that allows communications between parties located in different countries.[925] Indeed, usually the complainant party submits the claim through the Internet by filling an electronic form. The competent entity receives the request and puts in contact with the claimant and the other party. Subsequent communications

923 Chapter 5, Part 1, Section 8.
924 See Chapter 3, Section 2.1.2.
925 See Chapter 3, Section 2.3.

occur online, such as by an exchange of e-mails or video-calls. There are different kinds of ODRs. Some are adaptations of traditional ADRs, such as mediation or arbitration, to a virtual environment. Others are typical, such as Blind Negotiation[926] or Peer Pressure.[927]

In Europe, Article 17 of the e-Commerce Directive provides that 'Member States shall ensure that, in the event of disagreement between an information society service provider and the recipient of the service, their legislation does not hamper the use of out-of-court schemes, available under national law, for dispute settlement, including appropriate electronic means'.[928] In this respect, Regulation (EU) 524/2013 of the European

---

926 Blind Negotiation consists of exchanging proposals and counter-proposals to negotiate an amount of money in dispute. The offers are secret and are disclosed only if they match certain standards. More specifically, when the offers of both parties come within a predetermined range or a given amount of money, software settles the dispute in the midpoint of the offers.

927 Peer Pressure is a complaint against a supplier/service provider that the consumer/user can forward to the ODR provider. The ODR forwards the complaint to the provider. If the provider does not answer or denies any responsibility, the ODR publishes the dispute files on the website inviting the community to express an opinion.

928 The European Union has long expressed its interest in electronic out-of-court dispute resolution procedures. The Commission Recommendation of 4 April 2001 on the principles for out-of-court bodies involved in the consensual resolution of consumer disputes (2001/310/EC) [2001] OJ L 109/56 observes that 'The continuing development of new forms of commercial practices involving consumers such as electronic commerce, and the expected increase in cross-border transactions, require that particular attention be paid to generating the confidence of consumers, in particular by ensuring easy access to practical, effective and inexpensive means of redress, including access by electronic means' (recital 2). The Green Paper on alternative dispute resolution in civil and commercial law presented by the Commission on 19 April 2002 considers that 'ADR is a political priority, repeatedly declared by the European Union institutions, whose task is to promote these alternative techniques, to ensure an environment propitious to their development and to do what it can to guarantee quality. This political priority was specifically asserted in the context of the information society, where the role of new on-line dispute resolution (ODR) services has been recognised as a form of web-based cross-border dispute resolution'. Directive 2008/52/EC of the European Parliament and of the Council of 21 May 2008 on certain aspects of mediation in civil and commercial matters [2008] OJ L 136/3 affirms that it 'should not in any way prevent the use of modern communication technologies in the mediation process' (recital 9).
In Italy, Art. 141 of the Italian Consumer Code implementing Directive 2013/11/EU on Consumer ADR specifies that it also applies to electronic national or cross-border out-of-court dispute resolution procedures.

Parliament and of the Council on online dispute resolution for consumer disputes (Regulation on Consumer ODR) is important.[929] The Regulation applies to the out-of-court resolution of consumers' disputes against traders covered by Directive 2013/11/EU of the European Parliament and of the Council of 21 May 2013 on alternative dispute resolution for consumer disputes (Directive on consumer ADR).[930] The Regulation aims at giving consumers a simple, efficient, fast, and low-cost instrument to solve disputes arising from online transactions because they usually lack such mechanisms. The absence of electronic means of resolution of disputes acts as a barrier to cross-border online transactions and hampers the development of online commerce.[931] To this end, the European Commission has developed an ODR platform, an interactive website that can be accessed electronically and free of charge in all the official languages of the institutions of the Union.[932] The platform provides electronic complaint forms that the complainant can fill.[933] The form then reaches the trader.[934] Both the trader and the consumer have to agree on an ADR entity.[935] If the parties reach such an agreement, and the ADR entity agrees to deal with the dispute,[936] the ADR procedure starts and must be concluded within a specific time frame.[937] The outcome of the procedure varies according to the kind of ADR.[938]

One might suggest solving disputes arising from contracts concluded or performed through blockchain-based smart contracts using ODRs. ODRs might be suitable for the transnational and virtual nature of blockchain interactions. The following section focuses on this.

---

929 See Chapter 3, Section 2.3, n 543.

930 Recital 9.

931 Recital 8.

932 Art. 5.

933 Art. 8.

934 Art. 9.

935 According to Art. 9, the trader has 10 days to reply. Then, the reply is transmitted to the consumer, which has another ten days to answer.

936 Art. 9(7).

937 Art. 10(1)(a) by referral to Art. 8(1)(e) of Directive 2013/11/EU.

938 For instance, arbitration concludes with a binding decision, mediation with an agreement.

### 4.1. Blockchain and ODR.

According to Article 2 of the Regulation on Consumer ODR, the Regulation applies to the out-of-court resolution of disputes concerning contractual obligations stemming from online sales or service contracts. Article 4(1)(e) of the Regulation specifies that 'online sales or service contract' means a sales or service contract concluded online, on a website or other electronic means. The Regulation does not apply to disputes arising from contracts concluded offline.[939] From this follows that the Regulation may apply to contracts concluded on-chain, or off-chain with other electronic means. It may not apply to contracts concluded off-line and performed through the record and execution of a smart contract on a blockchain.[940]

The Regulation applies to disputes between a business and a consumer. The consumer has to be resident in the Union and the trader has to be established in the Union.[941] These rules imply the identification of the parties and are conceived on a territorial basis. The intervention of an ADR entity solves disputes according to Directive 2013/11/EU on Consumer ADR. Article 8(2) establishes that the complainant party must submit to the ODR platform the information to determine the competent ADR entity. Such competence can be geographically defined, according to the consumer's domicile or the place of fulfilment of the contract.[942] Lastly, the applicable law in cross-border disputes is determined according to the Rome I Regulation.[943]

---

939 Recital 15.

940 The various ways of contract conclusion in the blockchain realm were illustrated in Chapter 4, Section 2.

941 The place of establishment of the trader is his place of business, in case he is a natural person; if the trader is a company or other legal person or association of natural or legal persons, the establishment is where it has its statutory seat, central administration or place of business, including a branch, agency or any other establishment (Art. 4(2) by referral to Art. 4(2) of Directive 2013/11/EU).

942 Morais Carvalho, Campos Carvalho (n 543) 258. For instance, Article 4(1) of the Italian Legislative Decree No. 28 of 4 March 2010 on mediation establishes that the competent body is that of the place of the court with territorial jurisdiction.

943 Art. 11(1)(b) states that 'in a situation involving a conflict of laws, where the law applicable to the sales or service contract is determined in accordance with Article 6(1) and (2) of Regulation (EC) No 593/2008, the solution imposed by the ADR entity shall not result in the consumer being deprived of the protection afforded to him by the provisions that cannot be derogated from by agreement by virtue of the law of the Member State in which he is habitually resident'; Art. 11(1)(c) dictates that 'in a situation involving a conflict of laws, where the law applicable to the sales or service contract is determined in accordance

In light of the above and the absence of an agreement of the parties, the recourse to ODR resolution systems does not solve the alleged problem of anonymity and a-territoriality of blockchain technology to resolve cross-border disputes. Like the rules concerning the choice of jurisdiction and applicable law when the claim is activated in front of a court, the identification of the parties and other territorial parameters are important to establish the competent ODR entity and set the procedural and substantial rules that the latter has to consider.[944]

In addition, ODR resolution procedures do not prevent parties to address their claims in front of a jurisdictional court.[945]

In summary, also ODR procedures are based on national law. So, they are constraint within territorial borders, which can lead to complications in transnational situations.[946] To face this, in 2010 the UNCITRAL created the Working Group III on ODR, which in 2016 developed the Technical Notes on Online Dispute Resolution. However, the latter only contains some general concepts and elements of ODR proceedings. Indeed, the UNCITRAL did not pursue its initial aim to develop an international set of procedural rules including guidelines and minimum standards for ODR entities, substantive legal principles for resolving disputes, and a cross-border enforcement mechanism.[947] Moreover, they have a non-binding nature.

---

with Article 5(1) to (3) of the Rome Convention of 19 June 1980 on the law applicable to contractual obligations, the solution imposed by the ADR entity shall not result in the consumer being deprived of the protection afforded to him by the mandatory rules of the law of the Member State in which he is habitually resident'.

944 Clément (n 720) 285, discussing the possibility of alternative dispute resolution mechanisms for smart contracts argues that 'the selection and institution of panels in charge of arbitration and more generally the rules followed by these panels are difficult to create without reference to a legal system'.

945 According to recital 26 of the Regulation on Consumer ODR, 'ODR is not intended to and cannot be designed to replace court procedures, nor should it deprive consumers or traders of their rights to seek redress before the courts. This Regulation should not, therefore, prevent parties from exercising their right of access to the judicial system'.

946 R. Koulu, 'Blokchains and Online Dispute Resolution: Smart Contracts as an Alternative to Enforcement' (2016) 13 SCRIPTed 40, 43.

947 The Working Group changed its initial mandate because of disagreements on the nature of the final phase due to the differences between the national jurisdictions. The steps of the work are illustrated in the reports of each session and are available at the following link <https://uncitral.un.org/en/working_groups/3/online_dispute> accessed 1 October 2021.

## *5. Findings and conclusions.*

The chapter focused on the choice of jurisdiction and applicable law in disputes concerning cross-border contracts whose conclusion or performance occurs through blockchain-based smart contracts. Some scholars have identified some incompatibilities between blockchain characteristics and existing rules. More specifically, the anonymity of the parties and problems in the exact localisation of the nodes would hinder identifying the connecting factors.

The study was conducted by considering the current criteria of determination of jurisdiction and applicable law set down in the European and Italian legal framework, as illustrated in Chapter 3, Section 2.3. Namely, those criteria were grouped in the location of contract formation, location of contract performance, and place of residence, domicile, business, and administration.

It first resulted from the above that in some cases blockchain technology does not pose any obstacles. The location of contract formation is easily determinable when the parties conclude their contract offline and use a smart contract to perform it. Indeed, addresses are physical. As concerns the location of contract performance, there are no impediments when the execution of the contract has to take place outside the blockchain and in the real world. Finally, the assumption that in blockchain the contracting party cannot identify the other is incorrect. Anonymity is not an essential feature of blockchain technology. Moreover, it depends on the modality of contract conclusion. For instance, if the contract is concluded off-line, it is more likely that the parties will have the chance to identify each other.

Secondly, it was observed that the problematic issues do not diverge from those related to electronic commerce on the Internet. When parties conclude their contract using a blockchain, one could compare such a conclusion to exchanging data messages through e-mails. Every contracting party sends messages using a system of double-keys and after having opened a blockchain account. Blockchain accounts, like e-mail addresses or IP addresses, are logical and not physical. Blockchain nodes, like servers, may be located everywhere. Therefore, as happened with the Internet, one should consider the party's location as the place of dispatch or receipt of electronic messages to identify the place of contract conclusion.

However, parties's identification is not always possible. Thus, one cannot even establish residence, domicile, business, or administration of the party. In reality, the matter falls within that of digital identities in distance contracts. As already seen, there are legal instruments to allow or favour identification that were conceived for electronic commerce on the Internet. Lastly, contract performance location might be a difficult task because, like the Internet, blockchain is not a place but a medium.

In summary, it does not seem that blockchain technology raises new issues. Old problems do not need new legal solutions and rules.

Alternatively, one might suggest the adoption of ODR mechanisms as a mean to solve disputes. ODRs might be suitable for the transnational and virtual nature of blockchain interactions. Nonetheless, the rules that govern ODRs are also conceived on a territorial basis, like private international law rules on jurisdiction and applicable law in cross-border contracts. ODRs may instead help to resolve controversies in a simple, efficient, fast, and low-cost way.

# CHAPTER 7: CONCLUSIONS

## *1. Summary of preceding conclusions.*

The study aimed at investigating the impact of blockchain-based smart contracts on contract law. In particular, the analysis considered contract formation, contract performance, jurisdiction, and applicable law in cross-border contracts.

As concerns the former, the main question was whether smart contracts could be considered legally binding contracts. Contract law requirements were correlated to the characteristics of these kinds of applications to answer the question. As clarified in the section on methodology, it was referred not to the technology as such, but to four scenarios of use of blockchain in the realm of contracts. Here, the primary discussions had regard to the possibility to conclude a contract in the form of lines of code. On this point, it was concluded that there are no legal obstacles to recognise such contracts, according to the principles of non-discrimination, freedom of form, and technological neutrality. Instead, the issue is not related to blockchain but applies to any contract. Contracts could be invalid because of a lack of contractual intention or fundamental mistake if the case circumstances hindered the party from understanding that she would conclude a contract or the contractual terms. In electronic contracts, this is even more important given that parties conclude contracts with no traditional means. For this reason, international, European, and national regulators pay colossal attention to provide the contracting party with transparent and clear information, especially in the case of unilaterally drafted B2C contracts. For the above reasons, and not counting the actual impossibility to technically embed the complexity of entire contracts into a computer program, it was argued that a natural language version of the contract should accompany the encoded one, at least until the spread of negotiations by machines.

Also, the written form has a warning function. Legal systems usually prescribe the written form in particularly relevant contracts, which require the identification of the parties and guarantees of provenance and integrity of contractual declarations. In electronic contracts, this can be achieved thanks to technical arrangements. Therefore, adequate design solutions would allow reaching compliance of blockchain-based smart contracts with contract law.

Lastly, the exchange between offer and acceptance, their revocation, and the time of conclusion of the contract acquire relevance when contracts are concluded on-chain. Indeed, blockchain is not a mere database to record pre-existing agreements but a mean of contract conclusion. In the latter hypothesis, it was found that contracts formed on-chain are nothing more than distance contracts concluded by electronic means through the exchange of data messages.

Moving to contract performance, it was deepened the matter of self-enforcement of smart contracts and the suitability of existing rules on contractual liability. The latter has the function to induce the other party to perform the contract under the threat of law enforcement. Instead, in blockchain-based smart contracts, the creditor has not to trust that the other party performs the contract. The obliged party is not in control of the execution of the code. The creditor trusts that the code executes properly. It is said that there is a shift from trust in the other party to trust in the code. This view was criticised.

First of all, it was demonstrated that the decentralisation and immutability of the blockchain, combined with the self-execution of smart contracts, cannot give rise to breach-less contracts. Furthermore, thanks to some clarifications on the real meaning of some terms and the functioning of the technology, and by taking into account the four scenarios, it was ascertained that trust is still in the other party. The real difficulties derive from the multiple components of blockchain applications and the unknowledge on the identity of the involved parties, which complicates to identify where actual responsibilities lye, mainly in permissionless blockchains. However, this is not peculiar to the blockchain. As seen in Chapter 3, the same problems affect computer contracts. It is essential to correctly classify the contract, carefully analyse the contractual conditions, and verify the validity of potential clauses limiting or excluding liability.

Part 2 of Chapter 5 was dedicated to the immutability of blockchain and the impossibility to stop or modify the smart contract in case of a need of ex-post interventions on the contract, such as invalidity, termination, rescission, withdrawal, or renegotiation. After having specified that blockchain is not exactly immutable, and the techniques to amend it that are under development, it was argued that the impossibility to stop the execution of the smart contract on the blockchain does not always imply that the party cannot halt the performance of the contract. It depends on the subject matter of the obligation and on the capability to govern the system. Indeed, as also clarified in Part 1 of Chapter 5, blockchain has a closed nature, and cannot manage what happens outside of it. Besides, decentralised technology does not necessarily mean decentralised governance.

Even though the smart contract continues to execute, it was noticed that the other party could claim for the restitution of what performed *sine causa* under existing rules; if restitution in kind is impossible, the law provides the payment of a sum of money. Alternatively, the parties may *ex-ante* agree to renounce to ex-post interventions on the contract under the principle of contractual autonomy. However, the limitations to the latter principle in favour of other overriding values have been put in evidence. Even when the law admits derogations, the renounce has not to be contrary to the principle of good faith and fair dealing. More specifically, it must be ensured that the party that is negatively affected by the renounce expressed informed consent. It has to be ensured that the disadvantaged party understood or ought to have understood the terms of the exclusion of the right to ask the modification or elimination of the contract.

Finally, about jurisdiction and applicable law in cross-border contracts, the overall conclusion was that blockchain technology does not raise further issues than those related to electronic commerce on the Internet. Again, problematic issues are not specific to blockchain but rather apply to open networks in general, where users communicate at a distance, identities are unknown, and operations occur virtually.

Alongside this, it was highlighted that in some cases, blockchain technology does not pose any obstacles. Namely, the location of contract formation is readily determinable when the parties conclude their contract offline and use a smart contract to perform it because addresses are physical and not logical. There are no impediments to identify the location of contract performance when the execution of the contract takes place in the real world, outside the blockchain. Then depending on the modality of contract conclusion, it might be that the parties had the chance to identify each other (e.g. the contract is concluded off-line).

This section has summarised the conclusions made above in Chapters 4, 5, and 6. The next sections start from such considerations to make some concluding remarks.

*2. False myths surrounding blockchain and smart contracts.*

The study showed some false myths surrounding blockchain and smart contracts, which might determine some confusion among legal experts. It was attempted to clarify them to make a proper legal analysis. It is believed that such misunderstandings mainly derive from the use of some terms that can have different meanings in different fields and the anarchist ideology of the group that first promoted the development of this new technology.

The first false myth is that blockchain technology is characterised by an absence of any form of central control because of its 'decentralisation'. Instead, decentralisation means that the nodes where the copies of the database are distributed can independently verify and validate transactions that update the database state and independently recreate the entire transaction history by sharing a consensus protocol. The consensus protocol is a software run by all network nodes that pre-establishes the rules to update the ledger. There is not a central 'master copy' of the database.

Decentralised technology is not synonymous with decentralised management and control over the technology. For instance, if a company decides to invest and build its blockchain, it controls the nodes of the network (the hardware) and the consensus protocol (the software).

In the contractual domain, because of blockchain decentralisation, it is affirmed that the parties cannot control the execution of the smart contract. This assumption is not accurate. For example, in scenario 4 the smart contract code is recorded and executed in a permissioned database that the obliged party uses as back end. So, the obliged party can influence the execution of the code because it holds the entire infrastructure (both hardware and software). The same example is also valid to admit that blockchain decentralisation does not always imply an impossibility to intervene on the blockchain to stop or modify the code when the contract has to be eliminated or amended.

The second false myth is that blockchain technology solves a lack of trust in legal relationships because trust is in the system. In contracts, it is argued that with blockchain, the aggrieved party has no more need no trust that the obliged party performs the contract because trust is in the code.

Blockchain is reliable because it guarantees data integrity and provenance thanks to the combination of concatenated hash, asymmetric cryptography, and distribution. For this reason, smart contracts (codes) cannot be altered, and the blockchain guarantees reliable execution of the smart contract code. However, secure execution is not the same as a secure performance of the contract.

First of all, blockchain technology cannot avoid malfunctions of the code or erroneous translations of the parties' will. Malfunctions may also affect other components of the blockchain application. Secondly, the execution of the code and execution of the contract do not coincide. Technically speaking, execution of code means that a computer follows the instructions of a computer program. So, the execution of the code might be reliable, but not match with the operations needed to perform the agreed contract. Moreover, blockchain is a closed database that has not the ability to manage what happens outside. Thus, the smart contract could give the right output, but the necessary actions do not follow the latter in the off-chain world. All these circumstances have in common the breach of the contract because of someone else's unreliability.

The third false myth is that in blockchain, participants are anonymous. Apart from permissioned blockchains where access is subject to preselection and identification, it should be better to talk about pseudonymity. According to the definition of the GDPR, "pseudonymisation' means the processing of personal data in such a manner that the personal data can no longer be attributed to a specific data subject without the use of additional information, provided that such additional information is kept separately and is subject to technical and organisational measures to ensure that the personal data are not attributed to an identified or identifiable natural person' (Article 4(1)(5)). In the blockchain, it is not unusual that the keys are ascribable to precise identities. There are some techniques, some trivial, other more complex, to trace back to the data.

Anonymity is not an essential blockchain characteristic. Asymmetric cryptography for blockchain inventors had the political scope to transact anonymously to escape from the control of traditional institutions. Of course, if permissionless blockchains are also public, i.e. everyone can see the transactions, there is an interest in maintaining users' privacy. However, anonymity is not a prerequisite to taking advantage of blockchain potentials. Asymmetric cryptography only serves to guarantee data provenance and integrity. Nothing hinders to connect public keys with corresponding identities. As was seen from the analysis of the scenarios, sometimes the contracting parties already know each other.

### 3. *Applicability of existing rules.*

The second main result of the research is that existing rules apply to blockchain-based smart contracts. It emerged thanks to a careful attempt to understand the technology, the recalling of the evolution of contract law with the development of the technology, the clarifications of the above false myths, and the focus on some concrete scenarios of use of such applications for the conclusion/performance of contracts.

Concerning Chapter 4 on contract formation, it was outlined that, according to the definition of contract, the agreement can occur off-chain or on-chain. In the former case, traditional rules apply. In the latter, the parties exchange their offer and acceptance using data messages. These data messages are sent from electronic addresses and signed with cryptographic keys. The parties do not use an instantaneous means of communication (such as the telephone), but they are absent and a specific time passes between offer and acceptance. There is no difference in electronic commerce. Therefore, the interpretation given to traditional rules to suit the electronic context also applies to blockchain-based smart contracts to identify the offer, the acceptance, and the time of conclusion of the contract. The on-the-chain conclusion of contracts also falls within the scope of the e-Commerce Directive, the Consumer Rights Directive, and the international, European, and national rules on electronic documents and signatures.

The matters of contractual intention and understandability of the contractual conditions also belong to electronic commerce. Similarities have been found between on-chain and wrap contracts because of the non-traditional way of presenting the offer and expressing assent. For this reason, information requirements laid down in the e-Commerce Directive and Consumer Rights Directive are useful to ensure awareness and comprehensibility of contract terms, especially for the weakest party, even in this context.

Regarding contract performance, it was argued that trust is still in the other party. Indeed, the breach of the contract is ascribable to problems in the functioning of the blockchain application of which the contracting party is responsible: or directly because the contracting party provided the application; or indirectly, because the contracting party assumed the risk of adopting such an instrument. In the latter case, the debtor can turn to the third-party service provider.

Regarding *ex-post* interventions on the contract, it was observed that the immutability of blockchain and the impossibility to modify or stop the code of the smart contract do not hinder the application of the existing discipline. If the smart contract cannot directly perform the contract because there is a need for interactions with the off-chain world, the fact that the smart contract code continues to execute is irrelevant. The execution of the smart contract code cannot determine any consequences if other actions do not follow its outputs. Consequently, ex-post interventions on the contract are practicable. When the smart contract can directly perform the contract because it can take place entirely inside the chain (such as a payment in virtual currencies), it was nevertheless considered that the performance of an invalid, terminated, rescinded, withdrawn, or renegotiated contract is unjustified. When performance occurs *sine causa*, the recipient of the undue performance must return it, and the performing party has a corresponding right to ask for the restitution of what performed. If restitution is not possible, she has the right to receive a reasonable sum of money.

Regarding the choice of jurisdiction and applicable law in cross-border contracts, legal experts do not suggest adopting different rules, even though they highlight some difficulties of application of existing ones, which are approached in the next section.

## 4. *Open issues.*

Acknowledged that existing rules seem to be suitable to blockchain-based smart legal contracts, some issues remain open. However, they are not peculiar to the blockchain.

The first one is the difficulty to identify blockchain users. There might be some cases where the contracting parties do not know each other, as seen from the analysis of the scenarios. Identification is difficult because negotiations occur at a distance behind the veil of anonymous accounts. It prevents identifying the subject against which to start a dispute for the breach of the contract or to address a claim for restitution of what received *sine causa*, as discussed in Chapter 5, Part 1 and 2. Moreover, it hinders the application of the rules that state the place of residence, domicile, business, or administration to determine the jurisdiction or applicable law in cross-border contracts. The matter does not diverge from digital identity in electronic commerce addressed in Chapter 3, Section 2.1.2. Consequently, it must be tackled with the same legal instruments, such as the duty to give some information as laid down in the e-Commerce Directive or Consumer Rights Directive, electronic signatures and other digital identification means. On the latter, the study mentioned the European e-IDAS Regulation and the commitments of the UNCITRAL Working Group IV on Electronic Commerce.

As explained in Chapter 6, localising the place of contract formation and performance may be difficult in the blockchain. Again, such obstacles involve overall virtual networks. A comparison between Chapter 3, Section 2.3, and Chapter 6, Sections 3 and 3.1 corroborates this affirmation.

### 5. *Research question answers.*

In light of the above results, it is argued that blockchain-based smart legal contracts do not generate any new questions that require further regulatory responses. Current contract law applies. The study revealed that existing rules are still suitable and also fix the blockchain context. It is believed that most of the legal questionings that have arisen among legal experts are only apparent and can be removed through the clarifications of some false myths surrounding blockchain and smart contracts. The remaining ones are not particularly peculiar of blockchain but rather are comparable to some problematic issues concerning electronic commerce and smart contracts in general, even without the blockchain. Thus, they can be addressed together.

From this follows that the legislators do not need to implement a specific legal regime. Instead, Italy has introduced Article 8-*ter* of Law no. 12/2019. Article 8-*ter*(2) defines 'smart contract' as a computer program that runs on distributed ledger technologies and whose execution automatically binds two or more parties on the base of predefined effects. Moreover, as seen in Chapter 4, Section 5, smart contracts satisfy the requirement of the written form upon prior IT identification of the interested parties through a process that meets the requirements set by the *Agenzia per l'Italia Digitale* (AGID) with guidelines. This article has been criticised because it gives a restrictive definition of 'smart contract', which is confined to DLTs and does not consider that smart contracts can also rely on other technologies. Furthermore, while they are defined as mere 'computer programs', it is established that they can 'bind' the parties, thus making one wonder whether to interpret a smart contract as an execution tool of a pre-existing contract or also as a 'contract' in the civil law meaning.[948]

948 European Commission, 'Study on Blockchains: Legal, Governance and Interoperability Aspects' (n 11) 68.

About the written form, it has been already affirmed that the Article is very similar to Article 20 of the Italian Code of the Digital Administration (Codice dell'Amministrazione Digitale, CAD), even though it generically refers to a process upon prior identification of the parties without setting any requirements. The latter determination is left to the AGID that has not issued any guidelines yet. The absence of guidelines, combined with the fact that the article does not refer to electronic signatures, might inhibit the development of smart contracts in Italy.[949]

More generally, it is considered that a regulatory approach would be superfluous. As expressed in the Introduction, new rules might be counter-productive because they might generate overlaps, interpretational difficulties, and fragmentation. In sum, they might exacerbate legal uncertainty and discourage investments.

At most, enabling rules might boost entrepreneurs' reliance on legal compliance of blockchain solutions. For instance, the Arizona House Bill 2417 of 2017 prevents electronic records from being denied legal effects solely because they include a smart contract term. The already cited 2017 UNCITRAL Model Law on Electronic Transferable Records provides that its rules apply to various types of electronic transferable records, included those based on distributed ledger technology; besides, it recognises that the linking of a blockchain pseudonym with other elements that allow revealing the underlying identity, could satisfy the requirement to identify the signatory. Such rules do not add anything to existing ones, but they may orient interpretation.[950]

---

949 An overall critical analysis of Article 8-*ter* of Law no. 12/2019 can be found in C. Bomprezzi, 'Commento in materia di Blockchain e Smart contract alla luce del nuovo Decreto Semplificazioni' (2019) Diritto Mercato Tecnologia <https://www.dimt.it/news/breve-commento-alla-legge-11-febbraio-2019-n-12-di-conversione-del-decreto-legge-14-dicembre-2018-n-135-recante-disposizioni-urgenti-in-materia-di-sostegno-e-semplificazione-per-le-imprese-e-per-la-pu/> accessed 1 October 2021.

950 Taking into account general blockchain-based applications (apart from the use of smart contracts in the contractual realm), there are examples of enabling regulation. For instance, in France, Articles L.223 – 12 and L.223 – 13 of Ordinance No. 2016–520 of 28 April 2016 (*Ordonnance n° 2016–520 du 28 avril 2016 relative aux bons de caisse*) provide that saving bonds can be transmitted by means of a shared electronic registration device (in French: '*dispositif d'enregistremen électronique partagé*'). Then, France has approved the Blockchain Ordinance No. 2017–1674 (*Ordonnance n° 2017–1674 du 8 décembre 2017 relative à l'utilisation d'un dispositif d'enregistrement électronique partagé pour la représentation et la transmission de titres financiers*). It extends the list of the financial securities that can be registered in the blockchain (beyond saving bonds) and

Standards development can support the spread of compliant-by-design solutions, such as standard terms and conditions or model contracts that the regulation can subsequently endorse. Lastly, it would be desirable to address the matter at an International or European level. The sole definitions of blockchains and smart contracts are not uniform in the various countries, and there is a need for more clarity about that. The work of ISO/TC 307, which recently published a document providing fundamental terminology for blockchain and distributed ledger technologies,[951] goes in that direction.[952]

---

subjects the company issuing the securities to French Law. Luxembourg has licensed digital currency exchange platforms as financial institutions (the first European country to do so). The *Loi du 1er mars 2019 portant modification de la loi modifiée du 1er août 2001 concernant la circulation de titres* (known as 'Bill 7363') added Article 18*bis* to the Luxembourgish securities law to include tokens stored in a blockchain within dematerialised securities (<https://chd.lu/wps/portal/public/Accueil/TravailALaChambre/Recherche/RoleDesAffaires?action=doDocpaDetails&backto=/wps/portal/public/Accueil/Actualite/ALaUne/&id=7363> accessed 1 October 2021). For more details and to get an overall picture of similar regulations in European countries, see European Union Blockchain Observatory & Forum, 'EU Blockchain Ecosystem Developments', 20 November 2020 <https://www.eublockchainforum.eu/sites/default/files/reports/EU%20Blockchain%20Ecosystem%20Report_final_0.pdf> accessed 1 October 2021.

951 ISO 22739:2020 (n 779).

952 As already seen, the Proposal for a Regulation amending Regulation eIDAS provides a definition of electronic ledger (n 393).

# BIBLIOGRAPHY


## A) CASES

CJEU CASES

Case C-144/09, *Hotel Alpenhof GesmbH v. Oliver Heller* ECLI:EU:C:2010:740, [2010] ECR I-12527

Case C-585/08, *Pammer v. Reederei Karl Schlüter GmbH & KG* ECLI:EU:C:2010:740, [2010] ECR I-12527

ITALIAN CASES

Cassazione Civile, Sezione II, 18 October 2018, No. 26618

Cassazione Civile, Sezione III, 13 February 2015, No. 2868

Cassazione Civile, Sezione III, 18 June 1980, No. 3866

## B) LEGAL SOURCES

INTERNATIONAL LEGAL SOURCES

ISO 22739:2020 Blockchain and distributed ledger technologies – Vocabulary

ISO/TR 23244:2020 Blockchain and distributed ledger technologies – Privacy and personally identifiable information protection considerations

ISO/TR 23455:2019 Blockchain and distributed ledger technologies – Overview of and interactions between smart contracts in blockchain and distributed ledger technology systems

ISO/TR 23576:2020 Blockchain and distributed ledger technologies – Security management of digital asset custodians

Principles of European Tort Law (PETL)

UNCITRAL Model Law on Electronic Commerce (1996) with additional article 5 bis as adopted in 1998

UNCITRAL Model Law on Electronic Transferable Records (2017)

UNCITRAL Technical Notes on Online Dispute Resolution (2016)

United Nations Convention on Contracts for the International Sale of Goods (Vienna, 1980) (CISG)

United Nations Convention on the Use of Electronic Communications in International Contracts (New York, 23 November 2005)

United Nations Economic Commission for Europe Working Party on Facilitation of International Trade Procedures (WP4), Model Interchange Agreement for the International Commercial Use of Electronic Data Interchange (1991) Trade/ WP.4/R.697 <https://www.unece.org/tradewelcome/un-centre-for-trade-facilitation-and-e-business-uncefact/outputs/standards/unedifact/tradeedifactrules/part-2-uniform-rules-of-conduct-for-interchange-of-trade-data-by-teletransmission-uncid/part-2-uncid-chapter-4-annex.html> accessed 1 October 2021

## EUROPEAN LEGAL SOURCES

1980 Rome Convention on the law applicable to contractual obligations (consolidated version) [1998] OJ C 27/34

Answer of the Commission of the European Communities of 15 November 1988 to Written Question No. 706/88 by Mr. Gijs De Vries (LDR/NL) (89/C 114/76) [1989] OJ C114/42

Commission Implementing Decision (EU) 2016/650 of 25 April 2016 laying down standards for the security assessment of qualified signature and seal creation devices pursuant to Articles 30(3) and 39(2) of Regulation (EU) No 914/2014 of the European Parliament and of the Council on electronic identification and trust services for electronic transactions in the internal market [2016] OJ L 109/40.

Commission of the European Communities, Green Paper on alternative dispute resolution in civil and commercial law presented by the Commission on 19 April 2002 COM(2002) 196 final

Commission Recommendation of 19 October 1994 relating to the legal aspects of electronic data interchange (94/820/EC) [1994] OJ 338/98

Commission Recommendation of 4 April 2001 on the principles for out-of-court bodies involved in the consensual resolution of consumer disputes (2001/310/EC) [2001] OJ L 109/56

Communication from the Commission to the Council, the European Parliament, the Economic and Social Committee and the Committee of the Regions, A European Initiative in Electronic Commerce, COM(97) 157 final

Communication from the Commission to the European Parliament, the European Council, the Council, the European Economic and Social Committee and the Committee of the Regions, Artificial Intelligence for Europe, {SWD(2018) 137 final}

Council Directive (EC) 1999/93 on a community framework for electronic signatures [2000] OJ L13/12

Council Directive 93/13/EEC of 5 April 1993 on unfair terms in consumer contracts [1993] OJ L95/29

Council Directive of 25 July 1985 on the approximation of the laws, regulations and administrative provisions of the Member States concerning liability for defective products 85/374/EEC [1985] OJ L 210/29

DG Justice Guidance Document concerning Directive 2011/83/EU of the European Parliament and of the Council of 25 October 2011 on consumer rights, amending Council Directive 93/13/EEC and Directive 1999/44/EC of the European Parliament and of the Council and repealing Council Directive 85/577/EEC and Directive 97/7/EC of the European Parliament and of the Council

Directive (EC) 31/2000 on certain legal aspects of information society services, in particular electronic commerce, in the Internal Market [2000] OJ L 178/1

Directive (EU) 2019/2161 of the European Parliament and of the Council of 27 November 2019 amending Council Directive 93/13/EEC and Directives 98/6/EC, 2005/29/EC and 2011/83/EU of the European Parliament and of the Council as regards the better enforcement and modernisation of Union consumer protection rules [2019] OJ L 328/7

Directive (EU) 2019/770 on certain aspects concerning contracts for the supply of digital content and digital services [2019] OJ L 136/1

Directive (EU) 2019/771 on certain aspects concerning contracts for the sale of goods amending Regulation (EU) 2017/2394 and Directive 2009/22/EC and repealing Directive 1999/44/EC [2019] OJ L 136/28

Directive 2008/52/EC of the European Parliament and of the Council of 21 May 2008 on certain aspects of mediation in civil and commercial matters [2008] OJ L 136/3

Directive 2011/83/EU of the European Parliament and of the Council of 25 October 2011 on consumer rights, amending Council Directive 93/13/EEC and Directive 1999/44/EC of the European Parliament and of the Council and repealing Council Directive 85/577/EEC and Directive 97/7/EC of the European Parliament and of the Council Text with EEA relevance [2011] OJ L 304/64

European Parliament resolution of 16 February 2017 with recommendations to the Commission on Civil Law Rules on Robotics (2015/2103(INL)), P8_TA(2017)0051

European Parliament resolution of 20 October 2020 with recommendations to the Commission on a Digital Services Act: adapting commercial and civil law rules for commercial entities operating online (2020/2019(INL))

European Parliament resolution of 20 October 2020 with recommendations to the Commission on a civil liability regime for artificial intelligence (2020/2014(INL)), p9_TA(2020)0276

European Parliament resolution of 3 October 2018 on distributed ledger technologies and blockchains: building trust with disintermediation (2017/2772(RSP))

Proposal for a Regulation of the European Parliament and of the Council amending Regulation (EU) No 910/2014 as regards establishing a framework for a European Digital Identity COM/2021/281 final

Proposal for a Regulation of the European Parliament and of the Council laying down harmonised rules on Artificial Intelligence (Artificial intelligence Act) and amending certain union legislative acts COM/2021/206 final

Proposal for a Regulation of the European Parliament and of the Council on a Single Market for Digital Services (Digital Services Act) and amending Directive 2000/31/EC COM/2020/825 final

Regulation (EC) No 593/2008 of the European Parliament and of the Council of 17 June 2008 on the law applicable to contractual obligations (Rome I) [2008] OJ L177/6

Regulation (EU) 910/2014 of the European Parliament and of the Council of 23 July 2014 on electronic identification and trust services for electronic transactions in the internal market and repealing Directive 1999/93/EC [2014] OJ L 257/73

Regulation (EU) No 524/2013 of the European Parliament and of the Council of 21 May 2013 on online dispute resolution for consumer disputes and amending Regulation (EC) No 2006/2004 and Directive 2009/22/EC (Regulation on consumer ODR) [2013] OJ L 165/1

Regulation (EU) No. 1215/2012 of the European Parliament and of the Council of 12 December 2012 on jurisdiction and the recognition and enforcement of judgments in civil and commercial matters [2012] OJ L351/1

## US LEGAL SOURCES

2017 Ariz. HB 2417

2018 Cal. AB 2658

2018 Ohio. SB 220 1306.01

2018 Tenn. SB 1662 47–10–202

Nev. Rev. Stat. Ann. § 719.090

Uniform Electronic Transaction Act (1999)

## FRENCH LEGAL SOURCES

*Ordonnance n° 2016–520 du 28 avril 2016 relative aux bons de caisse*

*Ordonnance n° 2017–1674 du 8 décembre 2017 relative à l'utilisation d'un dispositif d'enregistrement électronique partagé pour la représentation et la transmission de titres financiers*

## ITALIAN LEGAL SOURCES

*Codice Civile*

*Codice di Procedura Civile*

*D.Lgs. 7 marzo 2005, n. 82*

*Decreto del Presidente del Consiglio dei Ministri 22 febbraio 2013, Regole tecniche in materia di generazione, apposizione e verifica delle firme elettroniche avanzate, qualificate e digitali, ai sensi degli articoli 20, comma 3, 24, comma 4, 28, comma 3, 32, comma 3, lettera b), 35, comma 2, 36, comma 2, e 71*

*Decreto legislativo 9 aprile 2003, n. 70 'Attuazione della direttiva 2000/31/CE relativa a taluni aspetti giuridici dei servizi della società dell'informazione nel mercato interno, con particolare riferimento al commercio elettronico'*

*Decreto legislativo n. 206 del 6 settembre 2005*

*Determinazione n. 116/2019 del 10 maggio 2019 – Istituzione di un Gruppo di lavoro per la predisposizione delle linee guida e standard tecnici relativi alle tecnologie basate su registri distribuiti e smart contract (art. 8ter, decreto legge 14 dicembre 2018, n. 135, Disposizioni urgenti in materia di sostegno e semplificazione per le imprese e per la pubblica amministrazione, convertito con modificazioni dalla legge 11 febbraio 2019, n. 12) (AGID)* <https://trasparenza.agid.gov.it/archivio28_provvedimenti-amministrativi_0_121975_725_1.html> accessed 1 October 2021

*Legge 11 febbraio 2019, n. 12, di conversione del decreto legge 14 dicembre 2018, n. 135, recante disposizioni urgenti in materia di sostegno e semplificazione per le imprese e la pubblica amministrazione*

Legge 31 maggio 1995, n. 218, *Riforma del sistema italiano di diritto internazionale privato*

*Linee guida contenenti le regole tecniche per la sottoscrizione elettronica di documenti ai sensi dell'art. 20 del CAD* (AGID) <https://www.agid.gov.it/sites/default/files/repository_files/linee_guida_per_la_sottoscrizione_elettronica_di_documenti_ai_sensi_dellart.20_del_cad.pdf> accessed 1 October 2021

OTHER LEGAL SOURCES

*Código civil* (Spain)

*Loi du 1er mars 2019 portant modification de la loi modifiée du 1er août 2001 concernant la circulation de titres* (Luxembourg)

Malta Digital Innovation Authority Act, 2018

UK Consumer Rights Act 2015

UK Electronic Commerce (EC Directive) Regulations 2002

## C) BOOKS

Abbate J. (ed), *Inventing the Internet* (MIT Press 2000)

Amadio G.(ed), *Lezioni di diritto civile* (Giappichelli 2018)

American Bar Association, Edi and Technological Division, Section of Science and Technology, *Model Electronic Payments Agreement and Commentary: For Domestic Credit Transfers* (American Bar Association 1992)

Amro I. (ed), *Online Arbitration in Theory and in Practice – A Comparative Study of Cross-Border Commercial Transactions in Common Law and Civil Law Countries* (Cambridge Scholars Publishing 2019)

Antoniolli L., Veneziano A. (eds), *Principles of European Contract Law and Italian Law* (Kluwer Law International 2005)

Antonopoulos A. M.(ed), *Mastering Bitcoin* (2nd edn O'Reilly 2017)

Auwers W., *Des Rechtsschutz der automatischen wage nach gemeinem Recht*, dissertation printed in 1891 by the bookseller of the University of Göttingen W. F. Kastner (Hansebook 2016)

Bashir I. (ed), *Mastering Blockchain* (2nd edn Packt 2018)

Beale H., Fauvarque-Cosson B., Rutgers J., Vogenauer S. (eds), *Cases, Materials and Texts on Contract Law* (3rd edn Hart 2019)

Bianca C. M. (ed), *Diritto civile. Vol. 4: l'obbligazione* (Giuffrè, 2019)

Bianca C. M. (ed), *Diritto civile. Vol. 4: l'obbligazione* (Giuffrè, 2019)

Bianca C. M. (ed), *Diritto civile. Vol. 5: la responsabilità* (2nd edn Giuffrè 2019)

Bianca C. M. (ed), *Il contratto* (3rd edn Giuffrè 2019)

Boss A. H., Kilian W. (eds), *The United Nations Convention on the Use of Electronic Communications in International Contracts: An In-depth Guide and Sourcebook* (Wolters Kluwer 2008)

Brunner C., Gottlieb B. (eds), *Commentary on the UN Sales Law (CISG)* (Wolters Kluwer 2019)

Cicu A.(ed), *Gli automi nel diritto privato* (Società Editrice Libraria 1901)

Clarizia R. (ed), *Informatica e conclusione del contratto* (Giuffrè 1985)

Cortada J. W. (ed), *The Digital Hand: Volume II: How Computers Changed the Work of American Financial, Telecommunications, Media, and Entertainment Industries* (Oxford 2006)

D'Amico G. (ed), *"Regole di validità" e principio di correttezza nella formazione del contratto* (Jovene 1996)

Dannen C.(ed), *Introducing Ethereum and Solidity* (Apress 2017)

De Filippi P., Wright A.(eds), *Blockchchain and the law – the rule of code* (Harvard University Press 2018)

De Franceschi A. (ed), *European Contract Law and the Digital Single Market – The Implications of the Digital Revolution* (Intersentia 2016)

De Franceschi A., Schulze R. (eds), Graziadei M., Pollicino O., Riente F., Sica S., Sirena P. (co-eds), *Digital Revolution – New Challenges for Law. Data Protection, Artificial Intelligence, Smart Products, Blockchain Technology and Virtual Currencies* (Beck, Nomos 2019)

De Nova G. (ed), *Il contratto ha forza di legge* (LED Edizioni Universitarie 1993)

De Nova G. (ed), *Recesso e risoluzione nei contratti* (Giuffrè 1994)

Delfini F. (ed), *I patti sulla risoluzione per inadempimento* (Ipsoa 1998)

Delfini F., Finocchiaro G. (eds), *Identificazione elettronica e servizi fiduciari per le transazioni elettroniche nel mercato interno, commento al regolamento UE 910/2014* (Giappichelli 2017)

Ertel P., *Der Automatenmissbrauch und seine Charakterisierung als Delikt*, dissertation printed by Wilhelm Pilz, Berlin, 1898

European Union, *The Principles of European Contract Law 2002 (Parts I, II and III)* (SiSU 2002) <https://www.jus.uio.no/lm/eu.contract.principles.parts.1.to.3.2002/portrait.pdf> accessed 1 October 2021

Finck M.(ed), *Blockchain regulation and governance in Europe* (Cambridge University Press 2018)

Finocchiaro G. (ed), *I contratti informatici* (Cedam 1997)

Finocchiaro G., Delfini F.(eds), *Diritto dell'informatica* (Utet 2014)

G. De Nova (ed), *Le clausole a rischio di nullità* (Cedam 2009)

Gallo P.(ed), *Trattato del contratto, 3* (Utet 2010)

Gambino A., *L'accordo telematico* (Giuffrè 1997)

Gazzoni F. (ed), *Obbligazioni e contratti* (Edizioni Scientifiche Italiane 2009)

Grundmann S. (ed), *European Contract Law in the Digital Age* (Intersentia 2018)

Günther F., *Das Automatenrecht*, dissertation printed in 1892 by the bookseller of the University of Göttingen W. F. Kästner (Kessinger 2010)

Gupta M. (ed), *Blockchain for dummies – IBM Limited Editions* (John Wiley & Sons 2017)

Hobbes T., *Leviathan* (1st ed 1651)

International Institute for the Unification of Private Law, *Unidroit Principles of International Commercial Contracts* (UNIDROIT 2016)

Kraus D., Obrist T., Hari O. (eds), *Blockchains, Smart Contracts, Decentralised Autonomous Organisations and the Law* (Edward Elgar 2019)

Lessig L. (ed), *Code: Version 2.0* (New York: Basic Books 2006)

Lloyd J. (ed), *Information Technology Law* (6th edn Oxford University Press 2011)

Lohsse S., Schulze R., Staudenmayer D. (eds), *Liability for Artificial Intelligence and the Internet of Things* (Hart Nomos 2019)

Lohsse S., Schulze R., Staudenmayer D. (eds), *Liability for Robotics and in the Internet of Things: Munster Colloquia on Eu Law and the Digital Economy IV* (Hart Nomos 2019)

Macario F. (ed), *Adeguamento e rinegoziazione nei contratti a lungo termine* (Jovene 1996)

Menichino C. (ed), *Le clausole di irresponsabilità contrattuale* (Giuffrè 2008)

Nicotra M., Sarzana di Sant'Ippolito F.(eds), *Diritto della blockchain, intelligenza artificiale e IoT* (Ipsoa 2018)

Nilsson J. (ed), *The Quest for Artificial Intelligence – A History of Ideas and Achievements* (Cambridge University Press 2010)

Perugini M. L.(ed), *Distributed Ledger Technologies e sistemi di Blockchain* (Key 2018)

Ricciuto V., Zorzi N. (eds), *Il contratto telematico* (Cedam 2002)

Roppo V. (ed), *Il contratto* (Giuffrè 2001)

Ruffolo U. (ed), *Intelligenza artificiale e responsabilità* (Giuffrè 2018)

Sacco R., De Nova G. (eds), *Il contratto* (Utet 2004)

Sacco R., De Nova G. (eds), *Il contratto* in *Trattato Sacco* (Utet 2004)

Sagaert V., Storme M. E., Terryn E. (eds), *The Draft Common Frame of Reference: national and comparative perspectives* (Intersentia 2012)

Schels K., *Der strafrechtlicheSchutz des Automaten*, Dissertation in Erlagen, München, 1897

Schiller F., *Rechtsverhältnisse des Automaten*, Dissertation in Zurich, 1898

Schlesinger P. (ed), *Il Codice civile. Commentario* (Giuffrè 2007)

Schreiber G. R. (ed), *A Concise History of Vending in the U.S.A.* (Vend 1961)

Schulze R., Staudenmayer D., Lohsse S. (eds) *Contracts for the Supply of Digital Content: Regulatory Challenges and Gaps* (Hart Nomos 2017)

Scialoja A. (ed), *L'offerta a persona indeterminata ed il contratto concluso mediante automatico* (S. Lapi 1902)

Segrave K. (ed), *Vending Machines: An American Social History* (McFarland & Company 2002)

Smits J. M. (ed), *Contract law-a comparative introduction* (Edward Elgar 2017)

Sorieul R. (ed), *The UNCITRAL Model Law and the Modernization of Legislation to Facilitate Electronic Commerce, Electronic Commerce Initiatives of ESCAP: Business Facilitation Needs/Economic and Social Commission for Asia and the Pacific* (United Nations 1998)

Stazi A. (ed), *Automazione contrattuale e "contratti intelligenti". Gli smart contracts nel diritto comparato* (Giappichelli 2019)

Study Group on a European Civil Code, Research Group on EC Private Law, *Principles, Definitions and Model Rules of European Private Law – Draft Common Frame of Reference (DFCR), Outline Edition* (sellier.european law publishers 2009)

Svantesson D. (ed), *Private International Law and the Internet* (3rd edn Kluwer Law International, The Hague 2016)

Swan M. (ed), *Blockchain. Blueprint for a new economy* (O' Reilly 2015)

United Nations Commission on International Trade Law, *Yearbook Volume XXXII: 2001* (United Nations 2003)

Valentino D. (ed), *Manuale di diritto dell'informatica* (Ed. Scientifiche Italiane 2016)

Vassalli F. (ed), *Trattato di diritto civile italiano* (Utet 1975)

Wagner B. *et al.* (eds), *Research Handbook on Human Rights and Digital Technology: Global Politics, Law and International Relations* (Edward Elgar Publishing 2019)

Zaccaria A., Schmidt Kessel M., Schulze R., Gambino A. M. (eds), *EU eIDAS Regulation – Article-by-Article Commentary* (Beck Hart Nomos 2020)

Zweigert K., H. Kotz (eds), *An introduction to comparative law*, (3rd edn Oxford University Press 1998)

## D) BOOK CHAPTERS

AE Martens S., 'Consequential Loss' in Schulze R., Staudenmayer D., Lohsse S. (eds) *Contracts for the Supply of Digital Content: Regulatory Challenges and Gaps* (Hart Nomos 2017)

Barrière F., 'The Payment with Bitcoins and other Virtual Currencies – Risks, liabilities, and regulatory responses' in De Franceschi A., Schulze R. (eds), Graziadei M., Pollicino O., Riente F., Sica S., Sirena P. (co-eds), *Digital Revolution – New Challenges for Law. Data Protection, Artificial Intelligence, Smart Products, Blockchain Technology and Virtual Currencies* (Beck, Nomos 2019)

Borgogno O., 'Usefulness and Dangers of Smart Contracts in Consumer Transactions' in Di Matteo L. A., Cannarsa M., Poncibò C. (eds), *The Cambridge Handbook of smart contracts, blockchain technology and digital platforms* (Cambridge University Press 2020)

Cannarsa M., 'Contract Interpretation' in Di Matteo L. A., Cannarsa M., Poncibò C. (eds), *The Cambridge Handbook of smart contracts, blockchain technology and digital platforms* (Cambridge University Press 2020)

Carnevali U., 'Della risoluzione per inadempimento, Artt. 1453–1454' in *Comm. Scialoja-Branca* (Zanichelli 1990)

Carron B., Botteron V., 'How smart can a contract be' in Kraus D., Obrist T., Hari O. (eds), *Blockchains, Smart Contracts, Decentralised Autonomous Organisations and the Law* (Edward Elgar 2019)

Castellani L., 'I testi dell'UNCITRAL in materia di diritto del commercio elettronico' in Finocchiaro G., Delfini F.(eds), *Diritto dell'informatica* (Utet 2014)

Chaum D., 'Blind Signatures for Untraceable Payments' in D. Chaum, R. L. Rivest, A. T. Sherman (eds), *Advances in Cryptology: Proceedings of Crypto 82* (Springer 1983)

Christandl G., 'Offer and acceptance', in Jansen N., Zimmermann R. (eds) *Commentaries on European contract laws* (Oxford 2018)

Clément M., 'Smart Contracts and the Courts' in Di Matteo L. A., Cannarsa M., Poncibò C. (eds), *The Cambridge Handbook of smart contracts, blockchain technology and digital platforms* (Cambridge University Press 2020)

Colombi Ciacchi A., von Schagen E., 'Conformity under the Draft Digital Content Directive: Regulatory Challenges and Gaps' in Schulze R., Staudenmayer D., Lohsse S. (eds) *Contracts for the Supply of Digital Content: Regulatory Challenges and Gaps* (Hart Nomos 2017)

Colombi Ciacchi A., von Schagen E., 'Conformity under the Draft Digital Content Directive: Regulatory Challenges and Gaps' in Schulze R., Staudenmayer D., Lohsse S. (eds) *Contracts for the Supply of Digital Content: Regulatory Challenges and Gaps* (Hart Nomos 2017)

Cuffaro V., 'Profili di tutela del consumatore nei contratti *online*' in Finocchiaro G., Delfini F.(eds), *Diritto dell'informatica* (Utet 2014)

Delimatsis P., 'When disruptive meets streamline: international standardization in blockchain' in Kraus D., Obrist T., Hari O. (eds), *Blockchains, Smart Contracts, Decentralised Autonomous Organisations and the Law* (Edward Elgar 2019)

Dely F., 'Lex Mercatoria (New Law Merchant): Globalization and International Self-Regulation' in Appelbaum R. P., Felstiner L. F., Gessner V. (eds) *Rules and Networks* (Oxford, Hart 2001).

Erler K., 'Article 29 Requirements for Qualified Electronic Signatures Creation Devices' in Zaccaria A., Schmidt Kessel M., Schulze R., Gambino A. M. (eds), *EU eIDAS Regulation – Article-by-Article Commentary* (Beck Hart Nomos 2020)

Finocchiaro G., 'Article 3 Definitions' in Zaccaria A., Schmidt Kessel M., Schulze R., Gambino A. M. (eds), *EU eIDAS Regulation – Article-by-Article Commentary* (Beck Hart Nomos 2020)

Finocchiaro G., '*Article 3. Definitions*', in Zaccaria A., Schmidt Kessel M., Schulze R., Gambino A. M. (eds), *EU eIDAS Regulation – Article-by-Article Commentary* (Beck Hart Nomos 2020)

Finocchiaro G., 'I contratti ad oggetto informatico' in Finocchiaro G., Delfini F. (eds), *Diritto dell'informatica* (Utet 2014)

Finocchiaro G., 'Lex mercatoria e commercio elettronico. Il diritto applicabile ai contratti conclusi su Internet' in V. Ricciuto and N. Zorzi (eds), *Il contratto telematico* (Cedam 2002)

Finocchiaro G., 'Lex mercatoria e commercio elettronico' in Ricciuto V., Zorzi N. (eds), *Il contratto telematico* (Cedam 2002)

Finocchiaro G., *Firme elettroniche e firma digitale*, in Finocchiaro G., Delfini F.(eds), *Diritto dell'informatica* (Utet 2014)

Galgano F. (ed), *Le obbligazioni in generale, il contratto in generale, i singoli contratti* in Galgano F. (ed), *Trattato di diritto civile*, vol. 2 (Cedam 2014)

Gambino A., Bomprezzi C., 'Blockchain e criptovalute' in Finocchiaro G., Falce V. (eds), *Fintech: diritti, concorrenza, regole – Le operazioni di finanziamento tecnologico* (Zanichelli 2019)

Gardella Tedeschi B., 'Art. 8:104–109' in Antoniolli L., Veneziano A. (eds), *Principles of European Contract Law and Italian Law* (Kluwer Law International 2005)

Gatteschi V., Lamberti F., Demartini C., 'Technology of Smart Contracts' in Di Matteo L. A., Cannarsa M., Poncibò C. (eds), *The Cambridge Handbook of smart contracts, blockchain technology and digital platforms* (Cambridge University Press 2020)

Gatteschi V., Lamberti F., Demartini C., 'Technology of Smart Contracts' in Di Matteo L. A., Cannarsa M., Poncibò C. (eds), *The Cambridge Handbook of smart contracts, blockchain technology and digital platforms* (Cambridge University Press 2020)

Gatti S., 'Article 35 Legal effects of electronic seals' in Zaccaria A., Schmidt Kessel M., Schulze R., Gambino A. M. (eds), *EU eIDAS Regulation – Article-by-Article Commentary* (Beck Hart Nomos 2020)

Granieri M., 'Technological contracts' in Monateri P. G. (ed) *Comparative Contract Law* (Edward Elgar 2017) <https://papers.ssrn.com/sol3/papers.cfm?abstract_id=2666191> accessed 1 October 2021

Graziadei M., 'Chapter III. Authority of agents' in Antoniolli L., Veneziano A. (eds), *Principles of European Contract Law and Italian Law* (Kluwer Law International 2005)

Gregory J. D., Remsu J., 'Article 14. Error in Electronic Communication' in Boss A. H., Kilian W. (eds), *The United Nations Convention on the Use of Electronic Communications in International Contracts: An In-depth Guide and Sourcebook* (Wolters Kluwer 2008)

Guillaume F., 'Aspects of private international law related to blockchain transactions' in Kraus D., Obrist T., Hari O. (eds), *Blockchains, Smart Contracts, Decentralised Autonomous Organisations and the Law* (Edward Elgar 2019)

Howells G., 'Reflections on Remedies for Lack of Conformity in Light of the Proposals of the EU Commission on Supply of Digital Content and Online and Other Distance Sales of Goods' in De Franceschi A. (ed), *European Contract Law and the Digital Single Market – The Implications of the Digital Revolution* (Intersentia 2016)

Iamiceli P., 'Art. 4:111–119' in Antoniolli L., Veneziano A. (eds), *Principles of European Contract Law and Italian Law* (Kluwer Law International 2005)

Iamiceli P., 'Art. 4:111–119' in Antoniolli L., Veneziano A. (eds), *Principles of European Contract Law and Italian Law* (Kluwer Law International 2005)

Jansen N., 'Art. 2:104: Terms not Individually Negotiated' in Jansen N., Zimmermann R. (eds) *Commentaries on European contract laws* (Oxford 2018)

Jansen N., Zimmermann R., 'General introduction European contract law. Foundations, Commentaries, Synthesis' in Jansen N., Zimmermann R. (eds) *Commentaries on European contract laws* (Oxford 2018)

Kleinschmidt J., 'Particular remedies for non-performance' Jansen N., Zimmermann R. (eds) *Commentaries on European contract laws* (Oxford 2018)

Lohsse S., 'Art. 4:103: Fundamental mistakes as to Facts or Law' in Jansen N., Zimmermann R. (eds) *Commentaries on European contract laws* (Oxford 2018)

Lohsse S., 'Art. 4:104: Inaccuracy in Communication' in Jansen N., Zimmermann R. (eds) *Commentaries on European contract laws* (Oxford 2018)

Loos M., 'Machine-to-Machine Contracting in the Age of the Internet of Things' in Schulze R., Staudenmayer D., Lohsse S. (eds) *Contracts for the Supply of Digital Content: Regulatory Challenges and Gaps* (Hart Nomos 2017)

Maniaci A., 'Le clausole di incontestabilità nei contratti di assicurazione' in G. De Nova (ed), *Le clausole a rischio di nullità* (Cedam 2009)

Memmo D., 'Il consenso nei contratti telematici' in Finocchiaro G., Delfini F.(eds), *Diritto dell'informatica* (Utet 2014)

Meneghetti M. C., 'Articolo 3' in Delfini F., Finocchiaro G. (eds), *Identificazione elettronica e servizi fiduciari per le transazioni elettroniche nel mercato interno, commento al regolamento UE 910/2014* (Giappichelli 2017)

Menichino C., 'Art. 19, d.lgs. 70/2003 (Composizione delle controversie)' in Finocchiaro G., Delfini F.(eds), *Diritto dell'informatica* (Utet 2014)

Mik E., 'Blockchains. A Technology for Decentralized Marketplaces' in Di Matteo L. A., Cannarsa M., Poncibò C. (eds), *The Cambridge Handbook of smart contracts, blockchain technology and digital platforms* (Cambridge University Press 2020)

Momberg R., 'Standard terms and transparency in online contracts' in De Franceschi A. (ed), *European Contract Law and the Digital Single Market – The Implications of the Digital Revolution* (Intersentia 2016)

Monti A., 'Art. 2:101–107' in Antoniolli L., Veneziano A. (eds), *Principles of European Contract Law and Italian Law* (Kluwer Law International 2005)

Morais Carvalho J., Campos Carvalho J., 'Online Dispute Resolution Platform – Making European Contract Law More Effective' in De Franceschi A. (ed), *European Contract Law and the Digital Single Market – The Implications of the Digital Revolution* (Intersentia 2016)

Newton J., 'System Supply Contracts' in Reed C. (ed), *Computer Law* (7th edn Oxford 2011)

Pollicino O., Bassini M., 'The Law of the Internet between Globalization and Localization' in Maduro M., Tuori K., Sankari S. (eds), *Transnational Law – Rethinking European Law and Legal Thinking* (Cambridge 2014)

Poncibò C., Di Matteo L. A., 'Smart contracts, Contractual and Noncontractual Remedies' in Matteo, Cannarsa, Poncibò

Ramberg C., 'Digital Content – A Digital CESL II – A Paradigm for Contract Law via the Backdoor?' in Grundmann S. (ed), *European Contract Law in the Digital Age* (Intersentia 2018)

Ratti M., '*La Convenzione sull'uso delle comunicazioni elettroniche: le principali disposizioni*' in Finocchiaro G., Delfini F.(eds), *Diritto dell'informatica* (Utet 2014)

Reed C., 'Electronic commerce' in Reed C. (ed), *Computer Law* (7th edn Oxford 2011)

RICCI A., 'I contratti di licenza d'uso di software in particolare: la licenza a strappo, licenze freeware, shareware e open source' in Finocchiaro G., Delfini F.(eds), *Diritto dell'informatica* (Utet 2014)

Sacco R. (ed), *Il contratto* in Vassalli F. (ed), *Trattato di diritto civile italiano* (Utet 1975)

Sacco R., 'I rimedi sinallagmatici' in Sacco R., De Nova G. (eds), *Il contratto* in *Trattato Sacco* (Utet 2004)

Schulze R., 'Supply of Digital Content. A new Challenge for European Contract Law' in De Franceschi A. (ed), *European Contract Law and the Digital Single Market – The Implications of the Digital Revolution* (Intersentia 2016)

Sicchiero G., 'Comm. All'art. 1453 cod.civ., La risoluzione per inadempimento' in Schlesinger P., *Il Codice civile. Commentario* (Giuffrè 2007)

Spindler G., 'Contracts for the Supply of Digital Content – The Proposal of the Commission for a Directive on Contracts for the Supply of Digital Content', in Grundmann S. (ed), *European Contract Law in the Digital Age* (Intersentia 2018)

Stazi A., Baldi A., 'Contratti di utilizzazione del software' in Valentino D. (ed), *Dei singoli contratti*, in Gabrielli E., *Commentario del codice civile*, vol. 2 (Utet 2016)

Svantesson D., 'Digital Contracts in Global Surroundings' in Grundmann S. (ed), *European Contract Law in the Digital Age* (Intersentia 2018)

Troiano S., 'Article 26 Requirements for advanced electronic signatures' in Zaccaria A., Schmidt Kessel M., Schulze R., Gambino A. M. (eds), *EU eIDAS Regulation – Article-by-Article Commentary* (Beck Hart Nomos 2020)

Wagner G., 'Robot Liability' in Lohsse S., Schulze R., Staudenmayer D. (eds), *Liability for Robotics and in the Internet of Things: Munster Colloquia on Eu Law and the Digital Economy IV* (Hart Nomos 2019)

Weber R. H., 'Smart contracts: Do we need New Legal Rules?' in De Franceschi A., Schulze R. (eds), Graziadei M., Pollicino O., Riente F., Sica S., Sirena P. (co-eds), *Digital Revolution – New Challenges for Law. Data Protection, Artificial Intelligence, Smart Products, Blockchain Technology and Virtual Currencies* (Beck, Nomos 2019)

## E) HARD COPY JOURNALS

Allen J. G., 'Wrapped and Stacked: 'Smart Contracts' and the Interaction of Natural and Formal Language' (2018) 14(4) European Review of Contract Law 307

Allen T., Widdison R., 'Can Computers Make Contracts?' (1996) 9(1) Harvard Journal of Law & Technology 25

American Bar Association Model Electronic Data Interchange Trading Partner Agreement and Commentary (1990) 45 Business Lawyer 1645

American Bar Association, Edi and Technological Division, Section of Science and Technology, 'Model Electronic Payments Agreement and Commentary: For Domestic Credit Transfers' (1992) 32 Jurimetrics Journal of Law, Science and Technology 601

Amidei A., 'Intelligenza Artificiale e *product liability*: sviluppi del diritto dell'Unione Europea' (2019) 7 Giurisprudenza Italiana 1715

Barcelo J., 'User Privacy in the Public Bitcoin Blockchain' (2007) 6 Journal of Latex Class Files 1

Bosco A. J., 'Blockchain and the Uniform Electronic Transactions Act' (2018/2019) 74 The Business Lawyer 243

Calvetti S., 'Si può rinunciare a far valere una nullità contrattuale?' (2018) 184 Diritto & Giustizia 9

Cappiello B., 'Dallo "smart contract" computer code allo smart (legal) contract. I nuovi strumenti (para) giuridici alla luce della normativa nazionale e del diritto internazionale privato europeo: prospettive de jure condendo' (2020) 2 Rivista del commercio internazionale 477

Casey A. J., Niblett A., 'Self-Driving Contracts' (2017) 43 Journal of Corporation Law 1

Chaum D., 'Security without Identification: Transaction Systems to Make Big Brother Obsolete' (1985) 28(10) Communications of the ACM 1030

Conte de Leon D. *et al.*, 'Blockchain: Properties and Misconceptions' (2017) 11(3) Asia Pacific Journal of Innovation and Entrepreneurship 294 <www.emeraldinsight.com/doi/full/10.1108/APJIE-12-2017-034> accessed 1 October 2021

Costanza M., 'L'intelligenza artificiale e gli stilemi della responsabilità civile' (2019) 7 Giurisprudenza Italiana 1686

Cuccuru P., 'Beyond Bitcoin: an early overview on smart contracts' (2017) 25 International Journal of Law and Information Technology 179

Cuccuru P., 'Blockchain ed automazione contrattuale. Riflessioni sugli smart contract' (2017) 1 Nuova Giurisprudenza Civile 107

Davola A., 'Blockchain e Smart Contract as a Service: Prospettive di mercato a criticità normative delle prestazioni BaaS e SCaaS alla luce di un'incerta qualificazione giuridica' (2020) 2 Il Diritto Industriale 147

De Graaf T. J., 'From old to new: from internet to smart contracts and from people to smart contracts' (2019) 35 (5) Computer Law & Security Review 105322

Delfini F., 'Autonomia privata e risoluzione del contratto per inadempimento' (2014) 3 Nuove Leggi Civili Commentate 577

Di Ciommo F., 'Smart contracts and (non)law. The case of financial markets' (2018) 7(2) Law and Economics Yearly Review 291

Di Sabato D., 'Gli smart contracts: robot che gestiscono il rischio contrattuale' (2017) 2 Contratto e Impresa 378

Durovic M., Janssen A., 'The Formation of Blockchain-based Smart Contracts in the Light of Contract Law' (2019) 6 European Review of Private Law 753

Evans J., 'Curb your enthusiasm: the real implications of blockchain in the legal industry' (2018) 11(2) Journal of Business, Entrepreneurship and the Law 273

Fasciano P., 'Internet Electronic Mail: A Last Bastion for the Mailbox Rule' (1997) 25(3) Hofstra Law Review 971

Fici A., *Il contratto incompleto* (Giappichelli 2005)

Finck M., 'Blockchains and Data Protection in the European Union' (2018) 1 European Data Protection Law Review 17

Finocchiaro G., 'Il contratto nell'era dell'intelligenza artificiale' (2018) 2 Rivista Trimestrale di Diritto e Procedura Civile 441

Finocchiaro G., 'Intelligenza artificiale e protezione dei dati personali' (2019) Giurisprudenza Italiana 1670

Finocchiaro G., 'La conclusione del contratto telematico mediante I 'software agents': un falso problema giuridico?' (2002) 18(2) Contratto e impresa 500

Finocchiaro G., 'La Legge Modello dell'UNCITRAL sui Titoli di Credito Elettronici' (2021) 1 Contratto e Impresa 38

Gambino A., Bomprezzi C., 'Blockchain e protezione dei dati personali' (2019) 3 Diritto dell'Informazione e dell'Informatica 619

Gambino F., 'Obbligo di rinegoziare e atto dovuto' (2006) XII Studium Juris 1374

Giancaspro M., 'Is a 'smart contract' really a smart idea? Insights from a legal perspective' (2017) 33(6) Computer Law & Security Review 825

Giang-Truong N., Kyungbaek K., 'A Survey about Consensus Algorithms Used in Blockchain' (2018) 1 Journal of Information Processing Systems 101

Gitti G., 'Robotic Transactional Decisions' (2018) 2 Osservatorio del diritto civile e commerciale 619

Giuliano M., 'La blockchain e gli smart contracts nell'innovazione del diritto del terzo millennio' (2018) 6 Diritto dell'Informazione e dell'Informatica 989

Goetz C. J., Scott R. E., 'Principles of Relational Contracts' (1981) 67 Virginia Law Review 1089

Grundmann S., 'The EU Consumer Rights Directive – Optimizing, Creating Alternatives or a Dead-End' (2013) 18 Uniform Law Review, 98

Hall H., Howells G., Watson J., 'The Consumer Rights Directive – An Assessment of its Contribution to the Development of European Consumer Contract Law' (2012) 8 European Review of Contract Law 139

Hart O., Moore J., 'Foundations of Incomplete Contracts' (1999) 66 Review of Economic Studies 115

Hultmark Ramberg C., ' The E-Commerce Directive and Formation of Contract in a Comparative Perspective' (2001) 26 European Law Review 429

Janssen A.U., Patti P., 'Demistificare gli smart contracts' (2020) 1 Osservatorio del diritto civile e commerciale 31

Johnson D. R., Post D., 'Law and Borders: The Rise of Law in Cyberspace' (1996) 48 Stanford Law Review 1367

Koulu R., 'Blokchains and Online Dispute Resolution: Smart Contracts as an Alternative to Enforcement' (2016) 13 SCRIPTed 40

Levy K., 'Book-Smart, Not Street-Smart: Blockchain-Base Smart Contracts and the Social Workings of Law' (2017) 3 Engaging Science, Technology, and Society 1

Macneil R. 'Relational Contract Theory: Challenges and Queries (2000) 94 Northwestern University Law Review 877

Macneil R., 'Relational Contract: What We Do and Do Not Know' (1985) Wisconsin Law Review 483

Maugeri M., 'Smart contracts e disciplina dei contratti' (2020) 2 Osservatorio del diritto civile e commerciale 400, 401

McKinney S. A., Landy R., Wilka R., 'Smart contracts, blockchain, and the next frontier of transnational law' (2018) 13 Washington Journal of Law, Technology & Arts 313

Meyer O., 'Stopping the Unstoppable. Termination and Unwinding of Smart Contracts' (2020) European Consumer and Market Law 17

Mik E., 'Smart contracts: terminology, technical limitations and real world complexity' (2017) 9 Journal of Law, Innovation and Technology 269

Mik E., 'The Effectiveness of Acceptances Communicated by Electronic Means, or – Does the Postal Acceptance Rule Apply to Email?' (2009) 26 Journal of Contract Law 1

Neumond H., '*Der Automat. Ein Beitrag zur Lehre über die Vertragsofferte*' (1899) *Archiv für die civilistische Praxis* 166

O' Shields R., 'Smart Contracts: Legal Agreements for the Blockchain' (2017) 21 N.C. Banking Inst. 177

Pearce G., Platten N., 'Promoting the Information Society: The EU Directive on Electronic Commerce' (2000) 6 European Law Journal 363

Pham V. A., Karmouch A., 'Mobile Software Agents: An Overview' (1998) 36(7) IEEE Communications Magazine 26

Piatti L., 'Dal Codice Civile al codice binario: *blockchain* e *smart contracts*' (2016) 3 Ciberspazio e diritto 325

Raskin M., 'The Law and Legality of Smart Contracts' (2017) 1 Georgetown Law Technology Review 305

Rawls A., 'Contract Formation in an Internet Age' (2009) X Columbia Science and Technology Law Review 200

Reidenberg J. R., 'Lex Informatica: The Formulation of Information Policy Rules Through Technology' (1998) 76 Texas Law Review 553

Ruffolo U., 'Intelligenza Artificiale, *machine learning* e responsabilità da algoritmo' (2019) 7 Giurisprudenza Italiana 1689

Scott R. E., Triantis G. G., 'Incomplete Contracts and the Theory of Contract Design' (2005) 56 Case Western Law Review 187

Sholz L. H., 'Algorithmic contracts' (2017) 20 Standard Technology Law Review 101

Sillaber C., Waltl B., 'Life Cycle of Smart Contracts in Blockchain Ecosystems' (2017) 8 Datenschutz und Datensicherheit 497

Sklaroff J. M., 'Smart contracts and the cost of inflexibility' (2017) 166 University of Pennsylvania Law Review 263

Solum L., 'Legal Personhood for Artificial Intelligences' (1992) 70 NC L Rev 1231

Surden H., 'Computable Contracts' (2012) 46 U. C. Davis Law Review 629

Tjong Tjin Tai E., 'Force Majeure and Excuses in Smart Contracts' (2018) 26(6) European Review of Private Law 787

Triaille J., 'The EEC Directive on Product Liability and its Application to Databases and Information' (1991) Computer Law and Practice 217

Vranken H. P. E., 'Sustainability of bitcoin and blockchains' (2017) 28 Current Opinion in environmental Sustainability 1

Weitzenboeck E. M., 'Electronic Agents and the Formation of Contracts' (2001) 9(3) International Journal of Law and Information Technology 204

Werbach K., Cornell N., 'Contracts Ex Machina' (2017) 67 Duke Law Journal 313

Winn J. K., Haubold J., 'Electronic Promises: Contract Law Reform and E-Commerce in a Comparative Perspective' (2002) 27 European Law Review 567

Wuyts D.,'The Product Liability Directive – More than two decades of defective products in Europe' (2014) 5(1) Journal of European Tort Law 1

## F) ONLINE JOURNALS

Bomprezzi C., 'Blockchain e assicurazione: opportunità e nuove sfide' (2017) Diritto Mercato Tecnologia <https://www.dimt.it/la-rivista/articoli/blockchain-e-assicurazione-opportunita-e-nuove-sfide/> accessed 1 October 2021

Bomprezzi C., 'Commento in materia di Blockchain e Smart contract alla luce del nuovo Decreto Semplificazioni' (2019) Diritto Mercato Tecnologia <https://www.dimt.it/news/breve-commento-alla-legge-11-febbraio-2019-n-12-di-conversione-del-decreto-legge-14-dicembre-2018-n-135-recante-disposizioni-urgenti-in-materia-di-sostegno-e-semplificazione-per-le-imprese-e-per-la-pu/> accessed 1 October 2021

Borselli A., 'Smart Contracts in Insurance. A Law and Futurology Perspective' (2019) SSRN Electronic Journal <https://ssrn.com/abstract=3318883> accessed 1 October 2021

Catchlove P., 'Smart Contracts: A New Era of Contract Use' (2017) SSRN Electronic Journal <https://ssrn.com/abstract=3090226> accessed 1 October 2021

Chohan U. W., 'The Double Spending Problem and Cryptocurrencies' (2017) SSRN Electronic Journal <https://ssrn.com/abstract=3090174> accessed 1 October 2021

Clack C. D., Bakshi V. A., Braine L., 'Smart Contract Templates: foundations, design landscape and research directions' (2016) arXiv: Computers and Society <https://arxiv.org/abs/1608.00771> accessed 1 October 2021

Cong L. W., He Z., 'Blockchain Disruption and Smart Contracts' (2017) SSRN Electronic Journal <https://ssrn.com/abstract=2985764> accessed 1 October 2021

Davidson S., De Filippi P., Potts J., 'Disrupting Governance: The New Institutional Economics of Distributed Ledger Technology' (2016) SSRN Electronic Journal <https://ssrn.com/abstract=2811995> accessed 1 October 2021

De Filippi P., 'The interplay between decentralization and privacy: the case of blockchain technologies' (2016) SSRN Electronic Journal <https://ssrn.com/abstract=2852689> accessed 1 October 2021

Finocchiaro G., Bomprezzi C., 'A legal analysis of the use of blockchain technology for the formation of smart legal contracts' (2020) 2 MediaLaws 111 <http://www.medialaws.eu/rivista/a-legal-analysis-of-the-use-of-blockchain-technology-for-the-formation-of-smart-legal-contracts/> accessed 1 October 2021

Finocchiaro G., 'Riflessioni sugli smart contract e sull'intelligenza artificiale' (2020) 11 Giustizia Civile.Com 1

Gambino A., Tuzzolino D, 'Il Digital Services Act tra responsabilità e governance. Commento alla proposta di Regolamento' (2020) Diritto Mercato Tecnologia <https://www.dimt.it/news/il-digital-services-act-tra-responsabilita-e-governance-commento-alla-proposta-di-regolamento/> accessed 1 October 2021

Goldenfein J., Leiter A., 'Legal Engineering on the Blockchain: 'Smart contracts' as Legal Conduct' (2018) SSRN Electronic Journal <https://ssrn.com/abstract=3176363> accessed 1 October 2021

Hileman G., Rauchs M., '2017 Global Blockchain Benchmarking Study' (2017) SSRN Electronic Journal <https://ssrn.com/abstract=3040224> accessed 1 October 2021

Madir J., 'Smart Contracts: (How) Do They Fit Under Existing Legal Frameworks?' (2018) SSRN Electronic Journal <https://ssrn.com/abstract=3301463> accessed 1 October 2021

Manente M., 'L. 12/2019 – Smart contract e tecnologie basate su registri distribuiti – prime note', Studio 1_2019, (2019) Notariato.it <https://www.notariato.it/it/content/studio-12019-di-legge-122019-%E2%80%93-smart-contract-e-tecnologie-basate-su-registri-distribuiti-%E2%80%93> accessed 1 October 2021

Meyer O., 'Stopping the Unstoppable. Termination and Unwinding of Smart Contracts' (2019) SSRN Electronic Journal <https://ssrn.com/abstract=3537477> accessed 1 October 2021

Mukherjiee A., 'Smart Contracts – Another Feather in UNCITRAL's Cap' (2018) Cornell International Law Journal Online <http://cornellilj.org/smart-contracts-another-feather-in-uncitrals-cap/> accessed 1 October 2021

Perugini M. L., Dal Checco P., 'Smart Contracts: A Preliminary Evaluation' (2015) SSRN Electronic Journal <https://ssrn.com/abstract=2729548> accessed 1 October 2021

Rauchs M. *et al.*, '2nd Global Enterprise Blockchain Benchmarking Study' (2019) SSRN Electronic Journal <https://ssrn.com/abstract=3461765> accessed 1 October 2021

Szabo N., 'Formalizing and Securing Relationships on Public Networks' (1997) 2(9) First Monday <https://firstmonday.org/ojs/index.php/fm/article/view/548> accessed 1 October 2021

Szczerbowski J. J., 'Place of smart contracts in civil law. A few comments on form and interpretation', Proceedings of the 12th Annual International Scientific Conference NEW TRENDS 2017, 335 (2017) SSRN Electronic Journal <https://ssrn.com/abstract=3095933> accessed 1 October 2021

Usman W. C., 'The Decentralised Autonomous Organisation and Governance Issues' (2017) SSRN Electronic Journal <https://ssrn.com/abstract=3082055> accessed 1 October 2021

Wright A., De Filippi P., 'Decentralized Blockchain Technology and the rise of Lex Cryptographia' (2015) SSRN Electronic Journal <https://ssrn.com/abstract=2580664> accessed 1 October 2021

## G) WORKING PAPERS

Bacon J., Michels J. D., Millard C., Singh J., 'Blockchain Demystified' (2017) Queen Mary University of London, School of Law, Legal Studies Research Paper No. 268/2017 <https://ssrn.com/abstract=3091218> accessed 1 October 2021

Chang H., 'Blockchain: Disrupting Data Protection' (2017) University of Hong Kong Falculty of Law Research Paper No. 2017/041 <http://ssrn.com/abstract=3093166> accessed 1 October 2021

Eenmaa-Dimitrieva H., Schmidt-Kessen M. J., 'Regulation through code as a safeguard for implementing smart contracts in no-trust environments' (2017) EUI Working papers LAW 2017/13 <http://hdl.handle.net/1814/47545> accessed 1 October 2021

McJohn S., McJohn I., 'The Commercial Law of Bitcoin and Blockchain Transactions' (2016) Suffolk University Law School Legal Studies Research Paper 16–13 <http://ssrn.com/abstract=2874463> accessed 1 October 2021

Pollicino O., Bassini M., 'Internet Law in the Era of Transnational Law' (2011) EUI Working Papers RSCAS 2011/24 <https://cadmus.eui.eu//handle/1814/16835> accessed 1 October 2021

Savelyev A., 'Contract law 2.0: 'smart' contracts as the beginning of the end of classic contract law' (2016) Higher School of Economics Research Paper no. WP BRP 71/LAW/2016 <https://ssrn.com/abstract=2885241> accessed 1 October 2021

Singh J., Michels J. D., 'Blockchain as a Service' (2017) Queen Mary University of London, School of Law, Legal Studies Research Paper No. 269/2017 <https://ssrn.com/abstract=3091223> accessed 1 October 2021

Tjong Tjin Tai E., 'Force Majeure and Excuses in Smart Contracts' (2018) <https://research.tilburguniversity.edu/en/publications/force-majeure-and-excuses-in-smart-contracts> accessed 1 October 2021

## H) CONFERENCE PAPERS

Cervone L., Palmirani M., Vitali F., 'The Intelligible Contract' (Proceedings of the 53rd Hawaii International Conference on System Sciences, Maui, Hawaii, USA, 7–10 January 2020) 1780 <https://hdl.handle.net/10125/63959> accessed 1 October 2021.

Juels A., Marino B., 'Setting Standards for Altering and Undoing Smart Contracts' in Alferes J. J. *et al.* (eds), *Rule Technologies: Research, Tools, and Applications*, Proceedings of the 10th International Symposium RuleML (Springer 2016)

Luu L. *et al*, 'Making Smart Contracts Smarter' in Proceedings of the 2016 ACM SIGSAC Conference on Computer and Communications Security, Vienna, October 2016, 254–269 <https://eprint.iacr.org/2016/633.pdf> accessed 1 October 2021

Mc Gregor C., Kumaran S., 'An Agent-Based System for Trading Partner Management in B2B e-Commerce' (IEEE Proceedings of the 12th International Workshop on Research Issues in Data Engineering: engineering e-Commerce/e-Business Systems RIDE-2EC, San Jose, CA, USA, 24–25 February 2002) <https://ieeexplore.ieee.org/document/995102?arnumber=995102> accessed 1 October 2021

Zheng Z, Xie S., Dai H., Chen X., Wang H., 'An Overview of Blockchain Technology: Architecture, Consensus, and Future Trends' (proceedings of the 2017 IEEE 6th International Congress on Big Data, Honolulu, 25–30 June 2017) 557 <https://www.researchgate.net/publication/318131748_An_Overview_of_Blockchain_Technology_Architecture_Consensus_and_Future_Trends> accessed 1 October 2021

## I) REPORTS AND STUDIES

'Discussion paper on blockchain and smart contracts in insurance: EIOPA invites comments' (EIOPA) <https://www.eiopa.europa.eu/media/news/discussion-paper-blockchain-and-smart-contracts-insurance-eiopa-invites-comments-0_en> accessed 1 October 2021

'EIOPA InsurTech Roundtable – How Technology and data are reshaping the insurance landscape. Summary from the roundtable organised by EIOPA on 28 April 2017' (EIOPA) <https://register.eiopa.europa.eu/Publications/Reports/08.0_EIOPA-BoS17-165_EIOPA_InsurTech_Roundtable_summary.pdf> accessed 1 October 2021

Bradgate R., 'Consumer Rights in Digital Products' (2010) Report prepared for the UK Department for Business, Innovation and Skills (BIS) < https://assets.publishing.service.gov.uk/government/uploads/system/uploads/attachment_data/file/31837/10-1125-consumer-rights-in-digital-products.pdf> accessed 1 October 2021

European Commission, 'Liability for Artificial Intelligence and other emerging digital technologies' – Report from the Expert Group on Liability and New Technologies – New Technologies Formation <https://op.europa.eu/it/publication-detail/-/publication/1c5e30be-1197-11ea-8c1f-01aa75ed71a1/language-en> accessed 1 October 2021

European Commission, 'Study on Blockchains – Legal, governance and interoperability aspects (SMART 2018/0038) <https://ec.europa.eu/digital-single-market/en/news/study-blockchains-legal-governance-and-interoperability-aspects-smart-20180038> accessed 1 October 2021

European Commission, Joint Research Centre, 'Blockchain now and tomorrow – assessing multidimensional impacts of distributed ledger technologies' (2019) <https://ec.europa.eu/jrc/en/facts4eufuture/blockchain-now-and-tomorrow> accessed 1 October 2021

European Parliamentary Research Service, 'Blockchain and the General Data Protection Regulation – Can distributed ledgers be squared with European data protection law?' (2019) <https://www.europarl.europa.eu/RegData/etudes/STUD/2019/634445/EPRS_STU(2019)634445_EN.pdf> accessed 1 October 2021

European Parliamentary Research Service, 'How blockchain technology could change our lives – In-depth Analysis' (2017) <https://www.europarl.europa.eu/RegData/etudes/IDAN/2017/581948/EPRS_IDA(2017)581948_EN.pdf> accessed 1 October 2021

European Union Blockchain Observatory & Forum, 'EU Blockchain Ecosystem Developments' <https://www.eublockchainforum.eu/sites/default/files/reports/EU%20Blockchain%20Ecosystem%20Report_final_0.pdf> accessed 1 October 2021

European Union Blockchain Observatory and Forum, 'Blockchain and digital identity' <https://www.eublockchainforum.eu/sites/default/files/report_identity_v0.9.4.pdf> accessed 1 October 2021

European Union Blockchain Observatory and Forum, 'Blockchain Ecosystem Developments and Trends' (2020) <https://www.eublockchainforum.eu/sites/default/files/reports/1st%20EUBOF%20Trend%20Report_November%202020.pdf> accessed 1 October 2021

European Union Blockchain Observatory and Forum, 'Blockchain in trade finance and supply chain' (2019) <https://www.eublockchainforum.eu/sites/default/files/report_supply_chain_v1.pdf> accessed 1 October 2021

European Union Blockchain Observatory and Forum, 'Convergence of blockchain, AI and IoT' <https://www.eublockchainforum.eu/sites/default/files/report_convergence_v1.0.pdf> accessed 1 October 2021

European Union Blockchain Observatory and Forum, 'Eu Blockchain Observatory and Forum 2018–2020 Conclusions and Reflections' (2020) <https://www.eublockchainforum.eu/sites/default/files/reports/report_conclusion_book_v1.0.pdf> accessed 1 October 2021

European Union Blockchain Observatory and Forum, 'Legal and Regulatory Framework of Blockchains and Smart Contracts' (2019) <https://www.eublockchainforum.eu/reports> accessed 1 October 2021

European Union Blockchain Observatory and Forum, 'Scalability, interoperability and sustainability of blockchains' (<https://www.eublockchainforum.eu/sites/default/files/reports/report_scalaibility_06_03_2019.pdf?width=1024&height=800&iframe=true> accessed 1 October 2021

Lauslahti K., Mattila J., Seppälaä T., 'Smart Contracts – How will Blockchain Technology Affect Contractual Practices?' (2017) ETLA Reports No 68 <https://www.etla.fi/wp-content/uploads/ETLA-Raportit-Reports-68.pdf> accessed 1 October 2021

Mainelli M., von Gunten C., 'Chain of a lifetime: how blockchain technology might transform personal insurance' (2014) Long Finance Report <https://papers.ssrn.com/sol3/papers.cfm?abstract_id=3676416> accessed 1 October 2021

Purcell B. *et al.*, 'Tech Radar: Artificial Intelligence Technologies and Solutions, Q1 2017' (2017) Forrester Report <https://www.forrester.com/report/TechRadar+Artificial+Intelligence+Technologies+And+Solutions+Q1+2017/-/E-RES136196> accessed 1 October 2021

Report from the Commission to the European Parliament, the Council and the European Economic and Social Committee, Report on the safety and liability implications of Artificial Intelligence, the Internet of Things and Robotics, COM(2020) 64 final <https://ec.europa.eu/info/sites/info/files/report-safety-liability-artificial-intelligence-feb2020_en_1.pdf> accessed 1 October 2021

United States General Account Office, *Electronic Fund Transfer, Information on Three Critical Banking Systems* (Briefing Report to the Chairman, Subcommittee on Telecommunications and Finance, Committee in Energy and Commerce, House of Representatives, February 1989, GAO/IMTEC-89–25BR)

World Economic Forum, Global Agenda Council on the Future of Software & Society, 'Deep Shift – Technology Tipping Points and Societal Impact (2015) <https://www.weforum.org/reports> accessed 1 October 2021

## J) WEB SOURCES

'A Practical Guide to Using Blockchain within the United Nations' (UN Innovation Network) <https://atrium.uninnovation.network/guide> accessed 1 October 2021

'AXA drops Etherum-based smart insurance platform' <https://coinrivet.com/axa-drops-ethereum-based-flight-insurance-platform/> accessed 1 October 2021

'Blockchain funding and investments' (European Commission) <https://digital-strategy.ec.europa.eu/en/policies/blockchain-funding> accessed 1 October 2021

'Blockchain standards' (European Commission) <https://digital-strategy.ec.europa.eu/en/policies/blockchain-standards> accessed 1 October 2021

'Can smart contracts be legally binding contracts?' (R3 and Norton Rose Fulbright White Paper) <https://sites-nortonrosefulbright.vuturevx.com/596/14051/uploads/r3-and-norton-rose-fulbright-white-paper-full-report-144581.pdf> accessed 1 October 2021

'Ethereum 2.0 Beacon Chain Goes Live as 'World Computer' Begins Long-Awaited Overhaul' (Coindesk) <https://www.coindesk.com/ethereum-2-0-beacon-chain-goes-live-as-world-computer-begins-long-awaited-overhaul> accessed 1 October 2021

'European countries join Blockchain Partnership' (European Commission) <https://digital-strategy.ec.europa.eu/en/news/european-countries-join-blockchain-partnership> accessed 1 October 2021

'Insurance companies start experimenting with blockchain technology' (Reply) <https://www.reply.com/en/content/insurance-companies-start-experimenting-with-blockchain-technology> accessed 1 October 2021

'MiSE and OECD on Blockchain: Italy is the first EU country to finance a study on startups and SMEs' (MISE) <https://www.mise.gov.it/index.php/en/news/2039990-mise-and-oecd-on-blockchain-italy-is-the-first-eu-country-to-finance-a-study-on-startups-and-smes> accessed 1 October 2021

'Nasdaq launches enterprise-wide blockchain technology initiative' (2015) <http://ir.nasdaq.com/news-releases/news-release-details/nasdaq-launches-enterprise-wide-blockchain-technology-initiative> accessed 1 October 2021

'New Deal: What benefits will I get as a consumer?' (European Commission) <https://ec.europa.eu/info/sites/info/files/factsheet_new_deal_consumer_benefits_2019.pdf> accessed 1 October 2021

'Nick Szabo' (Wikipedia) <https://en.wikipedia.org/wiki/Nick_Szabo> accessed 1 October 2021

'Press Release – Geneva Round Table on Electronic Commerce and Private International Law' (Hague Conference on Private International Law, 26 June 2003) < https://www.hcch.net/en/news-archive/details/?varevent=63> accessed 1 October 2021

'Smart insurance Contracts: A discussion paper by Pinsent Masons and Applied Blockchain' (Pinsent Masons) <https://www.the-digital-insurer.com/wp-content/uploads/2017/10/980-FinTech_Smart_Insurance_Contracts_Flyer.pdf> accessed 1 October 2021

Agenzia per l'Italia digitale <https://www.agid.gov.it/en/agency/about-us> accessed 1 October 2021

Atrium (Un Innovation Network) <https://www.uninnovation.network/blockchain> accessed 1 October 2021

Axoni core <https://axoni.com/technology/> accessed 1 October 2021

Barlow J. P., 'Declaration of Independence for Cyberspace' (1996) <https://www.eff.org/cyberspace-independence> accessed 1 October 2021

Bitcoin Block Explorer <https://www.blockchain.com/it/explorer> accessed 1 October 2021

Blockchain Insurance Industry Initiative (B3i) <https://b3i.tech> accessed 1 October 2021

Brodesser J., 'First Monday Interviews: David Chaum' (1999) First Monday <http://journals.uic.edu/ojs/index.php/fm/article/view/683/593> accessed 1 October 2021

Buterin V., 'A next-generation smart contract and decentralized application platform' (2013) <https://blockchainlab.com/pdf/Ethereum_white_paper a_next_generation_smart_contract_and_decentralized_application_platform-vitalik-buterin.pdf> accessed 1 October 2021

Buterin V., 'Ethereum Platform Review: Opportunities and Challenges for Private and Consortium Blockchains' (2016) <http://www.smallake.kr/wp-content/uploads/2016/06/314477721-Ethereum-Platform-Review-Opportunities-and-Challenges-for-Private-and-Consortium-Blockchains.pdf> accessed 1 October 2021

Chamber of Digital Commerce, Smart Contracts Alliance, 'Smart Contracts: Is the Law Ready?' (2018) <https://digitalchamber.s3.amazonaws.com/Smart-Contracts-Whitepaper-WEB.pdf> accessed 1 October 2021

Chamber of Digital Commerce, Smart Contracts Alliance, 'Smart Contracts: 12 Use Cases for Business & Beyond <http://digitalchamber.org/assets/smart-contracts-12-use-cases-for-business-and-beyond.pdf> accessed 1 October 2021

CoinMarketCap <https://coinmarketcap.com> accessed 1 October 2021

ColoredCoins.org <https://en.bitcoin.it/wiki/Colored_Coins> accessed 1 October 2021

Common Accord <http://www.commonaccord.org/> accessed 1 October 2021

Corda <https://www.corda.net> accessed 1 October 2021

Counterparty <https://counterparty.io> accessed 1 October 2021

Dax Hansen J., Reyes C. L., 'Legal Aspects of Smart Contract Applications' (2017) <https://www.virtualcurrencyreport.com/wp-content/uploads/sites/35/2017/05/Perkins-Coie-LLP-Legal-Aspects-of-Smart-Contracts-Applications.pdf> accessed 1 October 2021

Ethereum Foundation <https://ethereum.org/en/foundation/> accessed 1 October 2021

Ethereum/mist (GitHub) <https://github.com/ethereum/mist/releases> accessed 1 October 2021

Etherisc <https://fdd.etherisc.com> accessed 1 October 2021

EU Blockchain Observatory and Forum (European Commission) <https://www.eublockchainforum.eu/> accessed 1 October 2021

European Commission, Online Dispute Resolution platform <https://ec.europa.eu/consumers/odr/main/?event=main.trader.register#inline-nav-3> accessed 1 October 2021

Fizzy general conditions <https://fizzy.axa/fr/static/media/conditions-generales.38af84e2.pdf> accessed 1 October 2021

Fizzy, Axa <https://www.axa.com/en/magazine/axa-goes-blockchain-with-fizzy> accessed 1 October 2021

Global Blockchain Policy Centre (OECD) <https://www.oecd.org/going-digital/topics/blockchain> accessed 1 October 2021

Hughes E., 'A Cypherpunk's Manifesto' (1993) <https://www.activism.net/cypherpunk/manifesto.html> accessed 1 October 2021

Hyperledger fabric <https://www.hyperledger.org/projects/fabric> accessed 1 October 2021

Ibáñez L. D., O'Hara K., Simperl E., 'On Blockchains and the General Data Protection Regulation' (2018) <https://eprints.soton.ac.uk/422879/1/BLockchains_GDPR_4.pdf> accessed 1 October 2021

Insurance Blockchain Sandbox <https://www.insuranceblockchainsandbox.com/> accessed 1 October 2021

ISO/TC 307 <https://www.iso.org/committee/6266604.html> accessed 1 October 2021

Legalese <http://www.legalese.com/> accessed 1 October 2021

Lewis P. H., 'Attention Internet Shoppers: E-Cash Is Here' (1994) New York Times <http://www.nytimes.com/1994/10/19/business/attention-internet-shoppers-e-cash-is-here.html> accessed 1 October 2021

Lisk <https://lisk.io> accessed 1 October 2021

Loops (Wikipedia) <https://computersciencewiki.org/index.php/Loops> accessed 1 October 2021

Lumb R., Treat D., Jelf O., 'Editing the uneditable blockchain – Why distributed ledger technology must adapt to an imperfect world' (Accenture) <https://www.accenture.com/_acnmedia/pdf-33/accenture-editing-uneditable-blockchain.pdf> accessed 1 October 2021

May T. C., 'The Cyphernomicon: Cypherpunks FAQ and More, Version 0.666' (1994) <https://hackmd.io/@jmsjsph/TheCyphernomicon> accessed 1 October 2021

McCarthy J., Minsky M., Rochester N., Shannon C. E., 'A proposal for the Dartmouth Summer Research Project on Artificial Intelligence' (1956) <http://www-formal.stanford.edu/jmc/history/dartmouth.html> accessed 1 October 2021

Monax <https://monax.io> accessed 1 October 2021

Mou V., 'Blockchain Oracles Explained' <https://academy.binance.com/blockchain/blockchain-oracles-explained> accessed 1 October 2021

Nakamoto S., 'Bitcoin: A Peer-to-Peer Electronic Cash System' (2008) <https://bitcoin.org/bitcoin.pdf> accessed 1 October 2021

OB1 company <https://ob1.io/about.html> accessed 1 October 2021

Open Bazaar <https://openbazaar.org> accessed 1 October 2021

Principles of European Tort Law (PETL) < http://www.egtl.org/docs/PETL.pdf> accessed 1 October 2021

Provable <https://provable.xyz> accessed 1 October 2021

R3 <https://www.r3.com> accessed 1 October 2021

Realitio <https://realit.io> accessed 1 October 2021

Ricardian Contract <https://iang.org/papers/ricardian_contract.html> accessed 1 October 2021

Rikken O. *et al.*, 'Smart contracts as a specific application of blockchain technology' (2017) <https://dutchdigitaldelta.nl/uploads/pdf/Smart-Contracts-ENG-report.pdf> accessed 1 October 2021

Roberts J. J., 'Why Accenture's Plan to 'Edit' the Blockchain is a Big Deal' (Fortune) <https://fortune.com/2016/09/20/accenture-blockchain/> accessed 1 October 2021

SIX Digital Exchange <https://www.sdx.com/en/home.html> accessed 1 October 2021

Slock.it <https://blog.slock.it/> accessed 1 October 2021

Stark J., 'Making Sense of Blockchain Smart Contracts' (2016) <https://www.coindesk.com/making-sense-smart-contracts> accessed 1 October 2021

Stellar <https://www.stellar.org> accessed 1 October 2021

Swanson T., 'Consensus-as-a-service: a brief report on the emergence of permissioned, distributed ledger systems' (2015) 15 <http://www.ofnumbers.com/wp-content/uploads/2015/04/Permissioned-distributed-ledgers.pdf> accessed 1 October 2021

Szabo N., 'Smart Contracts' (1994) <http://www.fon.hum.uva.nl/rob/Courses/InformationInSpeech/CDROM/Literature/LOTwinterschool2006/szabo.best.vwh.net/smart.contracts.html> accessed 1 October 2021

The Digital Services Act package <https://ec.europa.eu/digital-single-market/en/digital-services-act-package> accessed 1 October 2021

Trakti <https://www.trakti.com/home/> accessed 1 October 2021

UNCITRAL <https://uncitral.un.org> accessed 1 October 2021

UNCITRAL Working Group III on ODR <https://uncitral.un.org/en/working_groups/3/online_dispute> accessed 1 October 2021

Vessenes P., 'Ethereum Contracts are Going to be Candy for Hackers' (2016) Vessenes <http://vessenes.com/ethereum-contracts-are-going-to-be-candy-for-hackers/> accessed 1 October 2021

Wood G., 'PoA Private Chains' (2015) GitHub <https://github.com/ethereum/guide/blob/master/poa.md> accessed 1 October 2021

Working Group IV: Electronic Commerce (UNCITRAL) <https://uncitral.un.org/en/working_groups/4/electronic_commerce> accessed 1 October 2021

## K) OTHER SOURCES

'Civil liability – adapting liability rules to the digital age and artificial intelligence' Inception impact assessment – Ares(2021)4266516 <https://ec.europa.eu/info/law/better-regulation/have-your-say/initiatives/12979-Civil-liability-adapting-liability-rules-to-the-digital-age-and-artificial-intelligence_en> accessed 1 October 2021

'Financial Markets, Insurance and Pensions: Digitalisation and Finance' (OECD) <https://www.oecd.org/finance/private-pensions/Financial-markets-insurance-pensions-digitalisation-and-finance.pdf> accessed 1 October 2021

De Poli M., 'Rescissione' in *Enc. Giur. Treccani Online* (2015)

Ferraro I., 'La pazienza della blockchain' (2019) Press release English version <https://bancaforte.it/articolo/un-e-book-sulla-pazienza-della-blockchain-RB97945k> accessed 1 October 2021

Gabrielli G., Padovini F., 'Recesso (dir.priv.)' in *Enc. Diritto* (1988) XXXIX

Mell P., Grance T., 'The NIST Definition of Cloud Computing. Recommendations of the National Institute of Standards and Technology' (2011) NIST Special Publication 800–145 <https://nvlpubs.nist.gov/nistpubs/Legacy/SP/nistspecialpublication800-145.pdf> accessed 1 October 2021

*Proposte per la Strategia italiana in materia di tecnologie basate su registri condivisi e Blockchain – Sintesi per la consultazione pubblica* (MISE) <https://www.mise.gov.it/index.php/it/consultazione-blockchain> accessed 1 October 2021

Rikken O., van Heukeolom-Verhage S. *et al.*, 'Blockchain and Distributed Ledger Technology: definitions' in UNOPS, 'The Legal Aspects of Blockchain' (2018) <https://insureblocks.com/ep-42-legal-aspects-of-blockchain/> accessed 1 October 2021

Scalfi G., 'Risoluzione del contratto, I), Diritto civile' in *Enc. Giur. Treccani* (1991)

Tomassini R., 'Invalidità (dir priv.)' in *Encicl. Diritto*, XXII, 1972, 586

UNIDROIT work and instruments in the area of Law & Technology (UNIDROIT) <https://unidroit.aedstudio.net/law-technology/> accessed 1 October 2021